THE HUNCHBACK OF NOTRE DAME

Books by
Philip J Riley

CLASSIC HORROR FILMS
Frankenstein, the original 1931 shooting script
Bride of Frankenstein, the original 1935 shooting script
Son of Frankenstein, the original 1939 shooting script
Ghost of Frankenstein, the original 1942 shooting script
Frankenstein Meets the Wolf Man, the original 1943 shooting script
House of Frankenstein, the original 1944 shooting script
The Mummy, the original 1932 shooting script
The Mummy's Curse the original 1944 shooting script (as Editor in Chief)
The Wolf Man, the original 1941 shooting script
Dracula, the original 1931 shooting script
House of Dracula, the original 1945 shooting script

CLASSIC COMEDY FILMS
Abbott & Costello Meet Frankenstein, the original 1948 shooting script

CLASSIC SCIENCE FICTION
This Island Earth, the original 1955 shooting script
The Creature from the Black Lagoon, the original 1953 shooting script (editor-in-chief)

THE ACKERMAN ARCHIVES SERIES - LOST FILMS
The Reconstruction of London After Midnight, the original 1927 shooting script
The Reconstruction of A Blind Bargain, the original 1922 shooting script
The Reconstruction of The Hunchback of Notre Dame, the original 1923 shooting script

CLASSIC SILENT FILMS
The Reconstruction of The Phantom of the Opera, the original 1925 shooting script
The Reconstruction of "London After Midnight" the original 1927 hooting script (2nd edition)

FILMONSTER SERIES - LOST SCRIPTS
James Whale's Dracula's Daughter, 1934
Cagliostro, The King of the Dead, 1932
Wolf Man vs. Dracula 1944
Lon Chaney as Dracula/Nosferatu
Robert Florey's Frankenstein 1931
Frankenstein - A play, 1931 (editor)
War Eagles (with David Conover)
Karloff as The Invisible Man 1932

AS EDITOR
Countess Dracula by Carroll Borland
My Hollywood, when both of us were young by Patsy Ruth Miller
Mr. Technicolor - Herbert Kalmus
Famous Monster of Filmland #2 by Forrest J Ackerman

FILM DOCUMENTARIES
A Thousand Faces - as contributor (Photoplay Productions)
Universal Horrors - as contributor (Photoplay Productions)

Mr. Riley has also contributed to 12 film related books by various authors
as well as numerous magazine articles and received the Count Dracula Society Award
and was inducted into Universal's Horror Hall of Fame adn
won the Halloween Book Festival 2011 award in the horror category

THE HUNCHBACK OF NOTRE DAME

Reconstructed and edited by
PHILIP J. RILEY

Foreword by
Patsy Ruth Miller

Introduction by
George Turner

Screenplay by
Edward T. Lowe Jr

Adapted by
Perley Poore Sheehan

An Imprint of Bearmanor Media
Ackerman Archives Series Volume III

MagicImage Filmbooks is an imprint of:

BearManor Media
P.O. Box 1129
Duncan, OK 73534-1129

Phone: 580-252-3547
Fax: 814-690-1559

©2012 Philip J Riley
For Copyright purposes
Philip J Riley is the author in the form of this book

Lon Chaney name and likeness are trademarks of Chaney Enterprises

Cover Art -Courtesy of Wes Shank
All photographs are from the Author's collection, The Wallace Worsley collection

The script, courtesy of Wallace Worsley Jr. and Sue Dwiggins, is director Wallace Worsley Sr.'s personal copy. It is now at the Academy of Motion Pictures Arts and Sciences Library. Original Theater program courtesy of Patsy Ruth Miller

Author's Note: I interviewed the producers, directors, stars, cast and crew in the early to late 1970s. They were recalling events that happened 35-45 years previous and sometimes memory fades or events are recalled from their perspective point of view.

First published by MagicImage Filmbook, 1988 together with "My Hollywood When Both of Us Were Young" - by Patsy Ruth Miller (Co-star of the 1923 Hunchback of Notre Dame)

First Bearmanor Media edition 2012

The purpose of this series is the preservation of the art of writing for the screen. Rare books have long been a source of enjoyment and an investment for the serious collector, and even in limited editions there are thousands printed. Scripts, however, numbered only 50 at the most. In the history of American Literature, the screenwriter was being lost in time. It is my hope that my efforts bring about a renewed history and preservation of a great American Literary form, The Screenplay, by preserving them for study by future generations.

**This volume is dedicated to:
JULIA TAYLOR WORSLEY
and
SUE DWIGGINS WORSLEY**

*For not making Wally Sr. & Jr.
clean out the garage.*

"THE HUNCHBACK OF NOTRE DAME" "I adore you," he whispered

"THE HUNCHBACK OF NOTRE DAME" "I'd rather see you dead than the plaything of an aristocrat!"

YOU HAVE TO ACT THE PART - by Patsy Ruth Miller

I did not appear in *A Blind Bargain* but I can recount my memories of the picture I made with Lon Chaney and Wallace Worsley, *The Hunchback of Notre Dame*, that same year. I don't remember when *The Hunchback* was released: we started shooting on it in December of 1922, and I worked on it until the end of June 1923. *

It was an epic, the only one I was ever in. It was known as an epic from its inception, but even better known as one of the first actual Million Dollar Movies. Today, a budget of a million dollars is hardly enough to make a two minute commercial, but in 1922, when the picture went into production, a million dollars was just what it sounds like. Those dollars were real, honest-to-goodness 100 cent dollars, and they were all spent on actual production, not on taxes, or labor disputes or politics. Of course salaries were included in the cost of production, but I assure you that no one, not even Lon Chaney received enough to make a dent in the million. My salary certainly didn't account for much of that sum, but on the other hand, what I received was mine, all mine. No deductions. Cigarettes were 15 cents a pack, two for a quarter. Gasoline was eight cents a gallon. You could get a good meal in a good restaurant for two or three dollars, and tips were five percent for really good service.

I knew that I was lucky to get the part of Esmeralda, the Gypsy girl, but I didn't dream that it was going to be the picture by which I was remembered. Sometimes I've been a bit annoyed by being introduced as Esmeralda. It's always: You remember "The Hunchback" don't you? She played the Gypsy girl in it. Then if the recipient of this world shaking news is under sixty, the response is generally, Oh Really? I thought it was Maureen O'Hara!

My memories of "The Hunchback" are good ones; the friendliness of everyone, the grips, the propmen, the cameramen, as well as the other members of the cast. And I remember Lon Chaney as being a very gentle and kind man.

He was completely dedicated to his art and approached it in a workmanlike manner. He watched every detail, not only of his own performance, but of the picture as a whole. He actually shared the direction of scenes with Wallace Worsley, and I couldn't help learning a great deal from him.

I had already been in eleven pictures, all in a matter of three years! But no one had coached me, or explained anything about acting. I had done western—well, I did learn

* *Miss Miller's foreword first appeared in "The reconstruction of "A Blind Bargain" MagicImage Filmbooks 1987*

Worsley, Chaney and Kerry preparing a scene in THE HUNCHBACK where Quasimodo buys Esmerelda clothes, while she is protected by the sanctuary of the Church—missing from most prints today.

how to ride a horse—and I had played comedy and tragedy and sill parts that took no ability, but it was all done by my own instincts; I lacked technique. I depended too much on my own emotion in dramatic scenes. I remember being terribly excited after filming a scene for "The Hunchback" because I had cried real tears. But Lon explained that crying real tears didn't make an actress good; it was making the audience cry that mattered, and that you didn't do if you emoted all over the set. He didn't believe that an actor should "lose himself" in the part; he should always be aware of what he was doing. There's a fine difference.

Norman Kerry, who played Phoebus in a curled wig and ornate costume, and who was completely irreverent, also gave me some advice. His was, "Don't look at the camera and try not to giggle in the love scenes." He added, "And don't forget to pick up your check every week.

Norman really wasn't really an actor at heart. He was just a fun-loving, handsome guy who made a living by "making faces in front of a camera," as he described acting. He took nothing, least of all himself, seriously. Much to the aggravation of Mr. Chaney who took his art quite serious. However once or twice Lon's sense of humor an occurrence which always took one by surprise, did endear him to me.

During the shooting of one of my close-ups, he stood off-camera, ostensibly to inspire me. As I raised my gaze, looking at Norman with wide-eyed innocence, he said in a girlish falsetto, "Oh, Mr. Kerry, are my eyes too big for pictures?" It broke everyone up, and the scene had to be taken over.

He did that sort of thing constantly throughout the shooting of "The Hunchback". But when it came to Norman's clowning, I don't think Lon ever quite understood it.

I also remember Ernest Torrence, who played Clopin, King of the Beggars, in a violent blustering manner. Actually he was a most charming, Scottish gentleman with a delightful, dry humor, as unlike his screen character as it is possible to be. I remember very little about the director, Wallace Worsley. Novice though I was, I was aware that he was not a very forceful man, and it seemed to me that Lon did as much directing of the personal scenes as Mr. Worsley. Although the responsibility of such as big budget picture and it's hundred of daily problems probably must have been a very big burden, the crowd scenes were handled by use of a then—innovative technique—an electric Loud Speaker system! Even in those scenes, Lon seemed to have a hand, and often a suggestion.

I also remember a young man just over from Europe, Alsace Lorraine, it might have been. I'm not sure now. Anyway, he and his brother, Robert, were nephews of Uncle Carl Laemmle, who was head of Universal. Willy was the other brother, and their last name was Wyler. Willy was put to work as sort of second assistant to the assistant director, and seemed to take to it with great enthusiasm. I don't remember what Robert did, but he was the one I'd have bet on; he was taller than Willy, and quite good-looking, although not blond and blue-eyed, which was my preference. No one could have called Willy good-looking, but he was very pleasant. I enjoyed chatting with him between scenes, in my fractured French, and I was impressed by how quickly he seemed to catch on to everything, the camera work, the set-ups, and all that.

Willy became completely Americanized; he changed his name from Willy to William, and became one of our finest directors.

Another memory returns to me, a little lecture from Lon one day. He was not in his terrible make-up, so he was free to chat, which was almost impossible when he was wearing that painful Hunchback outfit. He led up to the subject gradually, saying how pleased he was with my performance, going on to tell me that he was sure I would have a successful career, and he finally got to the point by saying, "It's all very well to be generous, but don't let people make a sucker out of you."

As was often the case, I didn't know what he was talking about. As was equally often the case, he looked at me with that "Are you for real?" look. Then he patiently explained that I was becoming known as a soft touch. Before I could protest that no one had been touching me, soft or otherwise, he gave a deep sigh and said, "What I'm trying to tell you is, don't fall for all those hard luck stories

you've been getting from some of the extras, Meg and Skeets, for instance."

Then I knew what he was talking about; how he knew I had lent them money I didn't know. Maybe he was just familiar with Meg and Skeets and their tactics. He ended his little lecture by saying, "You'll probably make a lot of money in this business, but just remember—you worked for it. So don't be a sucker."

I think it was very sweet of him to be concerned about me and my financial welfare. And I was careful from then on not to let him see me talking to any of the extras.

After six months of happy work, despite the daily drive from Beverly Hills to the Valley, the picture finally came to an end, and it was time to say goodbye to the cast, the crew and Lon. Most of us would never see each other again; friendships are formed on the set, but they usually don't carry over into "civilian" life. We might meet at parties—occasionally some of us worked together in other movies—but for the most part we went our own ways, in our own circle of friends. Romances also occasionally blossom, but seldom lasting ones.

Norman had given me a good hearty kiss, and said, "Let's work together again some day when you're grown up." Mr. Worsley had politely said it was a pleasure to work with me and I had replied that it was a pleasure to work with him. Then it was time to tell Lon goodbye.

He was in the projection room looking at the rushes. I knocked on the door. He opened with a look of annoyance, which changed into a smile when he saw me. Telling the projectionist to hold it, he came out into the hall, saying, "Well, you're leaving, eh?" When I thanked him for being so tolerant and so helpful, he smiled again, that rare, very sweet smile, and said that I looked fine in the rushes, and that he wished me the best of luck, but even as he was speaking, I had the feeling that he was no longer with me.

Permit me to tell about something that happened fifty years later. Some time in the Seventies, when my husband and I were in Edinburgh, we decided to fly to Glasglow to visit his Aunt Joan. We called her to say we'd be there on Sunday, and she said that she and Uncle George would meet us at the airport.

We arrived as scheduled, but there was no one at the airport to greet us. Worried that there might have been an accident, or that one of them was ill, my husband rushed to a phone. Her number rang and rang until it was answered by an apologetic Aunt Joan.

"Do forgive me, dear boy," she said. "We've been watching an old movie on the telly, and I'm afraid we completely forgot about you and Pat. It's "The Hunchback of Notre Dame" . . . it's still on as a matter of fact. . . do forgive us."

My husband said it didn't matter, to go back and watch the movie, we'd take a taxi, which we did. It's about a twenty minute drive to Bearsden, the suburb in which they lived, and by the time we got there TV show was over. I couldn't resist asking Aunt Joan whether seeing me on the screen hadn't reminded her that we would be at the airport.

"Not a bit of it, dear," she said. "In my mind I never connected the two of you at all."

That's about the way it was that summer day in 1923, at the Universal Studio, when I felt Lon Chaney drifting away from me.

I, Patsy Ruth Miller, was already gone, over and done with. She, Esmeralda, was just beginning to live, and in his mind he no longer connected the two of us at all.

Wallace Worsley, Patsy Ruth Miller and Lon Chaney reviewing the script of THE HUNCHBACK OF NOTRE DAME.

The Court of Miracles from THE HUNCHBACK as it exists today on the UNIVERSAL backlot. Notre Dame having burnt down about 20 years ago leaves only these surviving sets. The archway below was also used in THE GHOST OF FRANKENSTEIN where Lon Chaney Jr. saved the little girl trying to catch her balloon. (Sets can be seen as part of the Universal Studio's Tour).

Courtesy William K. Everson

PRODUCTION BACKGROUND
By
George Turner

The early 1920s were years of great artistic and technical growth for motion pictures. So man outstanding films were made during that time that it is virtually impossible to pick a single favorite.

Certainly a leading contender is the 1923 *The Hunchback of Notre Dame*, produced at Universal City under the benign dictatorship of the president, Carl Laemmle, and his youthful production executive, Irving G. Thalberg. It has spectacle in the best sense of the word, fine performances, cinematography which set new standards in several respects, steady direction which kept all the sprawling elements of the picture under control, magnificent settings and faithfulness to the spirit of a literary classic. It was one of the most expensive silent films, costing more than $1,250,000.

Universal at the time specialized in the making of inexpensive program pictures which were sold in packages to exhibitors. These were graded by Laemmle as to importance and quality, the top line products being designated as Universal Jewels, the Junior Jewels, Specials, etc. There was an occasional Super Jewel, meaning a picture so far above the ordinary as to demand special handling, higher rentals and longer playdates. Of this mere handful (which includes *Foolish Wives, Merry-go-round, The Phantom of the Opera* and *Uncle Tom's Cabin*), Laemmle's favorite and the company's biggest was *Hunchback*.

In adapting Victor Hugo's novel, "Notre Dame de Paris," Perley Poore Sheehan and Edward T. Lowe made many changes, some of the interest of paring the story down to a practical length for the screen, partly to relieve some of the gloom which permeates the novel but would hardly be acceptable to theater audiences of the time, and partly to eliminate Hugo's criticisms of the church.

The film centers around Quasimodo, the deformed bell-ringer of the Cathedral of Notre Dame in Paris, in 1482. He is ordered by Jehan, evil brother of the archdeacon, to kidnap Esmeralda, a beautiful Gypsy dancing girl and ward of the king of the underworld, Clopin. She is rescued by the dashing Captain Phoebus and Quasimodo is sentenced to be lashed in the public square. Esmeralda, taking pity, brings him water and stirs in him a hopeless love. Jehan jealously stabs Phoebus as he embraces Esmeralda. The girl is blamed and sentenced to be hanged in front of Notre Dame. Quasimodo climbs down from the cathedral tower and carries Esmeralda into the sanctuary of the church. Clopin leads his army of beggars, thieves and murderers from their quarter, known as the Court of Miracles, to storm Notre Dame. Quasimodo, thinking they are trying to return the girl to the gallows, hurls building blocks and beams down on them. He finally routs the attack by pouring molten lead onto the rabble. The King's guards disperse the mob as Clopin dies. Jehan now tries to attack Esmeralda in the tower. In rescuing her, Quasimodo is fatally stabbed before throwing Jehan from the tower. Esmeralda learns that Phoebus is alive and that she has been exonerated. As she leaves, Quasimodo tolls the church bells, then dies.

Laemmle and Thalberg agreed that only Lon Chaney could portray Quasimodo. Even while early research was being done by Sheehan in Paris and the physical aspects of the production were being planned, Thalberg was trying to sign the reclusive actor who was being difficult because of a grudge against the studio. And agreement was reached late in 1922.

A number of important directors had been considered. Chaney was instrumental in bringing in Wallace Worsley, who had directed him the Goldwyn production, *The Penalty*. A veteran actor and producer of the New York stage, he became a film director in 1917 and directed for most of the major studios. *Hunchback* was both his finest work and his last large-scale directional effort. After it was completed he devoted most of his efforts to the making of travel pictures.

Worsley was aware of Chaney's directional ability and allowed him to direct some of his own scenes. In staging the gigantic crowd scenes, in which as many as 2,500 extras appeared, Worsley utilized for the first time in motion picture production a public address system. This was the new Western Electric Public Address Apparatus, which made it possible for the director to give orders to actors and crew members in all parts of the vast set. An ex-army officer, George M. Stallings, and ten assistant directors, headed by Jimmy Dugan and Jack Sullivan, helped to control the mass of players. One of the assistant-assistants was a Laemmle relative from France, William Wyler.

Many modern critics have pondered Universal's choice of a comparatively little-known director for a picture which completed (successfully) with the outstanding historical epics of the silent screen. However, a study of the film reveals that *Hunchback* has all the virtures and few of the faults of pictures produced by the better known makers of this type of film: the crowds are handled with great skill, the individual performances are first rate (yet even Chaney is unable to reduce Hugo's concept to a star vehicle), the

Worsley and the first use of the P.A. System in a motion picture.

photographic technique is superior to any picture of its kind of the period, and there is a welcome absence of the dramatic excesses that marred Cecil B. DeMille's films or the exaggerated sentimentality that Griffith so often fell prey to. And if this be heresy . . .

Elmer E. Sheeley was in charge of set design, with Sidney Ullman as his first assistant. Archie Hall was the technical director in charge of set construction. Stephen Goosson—who designed Shangri La for *Lost Horizon* a dozen or so years later—worked with Ullman and several other artists in a special drafting room over the main stage. Their drawings, which combined the factual wit the fanciful, were based upon old prints of the architecture of the period, including a collection of sketches made by Victor Hugo. These designs were translated into plans which were blueprinted and delivered to Hall.

Meanwhile, 60 workman hauled in cobblestones from a river 20 miles away and laid them in cement beds—the streets of old Paris. Flagstones were molded in cement and laid in a long row in front of a string stretched between two poles to indicate the front line of the cathedral site. To lay out the cathedral place it was necessary to cut off one flank of a mountain and fill in a large swale.

Carl Laemmle told Hall that the sets should be built as solidly as the real thing, just as had been done previously with the Monte Carlo and Vienna sets for Erich von Stroheim's extravaganzas, *Foolish Wives* and *Merry-Go-Round*. It was his theory that the sets could be used in many other productions, and he was right. They remained in use for four decades, until the cathedral and most of the other buildings were destroyed in a disastrous fire.

The framework was set up by 200 carpenters while sections of the facade were cast in concrete. Finn Frowlich, a well known sculptor, was in charge of making the bas-reliefs, embellishments, saints, martyrs and gargoyles that cover the Gothic structure. Before completion the cathedral resembled a huge wooden shed, but when the lumber was removed it had become a replica of the original exterior—or, at least, the bottom 60 feet of it. After masons finished their work, 60 painters added the finishing touches.

At the time of the story, Notre Dame was 150 feet wide and 225 feet high (the spire was added at a later time). The cathedral ended at a point just above the huge arch over the center entrance. To show wider views of the cathedral, the upper portion was constructed as a large-scale miniature which was mounted between the camera and the building and lined up to blend perfectly with the full scale set. The complete cathedral, seen from several angles, defies detection.

Universal Studios in 1925 showing Chaney's dressing room, the Phantom stage and the Hunchback sets on hill in background.

Other parts of the building, for use in close-ups, were erected at different locations. Part of a tower was built full-scale on a hilltop about one mile away. The hill provided the elevation needed for low-angle shots but, as Patsy Ruth Miller says, "it was built so that you couldn't hurt yourself if you fell." The Bastille and drawbridge were built about a quarter of a mile from the courtyard. The gardens of the castle were located adjacent to the studio nursery, where the varieties of plants could be moved conveniently. Concrete arches were built over the Los Angeles River, which forms the northern boundary of Universal City, to represent the sewers of Paris. At that time the river bed was not concrete as it is today, and it was used in many pictures. When it appeared as the Seine, the Thames, the Danube or the Mississippi, the semi-arid river had to be dammed up or even irrigated by the studio fire department.

The principal sets covered 19 acres, 11 for the courtyard and cathedral and eight for streets and the Court of Miracles. The building included a castle, a hotel, shops, taverns and houses. Construction took six months. The settings and properties cost about $500,000—$342,869 of which was for the Place du Parvis set.

In *Movie Weekly* for April 21, 1923, Grace Kingsley describes a visit with Chaney to the set, where they "sat in the 11-acre-square of Notre Dame, facing that wonderful cathedral.

"We had driven up in Lon's cadillac! Image the humble hunchback driving a Cadillac! Around us sprawled or lounged a thousand extras . . .They were all in bright colors, and they formed a marvelous picture against the backgrounds of church, shops, old-fashioned houses of Paris, which themselves were silhouetted against the green hills of Universal City and the purple mountains in the distance."

Perley Poore Sheehan, co-author of the screenplay described the atmosphere more poetically in *Cinema Art* of January, 1924.

"The cathedral towers would shimmer in a blue radiance like that of a thousand moons and send back echoes of coyote calls. Wouldn't Victor Hugo have loved all this? I believe so. It was his sort of stuff. It was great and weird. I myself like to believe—and I do believe it—that the great Frenchman's spirit presided over the filming. . .from the very inception of the idea right up to the premiere opening on Broadway." Sheehan had lived in Paris for 10 years "under the very shadow of the old cathedral" and just around the corner from Hugo's house.

Jack Rumsey, recently returned from Hollywood, told the *New York Times* (July 1, 1923) that "the immensity of the sets and their accuracy was far beyond the ken of most persons" and that he "felt quite nonplussed when he stood before the great gate of Notre Dame in Universal City. . . All the atmosphere of Paris was near the cathedral, and every little detail has received attention in making the copy in far off California."

Sheehan, in addition to his writing duties, worked as a technical supervisor for Worsley. It was he who set the tone for the costuming with this directive:

"We don't think of Christopher Columbus discovering America 'in costume.' We don't allow ourselves to think for a moment of *Notre Dame's* fifteenth century people as wearing grotesque costumes and having queer costumes. No costumes were grotesque to the people who wore them. They were natural, everyday clothes. Our characters must wear their costumes as such. The costumes. . .will be incidental and the main object is to make them and use them so that the spectator will forget them. They must be incidental—accurate, correct, but inconspicuous."

Three thousand costumes had to be specially made. Planning and measurements were completed about a month before shooting was to begin. A building on the lot, which was 125 feet long with 18 windows, was enlarged to about double that size to handle the large number of costumes to be handed out to the extras at the windows. Around 200 men were necessary to handle wardrobe duties. Col. Gordon McGee, of Western Costume Company, supervised costume research and production. The fancier clothes were worn by characters of the court, the 50 men and 50 women attending the grand ball at the mansion of Madame Gaundalaurier, Esmeralda, and certain of the Gypsies. The more conspicuous extras were put on the payroll two days early so they could become accustomed to wearing their costumes in order that they would behave on camera as though they were wearing the normal clothes of their day.

The most unusual garb is that of the underworld denizens of the Court of Miracles. Because their home was surrounded by old palaces, these thieves and beggars wore garments pilfered from the nobility, especially during the plague when many of the rich abandoned their homes until the danger had passed. The beggars, therefore, wore the raiment of royalty, however soiled and tattered. The appearance of reality achieved in *Hunchback*, as opposed to the comic-opera look that contributed to the public's dislike of most historical epics, may be traced in large measure to the authentic drab costuming.

Director Worsley with Gypsies, Thieves and Beggars in the Court of Miracles.

Lon Chaney had been a colorful part of the ambience at Universal since its early days, first as an extra and bit player and eventually a featured actor and sometime writer and director. He was one of several actors (others were Jack Pierce, Cecil Holland and C.E. Collins) who stayed busy by bringing their own makeup kits to casting calls and making themselves up on the spot to fit whatever kinds of characters were being cast. Since Universal specialized in Westerns, serials and jungle melodramas, Chaney played many a scar-faced heavy, also appearing as elderly men and paunchy fathers in society dramas.

Chaney, after a salary dispute, left Universal and found greater fame at Paramount, Goldwyn and other companies. When he returned to do *Hunchback* he was a major star, earning the then-munificent sum of $2,500 per week. This picture brought him even greater stature and when the Metro-Goldwyn company was formed in 1924, he was their first star. He returned to Universal for the last time that year to make *The Phantom of the Opera*, thereafter working for MGM exclusively. He died in 1930 after making his only talking picture, *The Unholy Three*. Ironically, his two most popular pictures were Universal's *Hunchback* and *Phantom*.

Checking in at Universal, Chaney appropriated Dressing Room No. 5, a new one-room shack, with shower on the frontlot. Locking himself in with his makeup kit, two chairs, an iron cot, a wardrobe, a small table and a makeup mirror, he worked out the details of Quasimodo.

His personal manager, A.A. Grasso, had borrowed for him an old edition of Hugo's book which contained eight drawings of the hunchback by Hugo himself. Using these and Hugo's vivid verbal descriptions, Chaney emerged at length with a Quasimodo which seemed akin to the monstrous gargoyles of Notre Dame.

This initiated a studio tradition regarding No. 5 which persisted until it and similar cubicles made way for more modern structures. Chaney returned there to create *The Phantom of the Opera*. In 1928 the room was commandeered by Jack P. Pierce, head of makeup and a great friend and admirer of Chaney. Pierce created there Conrad Veidt's horror makeup for *The Man Who Laughs*. Later he worked in secrecy in No. 5 on Boris Karloff, Bela Lugosi, Lon Chaney Jr. and others who portrayed monsters of various sorts in the studio's popular horror movies of the 1930s and '40s. No 5 was known and the *Bugaboudoir* and engendered a certain superstitious awe among some of the old-time Universalites.

"When Chaney first put on his makeup—*The Hunchback* is his life's dream and every bit of his 5 year's intensive study of makeup goes into it—Jack Freulich, studio photographer; Henry Freulich, Graflex cameraman with the publicity department; Fred L. Archer, head of the art title department and internationally known for his prize-winning studies, and two other photographers shot photographs simultaneously of the remarkable Quasimodo," *American Cinematographer* reported in February, 1923.

This was the first photographic job for the youthful Henry Freulich (later ASC), son of Jack and a celebrated director of photography in later years.

The other major roles were assigned to Patsy Ruth Miller, an excellent young actress who already had played leads in more than a dozen pictures, as Esmeralda; Norman Keery (died 1956), who had been in pictures since 1919 and had just scored a big success in another spectacular production *Merry-Go-Round*, as Phoebus; and Ernest Torrence (died 1933), a tall, lantern-jawed opera singer, as the beggar-king, Clopin. All three are strong assets to the picture, and Torrence's characterization is almost as impelling as Chaney's. In fact, several who saw the original premiere engagement version have stated that Torrence's role was severely cut when the film was edited for release and that he dominated much of the long edition, which no longer is available.

Ernest Torrance

Patsy Ruth Miller

Wallace Worsley - Wallace Worsley Jr.

Robert E. Newhard, ASC, was named first cameraman (today he would be called director of photography). However, the magnitude of production was such over a long period that almost every other cameraman at Universal had a hand in it at various times, including Charles Stumar, ASC, Stephen S. Norton, ASC, Anthony Kornmann, ASC, Virgil Miller, ASC, Friend F. Baker, ASC, Philip H. Witman, ASC and perhaps a dozen others. Only Newhard received screen credit.

A founding member of the ASC in 1918-1919, Newhard had been a cinematographer for about 13 years, having begun as an assistant to Fred Balshofer at the 101 Bison Ranch. He then became one of the earliest special effects specialists, heading an experimental and research department for Thomas H Ince. Once of his most striking efforts was a Billie Burke feature filmed entirely without artificial light by use of mirrors and reflectors. After shooting 14 features for Ince in four years, he worked for Paralta, Frank Keenan, Selznick, Fox and Goldwyn. He teamed with aviator Frank Clarke in making aerial films, then was called to Universal for his biggest assignment: six months' work on *Hunchback*. It proved his *magnum opus*, a film whose photographic qualities (even in the much-copied 16mm prints which seem to be all that remain) are remarkable even today.

Newhard hailed from rural Pennsylvania and, since boyhood, had been fond of keeping snakes as pets. Snakes were abundant in the grassy and (then) largely undeveloped Universal backlot, and a six-foot gopher snake became Newhard's companion during the last two weeks of shooting. Most of the cast and crew gave the cameraman's friend a wide berth.

Anthony Kornmann ASC, also worked as a first cameraman on many scenes, although it is now impossible to determine which ones. Kornmann was a second unit specialist during most of his career. Hungarian-born Charles Stumar, the most famous of the cinematographers who contributed to the film, was another veteran of the Inceville studio and is believed to have shot some of the softly romantic scens between Esmeralda and Phoebus. At the height of his career, in 1935, Stumar was killed in an airplane crash while scouting locations. Stephen S. Norton ASC, a diminutive cameraman who at the time had photographed more than 160 features, several serials and innumerable short films, lent his expertise to some of the mob action.

Phil Whitman, another ASC founder, and Friend Baker had been working with designer Sheely in developing special effects techniques for Universal. They were responsible for the flawless glass shots and hanging miniature effects which expanded the scope of the setting enormously, completing the job of transforming the backlot into old Paris. They also filmed, at considerable expense, a fantasy sequence depicting Phoebus' fevered dreams during his delirium, which was not used in the final cut because studio executives found it confusing. (Whitman, who eventually switched to directing, is best known for his special effects for Douglas Fairbank' *The Thief of Bagdad* of 1926, and it was Baker who staged the earthquake for the 1927 *Old San Francisco*).

Virgil Miller, ASC, who died in 1974, considered Chaney "really one of the greatest." Miller said, "I remember when we were both working at Universal and I was getting $18 a week and he was getting $35. One day he said 'Virg, I'm going to hit 'em for a raise.' That encouraged me and I told him I would ask for a raise of $2 a week for myself. We went to Mr. Laemmle and he was refused his raise and so he left Universal. I got my increase and stayed.

"A few years later, with Chaney an established star, the studio wanted him and no one else for *The Hunchback*. He wanted me on camera, so I sat in on the conferences. I was delighted to hear my old friend hold out firmly for an added $35 to be called for in his contract. He got it, too. His checks were made out for $2,535 every week—quite a raise!"

Chaney demanded that Miller should do all of his close-ups. Miller had photographed Chaney in *The Trap* (1922), one of the earliest pictures to use panchromatic film, and Chaney liked the closeups better than those in his other films. Miller was also involved in some special effects and some of the large scale action.

"Once, when Chaney was at the top of the cathedral set and I was down below at the camera, I noticed that he was still wearing his wrist watch," Miller recalled. "I signaled wildly and spelled out 'wrist' in sign language, which he understood because his parent were deaf and he stuffed the watch out of sight. After that I always checked him out with the six-inch lens so I got a good close look before we started. I hated to see him have to do the rough scenes over if he didn't have to."

Chaney was himself an enigma. Secretive, uncommunicative and unfriendly much of the time. He could be a staunch friend as well. His first wife considered him an implacable and unforgiving enemy and his son suggested he could be terribly cruel.

Patsy Ruth Miller recalled "Lon did a lot of directing on his films. He wasn't a very social man. I *never* saw him out socially, anywhere.

Jackie Coogan, who worked with Chaney in *Oliver Twist* in 1922, described him as "very short, very tan, bowlegged—a rough man, a tough man. A real loner—he made Howard Hughes look like Pia Zadora."

Grace Kingsley found Chaney without makeup "very good-looking, very charming, very well-dressed. You'd never recognize him if you met him on the street.

"'In one way,' he explained, as we watched the extras flock over to the set, 'makeup helps you in putting a characterization over. It aids you in getting into the spirit of the part while you are looking into the mirror, and when you see the interest in the faces of your co-workers. But in another way it hinders.

"'When makeup is as painful as that which I wore as Blizzard in *The Penalty*, when I had my legs strapped up and couldn't bear it more than 20 minutes at a time—when I have to be a cripple, as in *The Miracle Man*, or have to keep a certain attitude of body as I did in playing Yen Sen in *Shadows*, it sometimes takes a good deal of imagination to forget your physical suffering. Yet at that the subconscious mind has a marvelous way of making you keep the right attitudes and make the right gestures when you are actually acting.

"'But there's another thing. Though makeup helps the illusion in the minds of the audience, too, still it sometimes requires ten times the concentration to get results when a grotesque makeup is used, inasmuch as the face in its set lines, must necessarily fail to register many expressions.

"'And when it comes to a character like the Hunchback, which demands that the audience sympathize, despite his repugnant looks—well, it is the hardest part I ever played, that's all.

"'You see, I am following as closely as possible the best-known illustrations of Hugo's novel. Therefore, I am hunchbacked, knock-kneed, have one eye almost entirely closed by a big wart, have a hairy skin, and am altogether repulsive to look at. But this isn't all. I wear a cast that weighs about 50 pounds, and which, doubled up as I am, it is nothing short of agony to carry around.'

"'Can't you take off your makeup and rest once in a while?' I asked.

"'What? When it takes me three hours and a half exactly to put it on?' demanded Lon. 'I should say not! But at that, I cannot stand the makeup longer than six hours at a time. Yet I must not only get interest in the Hunchback; I must get the deepest sympathy for him from my audiences, else he fills my onlookers only with revulsion and disgust. But the thing I dread most of all is not the putting on of the makeup, not even the wearing of it, but the taking it off. See all the hair gone from my eyebrows? Pulled it out taking off my false eyebrows. And my eyelid is all burned from the application of strong glue. Also I'm sure I'm permanently warped about the shoulders from carrying that hump on my back.'"

Actually, there is one major difference in Chaney's Quasimodo and that of Hugo. The author described a giant of a man who had been put together badly. Chaney, being of no more than average size, opted for a misshapen dwarf, a concept the public accepted without complaint.

His performance is above criticism, a masterpiece of pantomime investing an initially terrifying creature with endearing qualities. It should be noted that despite his many deformities, the hunchback possesses great strength and agility. Instead of 'hamming it up," as actors in heavy makeup often do, Chaney gives the impression that Quasimodo has learned to live with his condition.

Chaney was (secretly) doubled by Universal's serial star, Joe Bonomo, in some of the more athletic scenes on the tower and in the climb down the facade to rescue Esmeralda.

Historically, the most remarkable aspects of the picture are the lighting and photography of the night scenes, which are far more sophisticated than any previous efforts of this kind. As Harry D. Brown, who headed the lighting crew, said in *American Cinematographer* (*October*, 1923), 'the exact reproduction of the cathedral of Notre Dame on American soil at Universal City...was in itself a triumph for the motion picture technician, but in spite of all the faithfulness with which the reproduction was executed it could not have been brought to the screen if it were not amply illuminated so that it could be photographed properly.

There was no precedent by which the electrical engineer or the chief cinematographer could be guided. The entire illumination and proper photography were matters that they themselves had to figure out, and succeed or fail according to their own judgement." Brown stated that "success in filming this record-size set depended basically on the human angle; that is, all the artistic and technical attainment would have been naught had the cinematographic and electrical divisions not worked in harmony so that efficiency in the two departments aided rather than hindered.

"Bob newhard, a member of the American Society of Cinematographers,... is an artist of highest quality as proved by his splendid photographic achievement in *The Hunchback*. More than that, he is a prince among men, and during the six months that we worked on the picture there never was a controversy of any kind between the cinematographer and the electrical department, although at time the natural difficulties involved in the making of the picture were such as would test the evenest of tempers. As photography is one of the outstanding features in this production, Newhard cannot be given too much credit for his work.

"In the first sequence, that of the 'Festival of Fools,' the illumination had to be of such an intensity that would permit us to shoot the same shots with considerably less light and a great deal more in later scenes. Baskets of burning substances being the source of light, scenes were staged in the dead of night with the building all dark and no sign of life, when we had mobs to rush in suddenly from all sides with burning torches, starting bonfires and setting buildings on fire. To light this action atmospherically correct required not only a different intensity of light, but made it necessary to gradually raise the illumination as the mobs advanced on the palace and the cathedral.

Used in the filming the festival were 37 sunlight arcs, five GE spots, 154 Winfields and 47 overheads, plus 62 practical arcs for the baskets. Much more complicated was the lighting for the "moonlight and torches" scenes, described by Brown as follows:

"...We started with 15 sunlight arcs and 10 120-ampere spots, the 15 sunlights arcs burning full capacity with 37 sunlight arcs burning at very low voltage. As the mobs advance with their torches, the voltage was raised to a certain intensity, gradually increasing when they started the bonfires, again raising a little more when the buildings were set on fire, while in the meantime the windows in all of the buildings were lighting up. By the time the scene had progressed to its height all sunlight arcs were burning at their full capacity, every window was lighted and the entire set was one blaze of light for fully 10 minutes. The total amount of equipment burning was 52 sunlight arcs, 21 GE high intensity spots, 20 120 ampere spots, 47 overheads and 49 Winfields.

"To supply energy to this equipment required seven motor generators sets, two of which were of 300-kilowatt capacity, and three gas-driven power wagons, which gave a total of 24,000 amperes actual load. This energy was distributed to the various parts of the set over approximately five miles of stage cable and feeders, terminating in 16 locations switchboards, and from there to the different pieces of apparatus. Energy was transmitted from the main sub-station at the front end of the plant through one mile of 2200-volt feeders. Earl Miller was chief gaffer in charge of the electrical crew, consisting of 139 men working under nine divisional foremen. Separate crews handled lights and feeders to save time when changing setups. Miller noted that "All during the period of production we had 17 other companies shooting on the lot. We had to furnish them with men and equipment, too, bring the total to 230 electricians on the payroll and practically all the available equipment in Lon Angeles."

Harry Brown was one of the finest electrical experts in the studios. A Spanish-American War veteran, he built the first large electrical signs in America at Atlantic City in 1901, and later pioneered in designing animated signs in Los Angeles. He built the first portable generator and developed the first radioactive machine for the treatment of cancer.

The chief gaffer was Earl Miller, who reminisced about the picture 17 years later, when as chief electrical engineer of RKO-Radio Pictures he worked on a new version of *Hunchback* (In *American Cinematographer* for February, 1940):

"*What* a winter that was; rain, fog, wind and mud—days, weeks, months of it. 'The largest artificially lighted motion picture set in the world,' they told us.

"Believe me, when I recall those foggy cold nights and the miles we walked, night after night, up and down that cobblestone street and out in the mud, I wonder how the picture was ever completed.

"In 1923, incandescent lights were not used for motion pictures. The street set was a few feet longer and wider than the one used in the 1939 version. There were only 56 24-inch sun arcs in the entire industry in Hollywood

The Festival of Fools.

Release prints were printed on Eastman tinted base stocks. This type of color was not intended to resemble what was called *natural color* processes, such as Technicolor or Kinemacolor, but was designed to intensify the changing moods of the drama. The transparent colors of the film base provided a tint under the black and white images- amber for the candlelighed interiors, blue for night effects, peachglow for the romantic scenes, a garish green for the torture chamber and evil plotting of Jehan, and magenta for the flashback sequence about the kidnapping of Crazy Godule's child. In some instances the images were toned as well, producing a blue on blue for some of the night scenes, sepia on ambertone, and, for the torture scenes, a glue tone over a green tint that is appropriately hideous.

The premiere was held at Carnegie Hall on August 30, 1923. Proceeds were donated to the American Legion's fund drive for a mountain camp for veterans. Regular showings at advances prices began at the Astor Theater on September 2. The picture received excellent reviews and drew huge crowds. Laemmle was so pleased that he commissioned an Austrian sculptor, A. Finta, to make a bust of Chaney as Quasimodo, which was installed in the lobby in anticipation of a long engagement. A special program was held at the Astor to celebrate the 100th performance on October 22, and another for the 200th showing during an entire week of late December. The picture was about 12,000 feet long during this special engagement, with a running time of 320 minutes. It was later cut to about 10,000 feet.

On February 17, 1924, *Hunchback* left the Astor to begin its first regular price release. Carl Edouarde, musical director of the Mark Strand Theater in New York, assisted by composer-orchestrator Cecil Copping, arranged an entirely new score for a 50-piece orchestra, mixed chorus, soloist and chimes. Domenico Savino composed the "love theme," "Twilight Hour," and classics by Arcedelt, Suk, Delsaux, Fourdrain and others were utilized.

In 1929, plans were formulated to remake *Hunchback* as a talkie, utilizing the same sets and props that had been created for the original. Chaney, now under contract to MGM, was not available for the part. Conrad Veidt was considered, but he returned to his native Germany after hearing his heavily accented performance in the part-talking versions of two other films. The Depression had placed Universal in financial straits which made production of a picture of such scope impractical, so Laemmle had to content himself with a reissue of the original with a new musical score synchronized on disks. Recorded under the supervision of Roy Hunter, the orchestra was conducted by Heinz Roemheld with original music by Roemheld and Sam A. Perry augmented with library music.

Remake plans resurfaced in 1931 with Bela Lugosi as the prospective Quasimodo. A new script was written and during the next four years Boris Karloff, Henry Hull, Peter Lorre and Edward G. Robinson were mentioned as possible Quasimodos. The project was still pending at the time Universal was bought by a group of financiers in March 1936. With the departure of the Laemmle family and friends, the new owners set about establishing a new image in which Gothic spectacle had no place.

Three years later, *Hunchback* was remade, superbly by RKO-Radio, with Charles Laughton. RKO built a new cathedral and environs at the RKO ranch in Encino. A French version, released in the U.S. in 1957, featured Anthony Quinn and Gina Lollobrigida.

Universal's Paris set saw a great deal of use until the cathedral and most of the other buildings were destroyed by fire in the 1960's.

After more than eight decades, the 1923 film has attained almost legendary status. Laemmle's long-time right-hand man, Robert Cochrane, said an interesting thing about it a long time ago:

"The great pictures. . . were, almost without exception, productions which never would have been made if the question of whether or not they should be attempted had been left to a popular vote. You could count in a minute all the people who predicted the great success of *The Hunchback of Notre Dame*. "

Minature model of Notre Dame constructed for long shots.

Credits

Carl Laemmle *presents* The Hunchback of Notre Dame; *directed by* Wallace Worsley; *based on the book by* Victor Hugo; *adapted by* Perley Poore Sheehan; *scenario by* Edward T. Lowe; *photographed by* Robert Newhard, ASC; *film editors,* Sidney Singerman, Maurice Pivar *and* Edward Curtiss; *art directors,* Elmer E. Sheeley *and* Sidney Ullman; *added photography by* Tony Kornmann, ASC, Virgil Miller, ASC, Charles Stumar, ASC, Stephen S. Norton, ASC; *photographic effects by* Philip H. Whitman, ASC, *and* Friend F. Baker, ASC; *supervised by* Irving S. Thalberg; *production manager,* George M. Stallings; *scuptures by* Finn Froelich *and* Charles Gemora; *costume supervision,* Col. Gordon McGee; *assistant art directors,* Steven Goosson, Charles D. Hall; *technical director,* Archie Hall; *continuity,* Charlotte Woods; *production assistants,* Edgar Stein, Capt. Albert Conti; *unit manager,* William J. Koenig; *electrical engineer,* Arthur Shadur; *lighting effects,* Harry D. Brown, Earl Miller; *lighting crew,* Carl Gotham, Bud Barner, G.H. Merhoff, Soldier Graham, Fred Seelock, Eddie Barry, Bert Kohler, Eric von Miessel, Wayne West; *assistant directors,* Jack Sullivan, James Dugan, William Wyler; *art titles,* Fred W. Archer, ASC; *stillmen,* Jack Freulich, ASC, Henry Freulich, ASC; *casting,* Fred Dating; *music(1923)* arranged by Hugo Riesenfeld; *music(1924)* arranged by Carl Eduoarde and Cecil Copping, *featuring "Twilight Hour" by* Domenico Savino; *music(1928)* arranged and composed by Heinz Roemheld *and* Sam A. Perry; *length* c. 12,000 feet; released September 6, 1923.

Cast

Quasimodo, Lon Chaney; *Esmeralda,* Patsy Ruth Miller; *Phoebus,* Norman Kerry; *Clopin,* Ernest Torrence; *Mme. de Gondelaurier,* Kate Lester, *Jehan,* Brandon Hurst; *Gringone,* Raymond Hatton; *King Louis XI,* Tully Marshall; *Dom Claude,* Nigel de Brulier; *King's Chamberlain,* Edwin Wallock; *Justice of the Court,* John Cossar; *M. Neufchatel,* Harry L. Van Meter; *Crazy Godule,* Gladys Brockwell; *Marie,* Eulalie Jensen; *Fleur de Lys,* Winifred Bryson; *M. le Torteru,* Nicolai de Ruiz; *Josephus,* William Parke Sr.; *Charmolu's Assistant,* W. Ray Myers; *Charmolu,* Roy Laidlaw; *Hook-hand,* Robert Kortman; *Fat Man,* Harry Holman; *Double for Chaney,* Joe Bonomo; *and* Ethan Laidlaw, Al Ferguson, John George, George MacQuarrie, Albert MacQuarrie, Jay Hunt, Harrison DeVere, Pearl Tupper, Eva Lewis, Jane Sherman, Helen Brunneau, Gladys Johnston, Lydia Yeamans Titus, Alex Manuel, Arthur Hurni, Rene Traveletti.

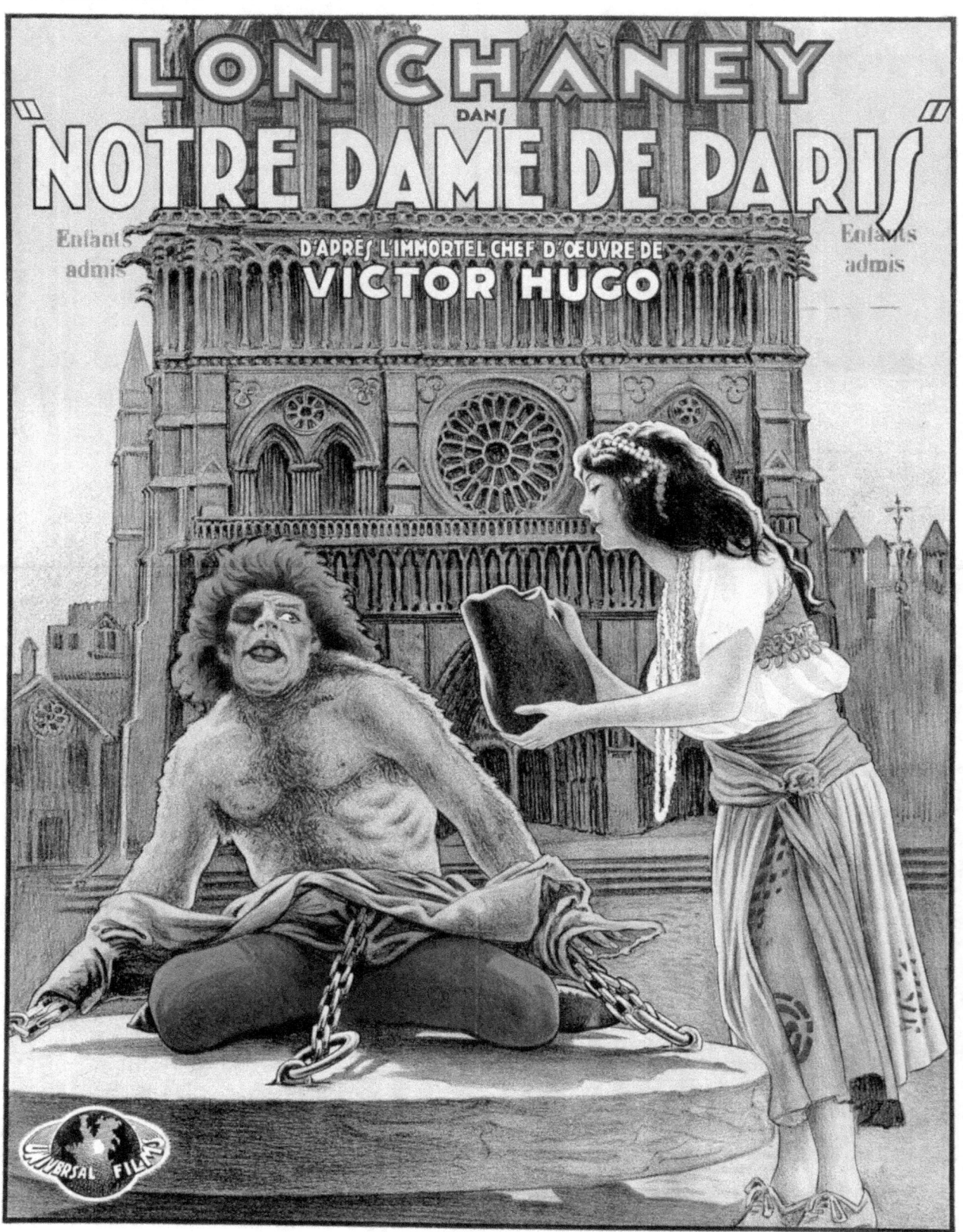

NOTES ON THE RECONSTRUCTION OF THE FILM

Unidentified, comedian Ed Wynn and Lon Chaney

Although it was Thalberg's genius that caused the existence of the film from it's first conception, he never got the chance to finish it for he left Universal Studios a few months after the filming began to become Louis B. Mayer's production manager. Also much of the credit goes to Chaney himself, for in the family files of Chaney's manager at the time, Albert Grasso there is documentation that Chaney himself was in New York seeking to get the rights to the book in 1922.

The supervision of the film was turned over to Wallace Worsley, also adding much stress to his duty as Director. He was actually relieved when Chaney took some of the directorial duties. Chaney even had a great deal of control of the final editing of the film. But the new General Manager of Universal, Julius Bernheim and Production Manager Homer A Boushy actually completed the production.

Julius Bernheim was, like Thalberg, a very young man when assigned the position of General Manager. He began his career in films with the old IMP Company as a studio helper and later went to the Distribution Department as a poster boy for Laemmle's Film Service in Minneapolis. He quickly moved up in position to assistant exchange manager and two years later joined the staff at Universal City as Business Manager

Two illustrations from Lon Chaney's personal copy of "The Hunchback" on which he based his makeup for Quasimodo.

Homer A. Boushey was a production manager for Essanay until it went out of business. The *Universal Weekly* from February 24, 1923 states: "Many of today's best known stars got their start under Boushey's direction, and a number of them owe their rise to his keen foresight. Such stars as Virginia Valli, Francis X. Bushman, Bryant Washburn, Henry B. Walthall and Ben Turpin did their first good work while Boushey was in charge at the Essanay Studio.

"Since Essanay quit producing, Boushey has been associated with George K. Spoor in the Spoor-Thompson Machine Company of Chicago, a concern handling projection appliances. His acquisition by Mr. Laemmle is considered of great promise to the Universal Company, since his unusual insight into production problems especially fits him for the control of such a large studio."

There is no true way of confirming if Irving Thalberg had worked behind the scenes on the completion of the film or if he advised or gave Chaney the benefit of his experience. But he did attend the premiere at Carnegie Hall, New York City, before its public opening at the Astor on Broadway.

From the *Universal Weekly*, September 15, 1923:

"Before an audience of prominent New Yorkers, society folks, stage and screen fold, editors, literary personages and artists, which vented its enthusiasm at the final fade-out by round after round of applause, *The Hunchback of Notre Dame*, Carl Laemmle's wonder picture adapted from Victor Hugo's immortal romance, had its premiere showing in the Astor Theatre last Sunday.

"The annals of picturedom never before chronicled an opening so colorful, amid settings so well calculated to establish the screen as a peer of all other arts. Mysteriously the words had gotten around among the cognoscenti of the great metropolis that there was something worth of the name of art, and so the Astor Theatre was crowded with the elite.

The unusual make-up of the audience emphasized all the more their outburst at the end—and outburst which did not lessen until Lon Chaney, the star, had been half pushed, half-dragged to the stage that he might stutter his thanks in the din, while the hundreds present voiced their approbation of his marvelous portrayal of Quasimodo, Hugo's repulsive but appealing hunchback bellringer."

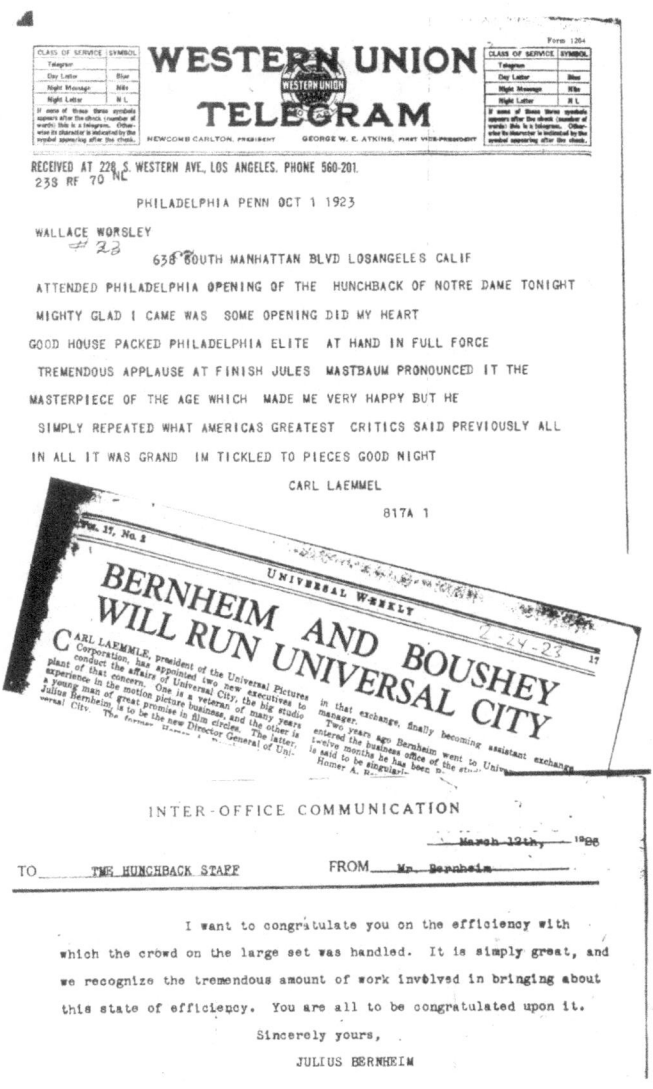

The premiere was a sterling tribute to Chaney, whose great acting made *The Hunchback of Notre Dame* human, to Wallace Worsley, whose directorial conception made the picture a masterpiece of setting and atmosphere, and to Carl Laemmle, the Universal chief, whose farsightedness envisioned Hugo's story as a great screen epic."

(No mention of Irving Thalberg at all. Apparently breaking his engagement to Rosabelle Laemmle could have been timed better but you have to admire his courage and principles)

"The ovation also accorded praise to Ernest Torrence, who handled a remarkable role in the picture and who was present at the premiere, and for Hugo Reisenfeld, who staged the production and gave to it its thematic musical setting. The public as well as the reviewers commented

favorably on the excellence of the work of practically every principal in the cast, especially that of Patsy Ruth Miller as Esmeralda, Raymond Hatton as Gringoire, Norman Kerry as Phoebus and Tully Marshall as Louis XI"

The reports of Lon Chaney's suffering for his art were not exaggerated—the harness and hump are in a storeroom of The Museum of Natural History in Los Angles (Among many articles and makeup boxes donated by his 2nd wife Hazel in the early 1930s)

But he did not perform all his own stunts. Following is an account recorded by the great stunt man Joe Bonomo from his book *The Strongman*, published by Bonomo Studios Inc. in 1968. (For Chaney fans, lucky enough to find a copy of the book, it also contains rare pictures from *A Light in the Dark* directed by Clarence Brown with interesting behind-the-scene stories during the shooting in New York City.)

[Joe Bonomo]

"When the cab pulled up at the studio entrance, you can picture my amazement at seeing thousands—actually THOUSANDS of people milling about

I went through the big arch to the front door of the Executive Building. As I started up the steps I was intercepted by a big Irishman in uniform—a studio cop.

"It's okay." I told him, "I'm Joe Bonomo."

"I don't care if you're Joe Eskimo," he retorted. "Wait over there with the rest of the mob."

"Mind telling me who they are? . . . I'm new here."

"You MUST be," he said, sizing me up. "They're extras. They'll be workin' in *The Hunchback of Notre Dame*—the new Lon Chaney picture."

"I'll probably be playing in that," I said, "I'm a personal friend of Lon Chaney's." and I started up the steps again. But he suddenly had me by the coat-sleeve and jerked me down.

"It won't work, kid. If you're after a job, get in that mob with the rest of 'em. Now start movin'."

"Oh, I've got a job," I said. "In fact, I've got a seven year contract."

"I'll BET you have." He was propelling me down the steps. "What are you—some kind of Nut or somethin'?"

"And here's my letter of introduction to Irving Thalberg," I said, showing it to him. He stared at the letter, bug-eyed.

"Pardon ME, Mister Bonomo. Right in there." He waved me back up the steps to the main door. I went through it feeling nine feet tall. I was ushered right into Mr. Thalberg's office.

Irving Thalberg, top producer for the studio, was a small man with sharp but sensitive eyes. He shook my hand warmly and welcomed me to Universal City.

"Is everything I've heard about you true, Joe?" he asked.

"Well I don't know, Mr. Thalberg," I laughed, "What did you hear?"

"Some fabulous things about your stunt work with Pathe. And I saw a film you made for Nathan Hirsh."

"Heck, Mr. Thalberg, I was only an amateur, then. You should see me *now*!"

He smiled, "Just don't try to do it all at once, Joe. We'd like to keep you around for a while."

Then he pushed a button for an assistant-assistant, and instructed him to show me around. I was introduced to a lot of big people, shown the dressing rooms, the special costume department, the make-up department and some of the studios. I noticed the stars all had their names on their dressing room doors. I wondered again if I shouldn't change my name to Vincent.

At the end of the tour I had a warm feeling of being "in". Then I was introduced to Fred Datig, the head casting director. He had adding machine eyes that were totaling me up as he shook my hand.

"As long as you're HERE, Mr. Bonomo..."

"Just call me Joe," I said.

"Well as long as you're here, Joe, you may as well go to work."

"The sooner the better," I said. . .and I meant it.

He called another assistant-assistant. "Fit Mr. Bonomo to a Lon Chaney costume. He may be doubling in the *Hunchback*. Then take him out to the Cathedral. So long and good luck, Joe."

Joe Bonomo on the Hunchback set

What a thrill! My first day in Hollywood and I was doubling the title role in *The Hunchback of Notre Dame*. It wasn't quite like playing the lead. . .but Rome wasn't built in a day and neither is a Hollywood star.

Properly costumed, I was taken to the back lot where a replica of Notre Dame Cathedral had been erected. Lon Chaney spotted me immediately and seemed overly pleased to see me.

"Hey, Wally," he called to Wallace Worsley, the director, "our troubles are over. Here's that Bonomo guy I've been telling you about."

You will recall Lon had been one of the stars of *A Light in the Dark* that I worked on with Hope Hampton

"Worsley seemed delighted. "Boy, are we glad to see *You*!"

I found out why as soon as he told me what my first assignment was to be. Whoever doubled for Chaney, as the Hunchback, had to slide down a rope, from the Cathedral tower to the ground—a good hundred and fifty feet. The slide had to be done fast, and they weren't sure it could be done successfully. At least, no one was willing to try. A long, fast slide down a rope may look easy, but actually it is one of the most difficult of stunts, and all stuntmen know it.

"But Joe'll do it, Chaney said, recalling my recklessness back East.

"Not so fast," I hedged, "let me see the equipment."

One of the other stuntmen eagerly handed me the heavy leather gloves that were to be used. I looked at them, then looked up at that hundred and fifty feet of rope, dangling from the tower window.

"And you want this done fast?" I asked

"Gotta be one continuous fast slide," said Worsley.

"Not in these gloves," I said, "it would be suicide."

"You've changed since New York," said Chaney. "Losing your nerve?"

"No," I said cheerfully, "I've just gotten a little smarter. I'll need a couple of hours to get some special gloves made."

At this Worsley exploded. I might have been fired on the spot had not another stuntman, (Harry, I heard someone call him,) stepped in.

"Let *me* have the gloves," he said, "I'll do it."

I suppose he figured this was his chance to gain a reputation, even though he must have known how dangerous the stunt was. He evidently was willing to gamble.

He got into the costume, went up in the tower, the cameras started turning and he started down. Those of you who saw the picture will remember that slide.) I knew he was going too fast. About two-thirds of the way down he let out a tortured groan, let go of the rope, and fell. When we reached him, he had a broken leg, to say nothing of serious hand and leg burns. The gloves were still smoking—they had burned right through.

A consultation followed and Worsley asked me how long it would take to make the special gloves. I said about two hours; so while I hustled off to the costume department they switched to another sequence.

I made the gloves myself. I got the heaviest leather ones I could find and lined them with special thick sheets of tin foil. . .the same stuff used on gum wrappers. . .to insulate against the heat. I also had long strips of foil sewed in the inside of my tights, from crotch to ankle. With this equipment the stunt was easy. We got perfect footage on the first attempt. The slide was sensational.

It never occurred to anyone that the already scorched rope might have broken while I was coming down—but it didn't—which goes to prove that stunting is more dangerous than putting your head in an alligator's mouth. Incidentally, a bit later on in this story I do that, too—again proving that if you insist on using your brain, you don't belong in this business.

Well, that was my first day in Hollywood. I had appeared in *The Hunchback of Notre Dame*. Though audiences would never know it was Bonomo, I was there just the same. I had gained a reputation as an efficient and safe stuntman."

The film is readily available in its shortened version on DVD, video tape and 16mm copies, the former Blackhawk films print from the Kit Parker collection being the best. Those familiar with the film will recognize immediately the cut scenes in the script portion of this book.

I had originally intended to present only these cut scenes. However the quality of Mr. Worsley's original nitrate key book from 8x10 negatives gave me an opportunity that I could not disregard as an historian, for if we never find an original 35mm complete print, the photographs deserve to be preserved as it might be the only chance we have to view the majestic quality achieved by the craftsmen who made the film.

Most of the cut footage dealt with Ernest Torrences' scenes and in still-form do not do justice to his acting ability. There were several outstanding scenes for Lon Chaney and Patsy Ruth Miller. While Esmeralda is protected by the sanctuary of the church Quasimodo goes to a merchant and buys her cloth for new clothes. The merchant tries to cheat him and you will see the results.

Also Quasimodo sneaks into Esmeralda's old room in the Court of Miracles and brings a caged bird to her room in the bell tower of Notre Dame in hopes of pleasing her.

Another theme that was cut was of Jehan's delving into the black arts. He was obsessed with alchemy and while plotting to steal the treasure of Notre Dame from the King, he spent his time in a primitive laboratory trying to turn lead into gold. Behind the laboratory was a black curtain concealing the symbols of the Satanic Cults.

Also scenes dealing with Jehan's jealousy of his saintly brother were deleted, including his attempted fratricide during the ending battle scenes, when he is refused the key to the King's treasure room.

Phoebus, unaware of Esmeralda's rescue by Quasimodo dreams of being reunited with his love and he serenades her with a lute.

Esmeralda, after being returned to the Beggar's court by Clopin from Phoebus' party is belittled by Clopin in front of the other gypsies, a frustrated lover, not as a protective father as the cut print seems to infer.

However as film historian/musician/Chaney expert Jon Mirsalis wrote in the last volume of this series, *A Blind Bargain* (Goldwyn, 1922), there is no way to determine the extent of the original release without a cutting continuity. (The film described and footage noted on paper) and even Mr. Worsley's script is missing a few scenes, giving an indication that the annotations were made for the editor and not the original photographer.

Philip J. Riley
April 29, 2012

Wallace Worsley (left 2nd row) began his film career at the Brunton Studios (later Paramount). Pictured are Robert Brunton, center—the stars, cast, crew and technicians.

Wallace Worsley, Elmer Sheeley, Sidney Ullman and Charles Hall begin construction of the sets.

Actual illustrations from which Universal's Art Department based their sets. Also shown on this and the following pages are Elmer Sheeley's drawings of the scenes as they finally appeared in the film.

PUBLICITY SECTION

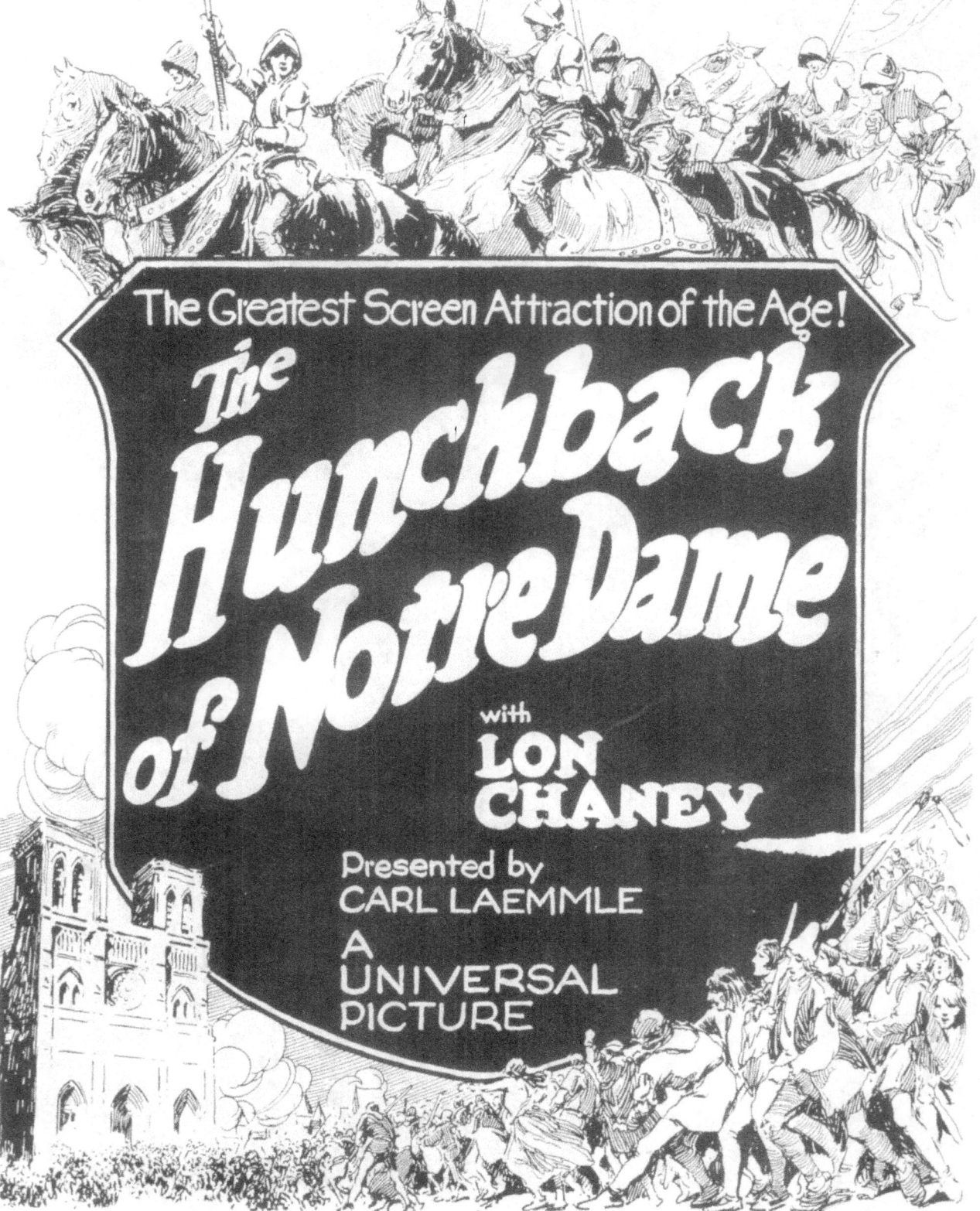

12 Pages of Smashing Publicity Material on the *Stupendous Universal Production* "The HUNCHBACK of NOTRE DAME"

AT A GLANCE

Title .... "THE HUNCHBACK OF NOTRE DAME"

Brand .... Universal Production.

Star .... LON CHANEY.

Supported by .... Patsy Ruth Miller, Ernest Torrence, Norman Kerry, Raymond Hatton, Tully Marshall, Brandon Hurst, Nigel de Brullier, Harry Von Meter, Caesar Gravina, Eulalie K. Jensen, Kate Lester, Winifred Bryson, and 62 other noted artists, with 3950 additional players.

Directed by ...... Wallace Worsley.

Written by ...... Victor Hugo.

Adapted by ..... Perley Poore Sheehan.

Scenario by ..... Edward T. Lowe, Jr.

Production Mgr .. George M. Stallings.

Head Cameraman, Robert Newhard.

Art Direction .... E. E. Sheeley and Sydney Ullman.

THUMB NAIL THEME

The story centers around the life of "Quasimodo," the deformed bell-ringer of the famous Cathedral of Notre Dame in Paris. He is prevailed upon by Jehan, the arch-deacon's evil brother, to kidnap the fair Esmeralda, the ward of the king of the underworld. Esmeralda is rescued by dashing Captain Phoebus and taken under his wing. Quasimodo is sentenced to be lashed in the public square. While he is suffering under the sting of the whip Esmeralda comes and brings him water. From that time on he is her devoted slave. Jehan and Clopin learn that Captain Phoebus plans to wed Esmeralda and do all in their power to break up the affair, but fail. Jehan then stabs Phoebus and lays the blame on Esmeralda. She is sentenced to die, but escapes to the Cathedral where she takes refuge. Clopin, egged on by Jehan, tries to storm the Cathedral while crafty Jehan uses the time to loot the treasure vaults. Quasimodo, single-handed, battles off the invaders with streams of molten lead, but gives his life in saving Esmeralda. Phoebus, who was only wounded, comes to the rescue and saves the church and his sweetheart. As they clasp each other to their hearts, Quasimodo rings their happiness and his own dirge.

Cash in on this Proven Publicity

There is one fact we want to stress right at the start, and that is that every story in this book is proven copy—copy that has passed the desks of dramatic and motion picture editors in New York, Boston, Chicago and half a dozen other large cities. It is a compilation of the work of half a dozen of the best press agents in the country and you should have no difficulty in "planting" it with your local editors, if you will only follow one simple rule:

Have the story you want to use typewritten, it only costs a few cents, and in the upper right hand corner write the name and title of the editor to whom you are submitting it. Pasted copy finds the waste-paper basket, as it deserves, six times out of ten. One more important thing—if you haven't got a press agent, take the copy to the newspaper yourself. Take only one story a day, don't slam down a press book on an editor's desk and expect him to make a choice for you. He's got plenty of work of his own to do.

Start work on this production just as soon as you book it. Get over the story about the negotiations and then follow it right up with short notes, feature stories and readers, and don't forget cuts. If your papers use Saturday or Sunday layouts, see that the editor has a number of photos from which to choose by the Tuesday preceding date of publication, and make it a point to get your Sunday copy in early.

Be sure that the Managing, City, Dramatic and Photoplay Editors all have seats for the opening night. Take them around yourself. Don't use a boy for this purpose.

Program Cut

Scene Cut No. 13

THE STELLAR CAST

QUASIMODO	LON CHANEY
Esmeralda	Patsy Ruth Miller
Phoebus De Chateaupers	Norman Kerry
Madame De Gondelaurier	Kate Lester
Fleur de Lys	Winnifred Bryson
Dom Claude	Nigel De Brulier
Jehan	Brandon Hurst
Clopin	Ernest Torrence
King Louis XI	Tully Marshall
Mons. Neufchatel	Harry Von Meter
Gringoire	Raymond Hatton
Mons. Le Torteru	Nick De Ruiz
Marie	Eulalie Jensen
Charmolu's Assistant	W. Ray Meyers
Josephus	Wm. Parke, Sr.
Sister Gadule	Gladys Brockwell
Judge of the Court	John Cossar
King's Chamberlain	Edwin Wallack

Data on Feature Players

LON CHANEY— born in Colorado Springs, Colo., has been connected with stage all his life, starting as boy of ten in stock company. Played in several musical comedies in Chicago and New York and then decided to seek fame in pictures. His career has been a succession of fights against natural obstacles but he won out and is now admittedly the screen's finest character actor. His first big hit was "The Miracle Man," followed by "The Penalty," "The Shock" and "Shadows." Critics unite in declaring that he has accomplished the greatest role of all time in this production.

PATSY RUTH MILLER—born in St. Louis, educated in convent in that city. She went into pictures because she was fascinated with the thought of being an actress. She appeared in minor roles for two years-and-a-half and then got her big chance in this Universal production.

ERNEST TORRENCE—born in Edinburgh, Scotland, started out to be musician, graduated from Stuttgart Academy of Music and Royal Conservatory. Was offered a chance to go on stage in England and has been on stage ever since. Featured comedian in some of Broadway musical comedies. He will be remembered as the star of the "Covered Wagon" and "Tolerable David."

BRANDON HURST—born in London, educated Broadstead College, has been on stage for twenty-five years, leading man for many famous stars, including Minnie Maddern Fiske and Lillian Russell, author of several successful stage playlets.

RAYMOND HATTON—born in Red Oak, Iowa, while father and mother were playing there with show. Has been in theatrical profession all his life. Plays the part of the sentimental poet in this production.

NORMAN KERRY—born in Rochester, N. Y., educated at St. John's Military Academy, Annapolis, Md. Called at studio one day with salesman friend and was hired as type. Has been in pictures as featured player ever since, notably in "Merry-Go-Round."

TULLY MARSHALL—born in Nevada City, Cal., has spent thirty-five years in business as call-boy, prompter, stage manager, actor, star and producer. Has been in pictures for six years. Makes a masterpiece of his role in "The Hunchback of Notre Dame."

Story of "THE HUNCHBACK OF NOTRE DAME" Will Be Found On Page Twelve

GENERAL ADVANCE

Start Plugging Weeks Before Your Play Date!

STRAND GETS HUNCHBACK NOTRE DAME

Production Which Has Taken Country by Storm Booked For Early Showing

Following lengthy negotiations between Carl Laemmle, president of Universal Pictures Corporation and Manager ..... of the ..... Theatre, contracts were signed yesterday for the early presentation here of "The Hunchback of Notre Dame." Booking of this wonder picture is one of the most important announcements in local theatrical circls in many weeks.

The fame of the Victor Hugo classic in its celluloid form has been so generally known that it is hardly necessary to dwell upon its greatness. During the first five months following its premier at the Astor Theatre in New York City it was shown only in the largest legitimate theatres of the United States. It established a record at the Astor by running for more than six months to capacity crowds.

Lon Chaney heads the notable cast of 3091 players which includes such brilliant artists as Patsy Ruth Miller, Ernest Torrence, Brandon Hurst, Tully Marshall, Nigel de Brulier and Winnifred Bryson. The majority of the seventy-five principals are as well known on the stage as they are on the screen. The production in its film form has been endorsed by the clergy of all denominations.

SCREEN BEAUTY — Patsy Ruth Miller, who plays the role of Esmeralda in Universal's superfeature, "The Hunchback of Notre Dame." Coming soon.

Scene Cut No. 18

COSTLY FILM IS COMING TO STRAND

"Hunchback of Notre Dame" is Changed to Avoid Offending Any Creed.

At the ...... Theatre ...... night will be held the local premier of "The Hunchback of Notre Dame," the picturized version of Victor Hugo's classic which has come down through the ages with untarnished lustre. Aside from the natural interest in the screening of such a notable masterpiece, there is a genral interest to see the prodgction which required more than a year to film and on which more than $1,500,000 was expended.

Liberties were taken with the story—being defend on the ground that a production intended for all classes could not afford to offend any particular religious denomination—but while many shook their heads and predicted dire failure as a result, the changes were all approved by the New York critics after the world premier in the Astor Theatre.

Certainly all the elements of success are contained in the production—Universal had the story, the title, the cast and unlimited funds. Local verification of the New York opinion will be watched with interest. The selection of Lon Chaney for the title role of "Quasimodo, the Hunchback," was a logical one. His amazing ability to portray characters such as he played in "The Miracle Man," "Outside the Law," and "Shadows," roles which required contortion ability as well as unusual dramatic training, is well known. It is claimed that Chaney required four and one-half hours daily to don the make-up of the deformed bell-ringer of Notre Dame.

The Cathedral of Notre Dame was reconstructed in its entirety at Universal City for the production, as were eight squares of Parisian streets of the period of Louis XI.

Script Change Lauded By Critics

"Hunchback of Notre Dame" In Film Form Held Superior To the Book.

The local premier of the widely heralded Universal production "The Hunchback of Notre Dame" will take place at the .... Theatre ...... night. Prior to the world premier at the Astor Theatre in New York City officials of the corporation were reticent in discussing the plot changes made in the immortal Victor Hugo masterpiece, beyond stating that certain changes had been made to avoid offending any religious denomination. A careful reading of the New York criticisms, however, divulges that the changes were generally endorsed and simply deleted some of the gruesomeness and switched the importance of some of the characters in order to make the ending more acceptable to theatre-goers. It is of interest to note that for the first time the critics approved changes in a masterpiece.

From all available sources of information Universal has reached the zenith with this production. Certainly no production was ever made with better ingredients of success. The producer had the story—one that is filled with action; he had the greatest of character stars, Lon Chaney; a capable director in Wallace Worsley, and unlimited funds and studio facilities not excelled anywhere in the world. The fact that the total cost was just a trifle under a million and a half dollars gives some idea of the greatness of the production.

The noted cast in addition to Lon Chaney includes Ernest Torrence, Patsy Ruth Miller, Norman Kerry, Nigel de Brulier, Tully Marshall, Brandon Hurst, Gladys Brockwell, and 67 other featured principals, as well as some 3500 extras.

ADVANCE NOTES

Lon Chaney, star of "The Hunchback of Notre Dame," the costly Universal production, which comes to the ...... Theatre for a limited engagement starting ......, spent three months in Parisian libraries and prowling throughout the city's highways and byways, in order to gather the right angle on his role. This explains one of the reasons why this sterling actor's work all stands forth above all other artists'.

Nigel de Brulier, former member of Henry Irving's company, and the Dom Claude of the Universal production, "The Hunchback of Notre Dame," which opens a limited engagement at the ...... Theatre on ......, is a student of ancient history and eastern theosophy. His natural quiet and unassuming demeanor admirably suits him for his part in this drama, but his work stands out in any company he may be cast with. It was he who played the symbolical character of Tohernoff in "The Four Horsemen," John the Baptist in Nazimova's "Salo- and Pir Kahn in Kipling's "Without Benefit of Clergy." De Brulier was noted as a gifted actor almost from the first day he stepped foot on a stage.

Many and most perplexing are the problems confronting the director of a large motion picture production. Mob scenes seem to be the ones that call for extraordinary talent in directing and this Wallace Worsley possesses. He proved it in connection with the filming of Universal's "Hunchback of Notre Dame" by using for the first time a radio amplification device which carried his voice to all sections during the scenes in which an army of 3000 storms historic Notre Dame Cathedral. This is the production which opens a limited engagement at the ...... Theatre, staring on ....

When one sees "The Hunchback of Notre Dame" on the screen of the ...... Theatre next ......, the realization of the tremendousness of the effort is bound to be brought home, but even at that one will have little idea of the work behind the scenes. One of the tasks that faced the technical staff was that of feeding 3000 persons daily on the lot. The problem was taken up with officers of the Quartermaster's Corps of the United States Army and experts were loaned Universal. It is interesting to note that the 3000 were fed lunch and were back at work in thirty minutes.

A consistent run of twenty years and still going strong. That is the remarkable record established by "A Stolen Kiss," a one-act play written by Brandon Hurst, who enacts the role of Jehan in Victor Hugo's masterpiece, "The Hunchback of Notre Dame," which Universal is presenting at the ...... Theatre for a limited engagement starting next .... Hurst won wide note as a playywright before he became an actor. In London, where he was born, he wrote a farce which scored a great success at the Trafalgar Theatre. He is the author of more than twenty one-act plays. Several of his works have been produced at the Lambs Club Frolics in New York City during the past two years.

Radio amplification was utilized by Universal to direct the 3000 odd players during the filming of "The Hunchback of Notre Dame," the stupendous spectacle which comes to the .... Theatre on .... The result is said to be mob scenes in which each player enacts his role in perfect harmony with the rest of the action. The director, Wallace Worsley, used a telephone instead of a megaphone. Lon Chaney is the star of the production.

Some idea of the immensity of "The Hunchback of Notre Dame," the Universal production which comes to the .... Theatre on ......, may be gained from the fact that the Cathedral of Notre Dame was reconstructed in its entirety at Universal City. Artists and students of architecture have marveled at the way each detail has been reproduced down to the last small gargoyle. Lon Chaney is the star of the production, which was filmed under the direction of Wallace Worsley.

During the filming of the Universal production, "The Hunchback of Notre Dame," each player was requested to fill out a sheet giving a history of their life and theatrical experience. One question was on what the player's most exciting experience. Patsy Ruth Miller, the Esmeralda of the production, answered by saying "Trying to make the dumb goat in this picture, act like an actor and a gentleman." One gathers that aforementioned animal got Patsy's goat. "The Hunchback of Notre Dame" will be seen at the ...... Theatre starting next ....

Lon Chaney, star of Universal's "Hunchback of Notre Dame," started life as a dancer in musical comedy, a fact that is not generally known. He was one of the main stays of the famous light opera organization gathered together by Mort Singer and Joe Howard at the La Salle Theatre in Chicago. He appeared in such famed shows as "The Time, Place and Girl," and "The Umpire." When the Universal production comes to the ...... Theatre on ......, he will be seen in the heaviest role ever essayed, surely proving the versatility of this remarkable actor.

There probably never lived an author with the dynamic power with which Victor Hugo invested his stories and of all his writings none contained more action or romance than the one that is admitted to be his masterpiece, "The Hunchback of Notre Dame," which has been made into a film supreme and is being offered by Universal at the ...... Theatre, starting next ...... afternoon. The love story that runs through the play is one that will have a special appeal to the women.

For once changes were made in a film version of a well-known masterpiece and the producer commended instead of condemned. The production which accomplished this hitherto impossible feat is "The Hunchback of Notre Dame," which Universal is offering at the ...... Theatre starting next ...... for an engagement of ...... days only. The changes were made to avoid giving offense to any particular religious denomination and the screen version has been endorsed by the clergy of every denomination. Critics admit that these changes were vital under the circumstances.

It is easy to understand the appeal that Universal's production, "The Hunchback of Notre Dame," has to women because it has probably the most thrilling of all romances interwoven throughout its stirring action. In each city where it has been presented the matinee business has been a revelation and a careful check up among patrons of the fair sex proved that it was because all were familiar with the love theme of the great Victor Hugo classic. The local engagement of the production starts at the ...... Theatre next ...... The engagement is limited to ..... days.

The musical score for "The Hunchback of Notre Dame" was probably the most costly ever written. It was prepared by Dr. Hugo Risenfeld, director of one of the largest musical organizations in New York, and a staff of six assistants. It took more than eight weeks to compile. The music is of vital importance in providing the proper "atmosphere" with a production of this kind and President Carl Laemmle, of Universal, spared no expense to insure a perfect presentation.

"Hunchback of Notre Dame" Most Widely Praised Film

ERNEST TORRENCE, one of the stellar players in Universal's great production of the Hugo classic.

Scene Cut No. 19

Unusual interest attaches to the presentation of the Universal special "The Hunchback of Notre Dame," at the ...... Theatre on ...... evening. For many months it has been widely heralded as the last word in cinema art, but this was taken with the proverbial grain of salt until after the world premier at the Astor Theatre in New York City. The Gotham critics shattered all precedent by using up more adjectives of praise than even the most intrepid press-agent would dare employ.

Carl Laemmle, president of Universal, realized the great risk he took in making changes in the masterpiece of Victor Hugo; changes which he defended, however, on the ground that as a drama must entertain all classes, anything offensive to any religious denomination must be deleted. And, strange to say, all of the changes were heartily endorsed by the critics.

Lon Chaney, one of the greatest character actors on either stage or screen, plays the difficult role of "Quasimodo," the hunchback. He is supported by such well-known players as Patsy Ruth Miller, Ernest Torrence, Norman Kerry, Nigel de Brulier, Tully Marshall, Brandon Hurst and Gladys Brockwell. There are 75 principals and 3500 extras in the cast.

The entire Cathedral of Notre Dame was reconstructed at Universal City as well as eight squares of Parisian streets and houses of the period of Louis XI.

Several curious persons have asked if it would not have been more feasible to have taken the company to Paris and "shoot" the scenes there rather than to go to the expense of rebuilding the costly sets at Universal City. There is no question but that this would have cut the cost of construction work in half, but what many persons fail to realize is that obtaining permission from the authorities of the French and church governments to photograph the Cathedral itself was something that was impossible. They have constantly refused similar requests.

The task of building the settings for this production was one of the most stupendous ever undertaken. Carl Laemmle sent a staff of twenty technical experts to Paris, where they spent six months in running through library files and prowling through dusky archives in order to get each detail true to the period of the picture. Incidentally, this is another reason why it was impossible to film the production in Paris. The French metropolis of today is not the same city it was in the days of Louis XI.

Probably no stage or screen drama has been given such uniformly high praise from critics from coast to coast as "The Hunchback." For the first five months after its world premier it was shown only in the largest legitimate theatres of the larger cities of the country. This was a severe test for any picture, and the fact that it came through with glowing colors, shows what a wonder film it must be.

Page Two

42

GENERAL ADVANCE

Each Story Is Written With A Real News Angle!

DEFIES ALL PRECEDENT, WINS OUT

President of Universal Pictures Proves It's Possible to Please with Classics.

Carl Laemmle, president of Universal, has achieved the impossible. He has taken one of the classics of all time, taken a blue pencil and made several decided changes in the story, filmed it without thinking of cost, and then brought the complete product to the screen, and—won the unanimous endorsement of every critic in New York City, and other large cities of America and England.

When he first announced his intention of filming "The Hunchback of Notre Dame," production experts declared it was impossible, first because the French would not permit the historic and sacred Cathedral to be used as a background, and secondly, that the cost of reconstructing it in this country was prohibitive. "C. L.," as he is popularly called, went right ahead. If he couldn't "shoot" in Paris, he could here and he did. He spent $500,000 alone and reconstructed the entire cathedral at Universal City.

Next the literary world took up the cudgels. Hugo's tale was too blood-thirsty, too gruesome, but C. L. smiled again, made changes and took New York by storm. The impossible had been accomplished, but the total cost was in excess of $1,500,000.

A week from Monday night at the ...... Theatre, local theatregoers will have a chance to see for themselves just what this production really is. Don Allen, writing in the N. Y. Evening World, calls it "the picture the world has been waiting for, the last word in art and entertainment." Lon Chaney heads the stellar cast.

"Hunchback" To Be Seen Here Tomorrow

All Who Have Seen Great Film Epic Predict Record Success Locally

...... tomorrow will have its first opportunity of seeing the massive production which swept into overnight fame in New York and made the critics so far forget themselves as to use up nearly the entire stock of laudatory adjectives in the English language in their reviews. As a general rule, success on Broadway does not always spell success here, but local theatre-goers who visited the Astor Theatre in New York, the first of the metropolitan runs, expressed the opinion that the hit will be even greater here, where Hugo's great work is so widely known. Seems like this is a reflection on Gotham's literary leanings.)

From all advance accounts Universal has all the ingredients of a great success—a story that is internationally famous, that is replete with action, albeit somewhat gruesome, the greatest of character stars in Lon Chaney, an excellent supporting cast, studio facilities, and unlimited funds. It may be divulging a trade secret, but it has leaked out that Universal, to guard against the least chance of adverse criticism, called in the director of New York's greatest cinema houses and one of the leading newspaper editors and had them do the final touches. The result is said to mark the dawn of a new day in cinema art and one that has made Carl Laemmle's slogan of "Better and finer productions" an absolute fact.

Lon Chaney, admittedly the finest interpreter of unusual character roles on either stage or screen, plays the stellar part of "Quasimodo," with Ernest Torrence as "Clopin, the underworld king," and Patsy Ruth Miller as "Esmeralda." Seventy-two other noted performers have featured parts, while two hundred players interpret smaller roles with the mob scenes numbering slightly in excess of 3500 persons.

Some idea of the immensity of the production can be obtained when it is stated that the entire Cathedral of Notre Dame was reconstructed at Universal City, as well as eight blocks of Parisian streets and houses of the time of Louis XI. The total cost was a trifle less than $1,500,000.

PHOEBUS, WAIT! cries Esmeralda, as her lover seeks to hold her in his arms despite the efforts of her underworld guardian to seize her.

Scene Cut No. 5

Big Advance Sale For Film Sets Record

If the advance sale is any criterion "The Hunchback of Notre Dame" is destined to be the most sensational success of any production that has ever appeared at the ...... Theatre. Of course, this unusual interest is easy to understand, as the wonderful criticisms that this production has received as a result of its five-month engagement in one of the leading Broadway legitimate theatres was widely discussed in the newspapers of the country. However, it is especially gratifying to Manager ...... and officials of the Universal Pictures Corporation.

No production—either stage or screen—ever received a tith of the praise that has been accorded Carl Laemmle's offering of the Victor Hugo classic. New York is still talking of the fact that Alan Dale, noted metropolitan critic, who seldom deigns to look at a picture, and more seldom fails to find a number of flaws for the consideration of his acrid pen, gazed upon "The Hunchback" and then wrote a review that was a masterpiece of English and in which he used 37 praiseworthy adjectives, more than the most rabid press agent would ever dare incorporate in any one article.

During the entire New York engagement seats were sold out for four weeks in advance and speculators reaped a young fortune on this production, despite all efforts of the management to keep the tickets out of their hands.

Victor Hugo's Greatest Work On The Screen

If Victor Hugo could but return to the world for one single night there is little doubt that he would gasp in amazement at the magnificence of the Universal production "The Hunchback of Notre Dame," adapted from his greatest masterpiece. Each tiny detail of the book and of the period was studied for months and faithfully reproduced on the screen, and the hardened critics of New York, Chicago and a score of other cities, united as one man in declaring that here, at last, "is the quintessence of perfection in screen art."

...... is eagerly awaiting the advent of the production at the ...... Theatre on the night of ...... The fame of the wonder picture reached here a few days after its opening at the Astor Theatre in New York City and there was general pleasure expressed when it was learned that Manager ...... of the ...... had "scooped" all opposition and landed the production for this city.

Lon Chaney is the star of the production. He is supported by a brilliant cast including Ernest Torrence, Patsy Ruth Miller, Tully Marshall, Norman Kerry, Brandon Hurst, Caesar Gravina and Gladys Brockwell. In all there are 75 principals and 3275 extra players. The entire Cathedral of Notre Dame was reconstructed especially for the production, as were eight blocks of Parisian streets and houses of the time of Louis XI.

The last detail that makes for the final bit of perfection and the ultimate in entertainment is the special musical score that was prepared by Dr. Hugo Riesenfeld and a half dozen other noted musical conductors. The music puts the audience in just the right mood for the various scenes, and conveys just that subtle shading that makes for perfect understanding.

"Hunchback of Notre Dame" Director Acted In Hugo Classic On Stage In 1901

At the ...... Theatre on Monday night will be held the widely heralded premiere of the Universal production, "The Hunchback of Notre Dame," which won the unqualified praise of New York critics, being generally hailed as the finest achievement of the age.

Throughout the Hugo masterpiece runs a beautiful love story—certain changes were made in the production in order to avoid offending any particular religious body, but these changes have been endorsed by all who have seen the production.

Lon Chaney heads the stellar cast of 3091, which includes such notables as Ernest Torrence, Patsy Ruth Miller, Tully Marshall, Brandon Hurst, Nigel de Brulier and Winifred Bryson. The majority of these are as well-known on the stage as on the screen.

Wallace Worsley, who directed the filming of "The Hunchback of Notre Dame," occupies the unique position of having produced in motion pictures a theme in which he once acted on the legitimate stage. A role in "The Hunchback of Notre Dame," when it appeared in legitimate drama was Worsley's first stage appearance. That was 22 years ago, but he remembered well the unfortunate handling of the theme that kept it from attaining the success that should have been its, and in the film production it need not be assured, the same mistakes were not repeated.

In other ways Worsley was peculiarly fitted as the director for this production. Worsley's favorite subject in Brown University was French history. His initial theatrical role revived this interest and through all of the intervening years he has been a student of French history. His knowledge is such that he could have been waked up in the middle of the night and he would have been able to direct from almost any period of French history.

NOTRE DAME LINKED WITH ROMANCE

Study For "Hunchback" Filming Brings to Light Many Interesting Facts.

Many interesting and little known facts about the romantic history of the ancient Cathedral of Notre Dame were brought to light during the exhaustive research work conducted as a prelude to the filming of Victor Hugo's classic, "The Hunchback of Notre Dame," which is booked for a limited engagement at the ...... Theatre, starting ......

One of the most interesting of these legends is concerned with the monarch Prudentius. Notre Dame stands on the site of the oldest basilica of the capital, constructed even before the Cathedral of Sainte Etienne Martyr, which was long considered to be the most ancient. Excavations made under the present Cathedral and on the Place de Parvis Notre Dame, especially those of 1847, confirmed this fact.

The original edifice consecrated to Notre Dame was built by Prudentius, and was a basilica without a transept, the roof being sustained by columns of marble and pavements decorated with mosaics. At the end of the sixth century, the both churches were standing, so near each other that they almost touched. The basilica of Sainte Pierre and Saint Paul, built by Clovis, was on the summit of the hill on the slopes of which stood the Palais des Thermes.

The legend relates that Prudentius, having selected the site, measured the ground to be devoted to the church by hurling his francisque, or double-headed battle axe, to the utmost point his strength permitted. He did not live to see it completed, but the work was finished by his widow, Clotilda. It was Maurice de Sauily, Bishop of Paris, who in 1163 demolished the ancient basilia and laid the first stone of the present structure. Pope Alexander III presided at the ceremony.

Premier Of 'Hunchback' Hectic One

Print Completed Just Eight Minutes Before Curtain Time on Opening Night.

Musical comedy producers have long ranted and raved over their sleepless nights just before the "premier," but they have nothing on the group of men that gave the final "rehearsals" to "The Hunchback of Notre Dame." It is common belief that when the studio of a motion picture company takes the last "shot" and sends the print on to New York, the play is ready for the public. Sometimes this is true, more often it is just the beginning.

Lifting the curtain a bit on the widely heralded production "The Hunchback of Notre Dame," the arrival of the film in New York was the beginning of a series of hectic days and nights. Wires were sent to the coast to send on parts of the production which had been "cut" at the studio. When these arrived work started on the rebuilding of the production, a score of Universal experts being aided by outside experts. At 5.30 in the morning, two days before the world premier at the Astor Theatre, the final O.K. was given and the print rushed to Fort Lee, N. J., to be completed, printed and tinted. The print was ready just eight minutes before curtain time. It was a world record for speed.

From first to last, expense has been a secondary consideration with this production. Carl Laemmle sent a staff of technical experts to Paris who worked for six months checking up detail and obtaining models of the Cathedral of Notre Dame and castles of the period of Louis XI. The settings alone cost $500,000, and the completed production $1,500,000. It opens its local engagement at the ...... Theatre on ......

"Hunchback" Cost As Much To Produce As Any Three Of The Biggest Musical Revues

During a discussion of dramatic and motion picture producers recently an interesting point came to light—namely, that the production of a picture like "The Hunchback of Notre Dame" costs as much as three of the editions of one of the most famed musical revues in the country, and that when advertising, transportation, and all other items of overhead are taken into consideration, it costs as much to present a super feature a year as it does the best of the spoken dramas, which charge two to four times what the picture does.

The public has demanded bigger and better pictures, but there is no doubt that if this demand is to be met that higher prices of admission are vitally necessary, else these bigger and better productions would soon bankrupt even the biggest companies. Reverting to "The Hunchback of Notre Dame," the Universal production which comes to the ...... Theatre next ...... for an indefinite engagement, the total cost was more than a million and a half.

According to all who have seen the production, not more than two hundred feet of film need be run before the spectator realizes that this is no idle statement, and begins to wonder how it was produced at that low figure. There were some 3091 actors employed in it, the time required was more than a year, and it was necessary to rebuild the entire Cathedral of Notre Dame and eight blocks of Parisian houses and streets of the period of Louis XI.

Aside from the love theme that plays on the heart strings like a bow does on a violin, there is action and thrills surpassing any in the most exciting production made heretofore.

The cast is one of the most noteworthy ever gathered under one banner and is headed by that pastmaster of character parts—Lon Chaney. Critics in New York and every other city where the production has been shown, have acclaimed Mr. Chaney's work as a piece of art of purest ray serene, a bit that cannot die. He is ably supported by such sterling artists as Ernest Torrence, of "Covered Wagon" and "Tolerable David" fame; Patsy Ruth Miller, Tully Marshall, Brandon Hurst, Nigel de Brulier, Harry Von Meter, Eulalie Jensen, Kate Lester and Winnifred Bryson.

DRAWING back the curtain on Patsy Ruth Miller in "The Hunchback of Notre Dame."

Scene Cut No. 4

Page Three

SPECIAL ADVANCE

Keep Cuts Travelling Along With Your Copy!

"Hunchback of Notre Dame" Is Laemmle's Reply To The Better Picture Movement

Local Theatregoers Expected To Endorse Verdict Of Hundreds Of Thousands In Cities From Coast To Coast

"The Hunchback of Notre Dame," the massive and much heralded film production of Victor Hugo's story masterpiece which swept into over-night fame in New York, will be given its local premier at the ...... Theatre ......, when it begins a limited engagement.

Never before, it is said, has there been offered a picture production representing so stupendous a cost—$1,500,000—never a film presentation so exact in its details, so artistic in its conception, so wonderful in the acting of its seventy-five principals, two hundred sub-principals, and in the handling of the mob scenes in which more than 3000 persons take part.

Lon Chaney, admittedly the finest interpreter of unusual character roles on either stage or screen, plays the stellar part of "Quasimodo," the deformed bell-ringer of Notre Dame, with Ernest Torrence as "Chupin," the under-world king, and Patsy Ruth Miller as "Esmeralda."

Carl Laemmle, who founded Universal City out in Southern California, it is said, has achieved something there which awakens the utmost admiration. He has taken Hugo's rather turgid melodramatic novel, and after building a replica of Paris' famous Cathedral, he has retold Hugo's story in pictures—vital, vivid pictures that hold the attention and excite admiration by their undeniable power and beauty.

The spirit of the story is "Quasimodo," the hunchback, an elemental creature, twisted in body and restricted in mind, who haunts the great church. "Quasimodo," as Mr. Chaney presents him, is said to be a grotesque monster, and yet under the forbidding aspect the actor succeeds in making the character human and pitiful. His daring poses on the projecting gargoyles of the Cathedral, his bold descent, stone by stone, of the front facade of the great church, his hazardous swinging on the great bells at the risk of his life, the gruesome scene of his castigation in the market place, and the pathos of his final act as, dying, he rings his own death knell on his beloved bells, are features, it is said, that make "The Hunchback of Notre Dame" the most noted film production to date.

In constructing the Cathedral of Notre Dame at Universal City an army of carpenters, masons and other mechanics, were employed. The building is an exact replica in every detail as the famous Cathedral looked in 1482. It is declared to be an extraordinary feat and an architectural and technical triumph. In addition to the Cathedral, other historical sets include exact reproductions of the Coura of Miracles, Place du Parvis, Palace de Justice, interior of the Bastille and the seven Noble Mansions. This may give a faint idea of this, the accredited most important screen production, not only in the history of the Universal Film Company, but of that of any producing concern in the world. Wallace Worsley was the director.

Among the other principals in the big cast are: Norman Kerry, who plays "Phoebus"; Tully Marshall, as "Louis XI"; Raymond Hatton, as "Gringoire"; Nigel de Brulier, as "Don Claude," and Gladys Brockwell as the crazy "Godule."

With "The Hunchback of Notre Dame," it is said, that "different picture" has arrived, one that marks the dawn of a new era in cinema art, and one that has made Carl Laemmle's slogan of "better and finer productions" an absolute fact.

Goat Gets Fair Star's Nanny By Butting Tactics

Animal Fails to Appreciate Value of Publicity Until Carrots Are Forthcoming.

Patsy Ruth Miller's goat got her "goat" coincident with the filming of the "Hunchback of Notre Dame" at Universal City. Throughout the scenes Miss Miller, as Esmeralda, is accompanied by the goat. The publicity department wanted some specially posed photos of Esmeralda and the animal. She was agreeable and it was assumed the goat would be also.

When the time came the photographer arrived and posed Miss Miller and then started in on the goat. Now it seems that Mr. Goat had been used to carrots as a delicacy and it insisted on mistaking the yellow tassels that hung from the actress' costume for the succulent vegetable. When the tassels failed to yield the proper flavor, the goat became peeved and evinced his ill-humor by butting.

After many unsuccessful efforts to induce the goat to abandon his ungentlemanly tactics, a hurry call was sent for carrots. Upon their arrival the goat was persuaded to pose between nibbles.

Miss Miller is a St. Louis girl who has had a quick rise in pictures. She went to Hollywood on a vacation and was ticked as a type by a director. Following her first bit she played extras for many weary months, then small parts, until thoroughly trained in her art. However, her selection for the important role in the Victor Hugo masterpiece came as a surprise. That the choice was a happy one, however, was proven by the unlimited praise she has received from all the critics. Lon Chaney is the "Quasimodo" of the production. It comes to the ...... Theatre on ......

The cast of "The Hunchback of Notre Dame" is one of the most brilliant ever gathered under one banner. Among the noted players, beside Chaney, are Ernest Torrence, Nigel de Brulier, Winnifred Bryson, Tully Marshall, Brandon Hurst, Norman Kerry, Gladys Brockwell, and 67 other noted artists. The entire Cathedral of Notre Dame was reconstructed at Universal City for this production. It is American made from start to finish and is a triumph for American filmdom.

"HELLO," says Patsy Ruth Miller, of the "Hunchback of Notre Dame" production.

Scene Cut No. 14

Plans Operatic Career, But He's Better Villain

Ernest Torrence Longs to Sing But Finds Acting Pays Better.

Fate sometimes plays strange pranks with men's ambitions.

Witness Ernest Torrence, who started forth blithely to become one of the leading operatic stars of the world and ended up by becoming "famous" as one of the most infamous characters in history, a man that ruthlessly wielded a knife to clinch arguments, a man that tried to kill his own brother and ransack the treasure vaults of a church.

Torrence hates himself for what he has become, but Fate—in the shape of motion picture directors—drives him ever on and on to new villainies. So great is his "infamous fame" that he was the first and logical choice of Casting Director Datig for the role of "Chopin" in "The Hunchback of Notre Dame," the stupendous Universal production which opens its local engagement at the ...... Theatre, on ......

Torrence was born in Edinborough, Scotland, 45 years ago, and early evinced a talent for music. He specialized in a piano course at the University of Stuttgardt. Returning home, he spent some time as an instructor and then went to London, where he took a course in voice culture at the Royal Academy. Soon after, he won the Westmoreland scholarship for singing, and also the gold medal for operatic rendition.

During the season of 1903-1904, he played romantic lover parts at the Savoy Theatre, London. This was followed by a wide range of character comedy roles, until 1911, when he came to America and appeared in musical comedy. He is best remembered for his excellent characterization in "The Only Girl" and "The Night Boat."

"The filming of 'The Hunchback of Notre Dame' is a classical triumph," Torrence stated. "I am proud to have had a part in this production, which must prove to be one of the epochal events in the history of the motion picture, for the story is one of the classics of the great master of the Romantic period. The amount of research for perfect verity of detail, the study and care given to the smallest things, stamp this as serious and successful demonstration in placing kinematic interpretation among the great arts. Here, indeed, is the convincing, compelling throb of flesh and blood and a reproduction of picturesque historical environment which seems little short of magical.

"I have long been a lover of Hugo. He is the king of romanticists and this great story of his—due to the splendid imagination and high ideals of an American producer—had been given a magnificent presentation, with the quality of truth and permanence, that give it the value of a volume de luxe, for entertainment today, and the years to come—for as the New York critics unanimously agree, it is the last word in the telling of the story."

1350 Hours To Don His Makeup For 'Hunchback'

Lon Chaney Devotes Record Time to His Characterization During Filming.

Thirteen hundred and fifty hours devoted to donning his make-up before the first performance, is the record of Lon Chaney, star of "The Hunchback of Notre Dame," which opens a limited engagement at the ...... Theatre on ...... The production was twelve solid months in the making and each day it took Chaney four and one-half hours to submerge his personality in that of "Quasimodo," the hunchback bell-ringer of Notre Dame. It was one of the most complicated pieces of make-up art ever attempted.

The fact that Victor Hugo was an artist (a fact not generally known) and that he had illustrated his own famous book, was of inestimable assistance to both the star and the other players, in visualizing the characters.

In a glowing description of the stupendous photo-drama Alan Dale, distinguished critic of the New York American, used fifty-seven laudatory adjectives to tell of the excellence of Chaney's work, ending up by saying: "This bit of work is art of the purest ray serene, it cannot die, it will live forever."

Universal spared no expense in the producing of the masterpiece. The entire Cathedral of Notre Dame was rebuilt at Universal City as were eight squares of Parisian houses and castles of the period of Louis XI. Seventy-five noted artists, including such famous players as Ernest Torrence, Patsy Ruth Miller, Brandon Hurst, Tully Marshall, Norman Kerry and Gladys Brockwell, support the star.

Photodrama So Real It Fools Expert

Spectator at Hugo Cassic Sure Cathedral Was Photographed Abroad.

Many amusing remarks are heard if one lurks in the dark of a theatre. One night at the Astor Theatre in New York, a woman was heard to whisper to her seat-mate:

"I wonder if they really built that Cathedral at the studio as they claim, or whether it was photographed in Paris?"

And the very wise young man who had escorted her to see "The Hunchback of Notre Dame" replied:

"Why, in Paris, of course. I saw the Cathedral of Notre Dame when there during the war and these scenes are too true to life to have been made anywhere else. Besides, it was much cheaper to send a cameraman across the water."

The young man was partly right. It would have been much cheaper to "shoot" in front of the original Cathedral, but what he didn't know was that permission to do so could not have been obtained by anyone. The spot is too sacred to the French people. In addition, the settings surrounding the Cathedral all had to be in the period of Louis XI, hence Universal spent $500,000 just to reconstruct the Cathedral and all the other eight squares of buildings in their entirety.

The patron's remark, however, showed how faithfully the reproduction was made. Critics everywhere have been astounded at the magnificence of the production. All unite in declaring that the production is the "last word" in picture art. It comes to the ...... Theatre here on ......

Lon Chaney's Hunchback Role Is Last Word In Stage Art

Lon Chaney, admittedly the finest interpreter of unusual character roles on either stage or screen and whose work as the fake cripple in "The Miracle Man" stands out as a bit of remarkable acting, to say nothing of his other wonderful impersonations, has added another striking characterization to his already long list in his appearance as "Quasimodo," the stellar role in "The Hunchback of Notre Dame," the massive picture production, based on Hugo's classic, which begins an engagement at the ...... Theatre ......

There is probably no actor behind the footlights, or before the camera, today who has mastered the art of make-up to the extent Lon Chaney has. His Fagin, in "Oliver Twist," was an example of his proficiency in this line. Besides being a player of intelligence, with a keen sense of the requirements of a role, Mr. Chaney is an acrobat and contortionist, abilities which he is often called upon to use in his characterizations.

Some idea of the regard Mr. Chaney has for detail of make-up and why his Quasimodo, in "The Hunchback of Notre Dame," is so remarkable and impressive in this line may be gathered from the fact he was on the "lot" at Universal City, where the mammoth production was made, each morning three and one-half hours before the remainder of the company, his work of transforming himself into Hugo's unique character requiring that amount of time. No effort was spared by Mr. Chaney to make the deformed bell-ringer of Notre Dame as near like what the famous novelist conceived him to be, as possible.

Incidentally, throughout the day Mr. Chaney was forced to carry 72 pounds on his back. It was another one of his torture roles for which he later paid the penalty by spending three weeks in a private hospital.

"Realizing that I had been chosen to play probably the most difficult role ever presented on the screen," Mr. Chaney said, "a role that called for the greatest artifice in facial transformation, contortion of the body, poetic, yet life-like impersonation, I put into my work all of the talent and capabilities I possessed. Never have I worked so hard or so faithfully in presenting a characterization.

"At all times I had the help and encouragement of Mr. Carl Laemmle, who had impressed upon me the fact that neither time, effort or money was to be spared in making 'The Hunchback of Notre Dame' the greatest picture production ever turned out. Not only were we to be supplied with the biggest and most artistic settings ever used in a film play, as near perfect atmosphere for the unfolding of Victor Hugo's story as possible, but we were cautioned that the portrayals of the various roles would have to be on the same high artistic plane. The perfecting of this exactness in every detail required a long time, and the cost was stupendous, but I believe the results have justified everything that was done."

PENSIVE Patsy Ruth Miller, in Universal's "Hunchback of Notre Dame" production.

Scene Cut No. 7

Starts Stage Career By Stepping On Train of Bernhardt's Gown

Stepping on Sarah Bernhardt's train is just about the most inauspicious way possible to start one's stage career, but that's just what Eulalie Jensen, one of the featured players in "The Hunchback of Notre Dame," did. She had answered a want ad. for girls for the "Divine Sarah's" play in Paris and was one of six girls selected. She was so frightened when she stepped out on the stage that she tripped over Bernhardt's gown. Madame let loose in her explosive French and then seeing the girl's dismay, relented and showered her with kisses.

From that day on, the two were the best of friends and Miss Jensen received her stage training under the "Divine Sarah." Her work in the big Universal production, which opens at the ...... Theatre on ...... shows how far she has progressed since. However, she acknowledges another debt to Lon Chaney, star of "The Hunchback of Notre Dame," for aiding her in evolving the difficult make-up she wears in the production.

Other players having featured roles in the $1,500,000 special are Ernest Torrence, of "Covered Wagon" fame, Patsy Ruth Miller, Norman Kerry, Nigel de Brulier, Tully Marshall, Brandon Hurst, Gladys Brockwell and Kate Lester.

SPECIAL ADVANCE

Find Out What Editors Want, Give It To Them!

"HUNCHBACK" SETS APPEAL TO TOURISTS

Academy of French Artists Ask Carl Laemmle to Keep Them Intact

One of the most unusual requests ever received by a motion picture company is contained in a letter which reached officials of the Universal Pictures Corporation from the Academy of French Artists and Authors. The distinguished body expressed the hope that the massive settings used in "The Hunchback of Notre Dame" be kept intact for at least six months to permit of a pilgrimage by members of the society and other students of the Victor Hugo and Louis XI period.

While Universal officials naturally were greatly pleased with this tribute, decision on the retention of the sets will be held in abeyance pending cabled advices from Carl Laemmle, president of the corporation, who is soon to be in Paris. He is expected to meet with officers of the Academy.

Photographs of the settings used in the production were sent to the International Congress of Motion Picture Arts in Paris some months ago and attracted great attention. In an address before the Congress M. Valentine Mendelstamm said:

"While touring America I visited Universal City where Victor Hugo's masterpiece was in the final stages of 'filming.' You would be astounded at the faithfulness with which the streets of Paris during the reign of Louis XI have been reproduced, but most of all by the remarkable reproduction of our beloved Cathedral of Notre Dame. I had the privilege of seeing some of the finished film and I feel safe in predicting that it marks the beginning of a new era in the art of the cinema.

"I think, also, that this great French classic, produced on such a scale as to make it stand alone in its class, will give a profound sentimental impulse to which the earnest friends of France and America are giving their heartfelt endeavor. Perley Poore Sheehan made the adaption of Hugo's work and having long been a resident of our great city, knows intimately the heart of France. It is men like him on both sides of the water who will hasten the intellectual and social entente to ideal fulness. Mr. Sheehan recently wrote me—and every Frenchman and sympathetic American will appreciate his mood—the following:

"'I have been keenly desirous of bringing Hugo unspoiled to the screen, because I have always loved him. I have always loved Paris, loved France, and, to me these were Hugo. He was their genius, he was their god. During the many years I lived in your wonderful city, I was, so to speak, a neighbor of Victor Hugo. He was dead, but his spirit still lived. And his house was there—now a public museum—right around the corner. I have brooded there for hours, communed with him in secret, learned of his great aspirations and found consolation and inspiration in his silent companionship. He was always with me when I walked near Notre Dame.'"

Undoubtedly this sympathetic understanding of the great author is responsible for the success scored by the Universal production, which opens its local engagement at the ...... Theatre on ......

French Solon Sends Watch To Director

Wallace Worsley, who directed Lon Chaney in Universal's "The Hunchback of Notre Dame," which comes to the ...... Theatre, is proudly displaying a handsomely engraved Swiss chime watch, the gift of a prominent French statesman who viewed the initial showing of the production at the Astor Theatre, New York. The watch was accompanied by a note setting forth the donor's great admiration for "a director who lost none of the inspiration or charm of Victor Hugo's great literary classic in transferring the novel to the screen."

Worsley's home on South Manhattan Place, Hollywood, was fairly deluged after the premier with letters and telegrams. All these admirers proclaimed it the outstanding cinema success of all times.

Lon Chaney, playing the role of Quasimodo in "The Hunchback of Notre Dame," is a stickler for detail in his make-up. He consumed three and one-half hours daily to don the complicated make-up he wears in the production.

FEAR NOT, Marie, Queen of the Gypsies, tells Esmeralda (Patsy Ruth Miller), as the girl voices her fear of the underworld forces.

Scene Cut No. 3

Holds Motion Pictures Will Be Text Books of Tomorrow

"Motion pictures will be the text-books of the schools of tomorrow," declared Professor R. S. Woodsworth, instructor in psychology, at Columbia University, after attending one of the performances of "The Hunchback of Notre Dame" in New York City. He had been keen to see the production, owing to the fact that he was a personal guest of Lon Chaney, the star, during the filming at Universal City, California.

"Educators," continued Prof. Woodsworth, "are daily realizing more and more the value of visual teaching. It is a cardinal rule of psychology that what one sees is most firmly affixed in the brain—literally photographed there. That is why advertisers use pictures to impress their wares in the public memory, and that is why teachers are coming to use motion pictures to impress historic facts and other information on the minds of children.

"Take the Cathedral of Notre Dame in the Universal production of Hugo's classic. Children will grow up and recall that masterpiece of architecture who otherwise would never know it from the personal standpoint, so to speak. When these children study French history or read books about that period they will connect incidents about the Cathedral with the edifice they saw in the picture.

"During my visit to Universal City while the picture was in making I was impressed by the fact that the director and star were close students of psychology. They studied every detail and how it would react on the public mind, and I honestly believe that the sensational success of the completed production is due in a large measure to their understanding and appreciation of the lessons of psychology."

Lon Chaney is the star of the production which comes to the ...... Theatre on ...... for a limited engagement of ...... days. Others of note playing leading roles are Patsy Ruth Miller, Norman Kerry, Ernest Torrence, Nigel de Brulier, Brandon Hurst and Gladys Brockwell.

"The Hunchback of Notre Dame" opened in New York in the face of terrific opposition and within ten days was forced to place tickets on sale four weeks ahead. It ran for five months in one of the leading Broadway legitimate houses, and duplicated its success in the same manner in Boston, Chicago, London, San Francisco, Philadelphia, and half a dozen other large cities, in the leading legitimate theatres of the country.

One of the points that has astonished astute showmen is the peculiar appeal this production seems to have for women, but this is easily understood when it is explained that the romance angle of the Hugo masterpiece has been featured in the screen version even above the multitude of dynamic thrills with which the feature abounds.

Actor Is Wealthy But Can't Resist Lure Of Spotlights

Caesar Gravina, who is one of the 75 principals in the cast of "The Hunchback of Notre Dame" which comes to the ...... Theatre on ......, is an actor who acts purely from love of his work. He is financially independent, being the owner of eight large theatres in Brazil and two in Chile. Each year he returns to South America for a few months to direct the destinies of his houses but as soon as possible he hurries back to Hollywood and his beloved character parts.

His engagement for a small role in "The Hunchback of Notre Dame" after he had been featured in "The Merry Go Round," "Foolish Wives" and other big specials, gives some idea of the care taken in casting even the smallest roles in the Victor Hugo masterpiece. There are 200 players in "extra parts" who are ordinarily "programmed names."

Not only does Caesar Gravina find music an absolute requisite for emotional acting on the set, but he chooses selections for scenes in which he appears with all the care he bestows upon his costume and make-up.

"It is not enough that sad music should be played during tragic scenes," says Gravina, adding: "There are different shades of tragedy as of all other emotions, and there is some particular piece of music which fits each scene as no other."

Gravina, who is Italian by birth, had selected a special list of compositions to be played during his scenes in the Victor Hugo picture, as follows: "Canta per Me" ("Sing for Me"), "Guardiana's Luna" ("Lonely Moon"), "Teresta che Lockse" ("The Closing Window"), "Cuore ingrato" ("Ungrateful Heart"), "Occhie Celeste" ("Blue Eyes"), "Perche?" ("Why?").

Lon Chaney is the star of the picture and other players include Patsy Ruth Miller, Norman Kerry, Kate Lester, Brandon Hurst, Winifred Bryson, Harry Van Meter, Tully Marshall, Jane Sherman, Gladys Johnstone, Nick de Ruiz,

HERE'S SPLENDID FEATURE STORY ON CHANEY PAPERS WILL LIKE

Chaney Adverse To Giving Interviews; Life Story Finally Obtained By Persistent Scribe

Rise To Stardom Has Been A Dominent Struggle Against Terrific Ods, But He Wins Out Thru Sheer, Grit and Nerve

When the average writer receives an assignment from his editor to go forth and interview an actor, he pats himself on the back and knows that the task is going to be easy, because whoever heard of an actor that did not relish publicity and was not willing to talk for hours for the edification of the reporter? But the writer recently received a shock when he sallied forth to talk to Lon Chaney. His article follows:

"In the first place it took me days and days of phoning and tearing around to corner Lon Chaney. Accustomed to all kinds of co-operation from actors, Chaney's disinclination to be interviewed only served to intrigue me all the more. I finally, after spending four months hanging around the set where he was making 'The Hunchback of Notre Dame,' wheedled from him, bit by bit, the story of his life.

"Chaney's rise to stardom has been a dominant struggle against tremendous handicaps, the kind of a story that has grit and stamina in every line of it. Chaney contends that there is nothing extraordinary in his life, that it's simply a very hard life. He will talk of men's things, of prize fights, races, business men's and fellow artists' success, but of Lon Chaney's early struggles he shows the voracity of a clam. Therefore, it was with a feeling of victory that I finally elicited the following facts.

"'I've fought—fought—fought—for everything that is mine,' said Chaney. 'I starved, I labored and hungered for the glad hand, for the companionship, that speeds so many young fellows on their way to success. I've often wondered when things seemed blackest, why I kept on, why I shouldn't give up and drift like I saw many others doing. But there was something in me that wouldn't let me stop.'

"Chaney spoke with the utmost sincerity. Not handsome, of a somewhat somber nature, his face is stern even in repose, and his words carry conviction because of the utter lack of affectation. He continued his story:

"'My parents were deaf-mutes, but perfectly normal in every other way and possessed perfectly splendid minds. So, as a child, I learned to express every wish with my facial muscles. I could talk with my fingers before I could speak, but as I grew older, I found that it was unnecessary, as we could converse with our faces, with our eyes. Those early years of pantomime are responsible for whatever skill I have at present.

"'When I was eighteen I landed a job as stage hand in a Colorado Springs theatre. Later I was a combination stage hand, chorus man and wardrobe mistress—yes, mistress, all for the stupendous sum of $14 a week. I was forced to support my parents and brother and sister.

"'I played in comic opera when I wanted to do tragic opera. I danced for the money, not for the joy. I danced in 'The Time, the Place and the Girl,' 'The Royal Chef,' and other operas. Nine years ago I went into pictures. My first part was the heavy in 'Hell Morgan's Girl.' I had no one to teach me how to make up. I had to teach myself by observing characters on the street and seeking to copy them.

"'After five years with Universal I decided to free lance. My wife stood back of me. I was determined to play only roles that I believed offered me real opportunity. My big chance came in 'The Miracle Man.' Then I went back to Universal to do the part of Blizzard in 'The Penalty.'

"'However, now I am through with cripple roles. I am too stove up through years of dancing. Though I have played practically every nationality, I prefer Orientals. The Latin races are too expressive; they talk with their hands, with gestures, but portraying the Oriental is, to my mind, an infinite art. He is passive, reserved, by thought alone have I put over my three Oriental characters.'

"Chaney's portrayal of 'Quasimodo, the Hunchback of Notre Dame,' in Hugo's masterpiece, at the ...... Theatre, is bound to be listed in the Hall of Fame of stars."

MUTE ADMIRATION by the "Hunchback of Notre Dame" (Lon Chaney), but it's lost on Esmeralda, who refuses to dance while he looks on.

Scene Cut No. 11

Page Five

SPECIAL ADVANCE

"Sell" The Public The Fact this is Classic

Ernest Torrence Wins Fame In Two Super Features All Within Space of Six Months

Fortunate indeed is the actor lucky enough to have a role in a production which scores one of the biggest hits in the history of the cinema art but when he comes right back as a featured member of the cast of another production hailed as greatest of all, he can surely be said to be a child of destiny. Such is Ernest Torrence, who plays one of the principal roles in "The Hunchback of Notre Dame," which opens its local engagement at the .... Theatre on ......

Torrence was given lavish praise for his work in "The Covered Wagon," but all who have seen him in the new Universal production, admit that he has accomplished a piece of art that will go down into history. In "The Hunchback of Notre Dame" his part is second only to that of Lon Chaney, the star, who portrays the role of "Quasimodo." Torrence will be seen as "Clopin, King of the Underworld." It is no reflection on either man to say that with any other man than Chaney in the title role Torrence would have "stolen" the stellar honors.

While every show that makes a decided hit in New York does not do so here, theatre-goers from this city who have seen the performance at the Astor Theatre in Gotham, have expressed the opinion that it will prove as great a success here. There is no question but that Hugo's story is so well known and liked that sectional likes and dislikes will play no part in determining its general popularity, and the unanimous praise given it by the New York critics has aroused a general attitude of interest.

Aside from Chaney and Torrence the cast is one of the most notable ever assembled, there being a total of 75 principals, including Tully Marshall, Brandon Hurst, Patsy Ruth Miller, Gladys Brockwell, Norman Kerry, Nigel de Brulier and Kate Lester. Two hundred players, ordinarily programmed names, played small parts, while the extras totaled in excess of 3500.

"Hunchback" is Masterpiece of Dramatic Art

"Well, it's done!"

With these three words, Director Wallace Worsley dropped wearily into a chair beside Carl Laemmle's desk in the producer's office in Universal City and the sigh of relief which escaped the lips of both of these men proved that the completion of "The Hunchback of Notre Dame" was a great event in the lives of each.

For more than a year the one thought uppermost in Mr. Laemmle's mind had been the making of this photodrama—the completion of a classic which would surpass everything previously attempted, not only at Universal studios, but also at any other.

That this has been done is the unanimous verdict of those fortunate enough to view it, and these same critics admit most freely that it even exceeds any ideas which they had formed regarding it, these being based on their knowledge of the extremes to which the producer had gone in his effort to make it a marvelous production.

In the first place, Victor Hugo's immortal masterpiece is so replete with dramatic action that never before has there been a picturization of a work of fiction which lends itself so perfectly to this form of drama. But the main idea back of Mr. Laemmle's intentions was that this motion picture classic would be made on the most lavish scale, a scale which the story truly deserved.

Accordingly, the best character actor of the day was secured for the part of "Quasimodo." Mr. Lon Chaney, and no expense was spared in the making—the total cost of the completed production being over a million and a quarter dollars. A cast of principals was then engaged which sounds like a "who's who"—in filmdom—and in addition over three thousand trained actors were secured for the scenes which require them.

The huge reproduction of the Notre Dame Cathedral is one of the most perfect ever conceived. This, together with the other sets, cost over half a million dollars, and there is every reason to believe that when "The Hunchback of Notre Dame" is shown to the public here it will astonish everyone with the dramatic quality of the story, which has all been retained, the enormity of the huge sets, perfect in every minute detail. "The Hunchback of Notre Dame" is admitted to be the greatest production ever attempted —the culminating effort in Mr. Laemmle's desire to produce a screen drama which would go down in history as the greatest ever made.

The production was eighteen months in the making; six in technical research and twelve in actual "shooting." The entire Cathedral of Notre Dame was reconstructed in its entirety at Universal City, as well as eight blocks of Parisian houses and squares of the period of Louis XI. It was directed by Wallace Worsley.

"Hunchback" of Notre Dame" Is Coming to Astor

A hundred pounds is a lot of weight to carry about for ten hours out of every twenty-four and to do that for a period extending over six months becomes even more of a "weighty" matter when one has to do it under the rays of a hot California sun.

Yet that is exactly what Norman Kerry underwent at Universal City, where he had to wear a full suit of armor in the making of "The Hunchback of Notre Dame," which Wallace Worsley directed and in which Lon Chaney is starred.

In using this garment of steel, Kerry first had to don a suit of mail which completely covers all portions of his body and over this he wore heavy breast steel, leg thigh plates. The entire outfit weighs a trifle over a hundred pounds and to add to his discomfort, the actor's body is kept perfectly rigid by the metal encasement.

Kerry's suit of armor was carefully selected by Perley Poore Sheehan, who supervised his adapion of Victor Hugo's immortal romance and Col. Gordon Magee, technical director, who are both authorities on fifteenth century Paris.

"The Hunchback of Notre Dame" is conceded by those who have seen it in the making, as the biggest screen drama ever made. It cost was well over a million and a quarter dollars, and principal players in the cast, which numbers over three thousand, are Patsy Ruth Miller, Ernest Torrence, Brandon Hurst, Winifred Bryson, Kate Lester, Tully Marshall, Jane Sherman, Harry Van Meter, Gladys Johnston, Raymond Hatton and Nick de Ruiz.

"The Hunchback of Notre Dame" is scheduled to open at the ......, Theatre on ......

MASTER ACTOR, Ernest Torrence, who achieves his greatest role as Clopin, King of the Underworld, in "The Hunchback of Notre Dame."

Scene Cut No. 8

Strangest Will Ever Made Found In Literary Search

"To my barber, Colin Caterne, who lives near Angelot, I will a big lump of ice from the Marne, to put on his chest (to match his cold heart!)"

That is one of the items from the strangest wills ever made—"The Grand Testament" of Francois Villon, notorious Parisian poet and thief, who consorted with cutthroats and came to his end on the gallows.

Villon ranks with the poet Gringoire as one of the most unique figures in literary history. Gringoire, whose life in many respects rivaled that of Villon's for color, is one of the principal characters in "The Hunchback of Notre Dame," the Universal production which is now holding forth at the ...... Theatre.

In his will Villon leaves various and fantastic items to strange friends. Mr. Sheehan, who spent many years in Paris, has translated portions of the will which retain much of the grotesque mixture of humor and pathos in which the original abounds.

In the latter part of his will, Villon thoughtfully leaves a loaf of bread to each of his executioners.

"I have found the study of the lives of Villon and Gringoire one of the most fascinating studies in all literature," declared Mr. Sheehan.

Raymond Hatton plays Gringoire in the picturized version of the Hugo classic.

Film Brings To Light Works of Scapegrace Poet

That genius sometimes walks in strange places is well illustrated in the careers of two French poets who were as infamous as they were famous.

Francois Villon, the more noted of Paris' two scapegrace poets, was a strange human incongruity. A thief and a drunkard, who spent his life in the underworld, consorted with cutthroats, and withal wrote some of the most beautiful verse in French literature. One of his best known poems is "A Ballad of Dead Ladies," touched with delicate beauty and tender pathos. Ultimately Villon was hung, and his picturesque career was the inspiration of Robert Louis Stevenson's great story "A Lodging For the Night."

Another poet who blossomed forth in the muck of darkest Paris was Gringoire. While probably less generally known in America because of the small number of his verses which have been translated, he vies with Villon for combining a life of debauchery with the noblest poetic expression.

Recently, Gringoire was the center of a literary controversy. It happened during the filming of "The Hunchback of Notre Dame," the Victor Hugo classic which is now playing at the ...... Theatre. In his classic Hugo credits the lines, "'Tis better to have loved and lost than never to have loved at all," to Gringoire, who is one of the chief characters in both book and drama.

Director Wallace Worsley insisted Tennyson wrote the lines, Hugo notwithstanding. A search showed that he was right. The question was put up to literary scholars and it was found that Gringoire's poems carried virtually the same lines, but with a shade different wording. So honors were settled evenly and the public can enjoy the picture without worry.

WHO COULD HELP loving Patsy Ruth Miller? Dainty starlet, as she appears in one of the scenes of "The Hunchback of Notre Dame."

Scene Cut No. 16

NUNS GUESTS OF HUNCHBACK MANAGEMENT

Many Sisters See Their First Motion Picture; All Are Enthusiasti.

Great discretion must be used in placing the following story. If you have a Catholic paper in your city, by all means see that the editor is provided with a typed copy of the article. If your community is to a large extent Catholic it will be safe to give it to the daily papers.

During the showing of "The Hunchback of Notre Dame" in Washington, D. C., a special invitation performance was given for four hundred nuns composing the sisterhood around the national capital. The nuns had not seen a theatrical performance of any kind since taking their vows, and to many it was their first view of any motion picture.

The performance was arranged through the courtesy of Carl Laemmle, president of Universal Pictures Corporation, in conjunction with the Knights of Columbus and officials of the National Welfare Council. It was necessary for the sisters to obtain special permission from Archbishop Michael J. Curley, of Baltimore. Their attendance is all the more remarkable when it is considered that this particular story of the great French master, Victor Hugo, is on the Index Prohibitorium at Rome. Changes were made in the motion picture version, however, that made it an acceptable entertainment for all creeds. As Mr. Laemmle so aptly said at the time:

"Pictures are made to entertain all persons and none should contain anything that would prove offensive to any race or creed. There is plenty of good things in the Hugo masterpiece, clean romance and thrilling action, without taking the darker and gloomier aspects."

The visitors to the beautiful Shubert-Belasco Theatre in the capital were welcomed by Mr. Laemmle's personal representative and every effort made for their comfort. It was interesting to watch the reaction of the members of the audience to the various big scenes; they were affected in exactly the same manner as a lay audience and were highly impressed with the reverential treatment of the great story by the producer.

While a strict rule of the various robed orders prevents speaking for publication and forbids the taking of pictures for newspaper purposes, one of the Mother Superiors did express her appreciation to those responsible for the entertainment, as follows:

"I think I can speak for everyone who attended when I say this visit was a real treat for the sisters. We enjoyed the picture—every minute of it—and found it clean, wholesome and a most interesting story. Truly it is marvelous how the art of the camera has developed, and to those of us who see such things seldom, the recreation of the great Cathedral of Notre Dame stands as modern miracle. We liked the actors also, and I am happy to put it down as a real memorable day in our lives. We thank you for it."

At Last, Feature Film Classic, To Be Shown Here

After months of reading of the greatness of Universal's "Hunchback of Notre Dame," ...... will have a chance to see this classic, as it is booked for showing at the ...... Theatre, starting on ......

The engagement will be limited to ...... days. Lon Chaney is the star and his interpretation of the role of "Quasimodo" is said to be the greatest piece of work that he has ever accomplished.

The cast is one of the finest ever gathered together and includes such well-known artists as Ernest Torrence, Patsy Ruth Miller, Nigel de Brulier, Brandon Hurst, Kate Lester, Gladys Brockwell, Eulalie Jensen, Tully Marshall and John Cossar.

The entire production was made at Universal City, California, and is the crowning achievement in a long list of superlatively fine film productions made by Carl Laemmle.

YOUR REVIEWS

Morning-After Notices Are Of Vital Importance!

Chaney Superb In Masterly Character Portrayal of Star Role of Hugo's 'Hunchback'

Universal Production at Strand Theatre Entitled to Designation of "Greatest of all"

According to an announcement made in connection with Carl Laemmle's screen version of "The Hunchback of Notre Dame," Lon Chaney is the best character actor in America today. I quote this, because I formed this opinion at least three years ago and I have never had reason to alter my opinion. Mr. Chaney has done the sort of work that has made screen acting a fine art. He has a technique that cannot be surpassed, he acts with intelligence that makes his work Mansfieldian, and it is probable that no one has ever exceeded him in the art of make-up.

These things have been brought home to us on many occasions, but never more strongly than yesterday afternoon when "The Hunchback of Notre Dame" was given its first local showing at the ...... Theatre. Here is a picture that is worthy of attention, for it has been screened so carefully it measures up so fully to one's expectations, that it comes near to occupying a place apart.

"The Hunchback" is a character study of the first water. The Cathedral is the most pretentious of the many settings and occupies a prominent place throughout the action. Other sets and scenes are of breath-taking immensity. Vaulted arches run back apparently hundreds of feet. The solemn air of the story is reverentially carried out. Director Wallace Worsley has done a rare bit of work. The picture sweeps from squalor to grandeur, from gilded ballrooms to dives and sewers of the underworld, always convincingly, always with force, above all—always superbly acted and directed.

Next to Chaney's "Quasimodo," undoubtedly the most striking figure in the film is Ernest Torrence's "Clopin, King of the Underworld." His impersonation is a masterstroke of acting. Patsy Ruth Miller was questioned as a choice for the role of "Esmeralda," but after one sees the production, all doubt as to the wisdom of the choice vanishes in thin air. She is ideally cast and we predict great things for this talented young St. Louis girl in the future. Norman Kerry makes a handsome and dashing character in the part of Capt. Phoebus, who loves the fair Esmeralda, even though she be far below his station in life.

The story, briefly, takes place during the turbulent days of Louis XI, the ruthless ruler of France. It opens with a fool's festival in the public square in front of the Cathedral of Notre Dame. Quasimodo, disdainfully, watches the revelry from one of the church towers.

Jehan, who exercises a strong influence at first over Quasimodo, urges the hunchback to kidnap Esmeralda, a gypsy dancing girl. Esmeralda is rescued by Capt. Phoebus, who has fallen in love with her on seeing her in the square dancing. Quasimodo is captured and sentenced to be lashed in the public square.

After his beating, the hunchback, in agony from thirst, is given a drink by Esmeralda, whom he worships from that time on. His only other favorites are the bells of the Cathedral, the Cathedral itself, and its saintly archdeacon, Dom Claude. He has lost faith in Jehan. Later Phoebus is stabbed by Jehan while he sits with Esmeralda. The dancing girl is arrested for the crime and is about to be executed when the hunchback, seeing her in the hands of the executioners, rushes forth and carries her to safety within the walls of the church.

Clopin's followers now seek to rescue her and plan to take her back to the underworld. But Phoebus, now recovered, learns of her presence in the church and heads the rescue. The mob is held off by Quasimodo, who gives his life, however, in protecting Esmeralda from Jehan, who covets her. The final scene finds the happy Esmeralda and Capt. Phoebus in each other's arms, while the dying Quasimodo plays their happiness in chimes upon the Cathedral bells and then rings out his own funeral dirge.

"Hunchback of Notre Dame" Magnificent Entertainment

The audience which assembled at the ...... Theatre last night to see the first presentation here of the widely heralded Universal production "The Hunchback of Notre Dame," witnessed a picture as beautiful, as profoundly stirring, as anything ever hoped for. Universal has taken Victor Hugo's famous novel and converted it into a production that will reach a great many more people and impress them more deeply than the book ever did. It is an indisputably fine achievement.

The conversion process has not been a polite one, in that many changes were made, but they are changes that were decidedly for the better. Entertainment is for all people and it is only right to make changes in points that were offensive to a religious creed.

"The Hunchback of Notre Dame" has been produced on a magnificent scale. The settings are magnificent beyond words and stamped with authenticity and fidelity to detail that places them far above anything that has come out of Hollywood heretofore. So much for the mechanical details of the production.

Turning our attention to the flesh and blood element in the ensemble, we find that two names stand out boldly—Lon Chaney, the star; and Wallace Worsley, the director. Mr. Worsley has done his job so thoroughly that he climbs to a place among the movie great. He has made a magnificent job of this picture, displaying a positive genius for composition, for mass effect and for the development of drama by pictorial methods.

Mr. Chaney, who up to now has been far from an obscure player, impersonates "Quasimodo," the poor twisted dwarf who rang the bells of Notre Dame and served as a fulcrum on which Victor Hugo balanced the plot of his novel. This performance transcends anything that Mr. Chaney has ever done before. His make-up is uncanny and his spiritual realization of the role unusual. In creating this weird character he has used both his make-up box and his head to tremendous advantage.

That great actor, Ernest Torrence, is also present, appearing as Clopin, the King of the Underworld, and does some remarkable work. Every member of the cast deserves praise for their excellent work. There is Patsy Ruth Miller, an adorable creature, playing the role of Esmeralda, the dancing girl; Norman Kerry, Tully Marshall, Nigel de Brulier, Brandon Hurst, John Cossar, Kate Lester, Gladys Brockwell and Eulalie Jensen.

The picture opens exactly as does the book, with the Festival of Fools. Of course in the book Mr. Hugo did the best he could, and he never dreamed how cold and ineffectual words could be in portraying a mob scene or in picturing a dark vision like Esmeralda.

Universal claims that $1,500,000 was expended on the production and after seeing the picture one wonders that all that is in it could have been obtained for this sum—truly it can be said that not one cent was wasted. Months of research work went into the production and it is evident from start to finish. Nothing more thrilling has ever been screened than the scenes in connection with the storming of the Cathedral.

ALL DRESSED UP.—Patsy Ruth Miller, featured feminine player in Universal's super-production, "The Hunchback of Notre Dame."

Scene Cut No. 1

America's Greatest Critic Calls 'The Hunchback' The Superlative Of Pictures

NOTE TO EXHIBITOR.—Herewith is given the famous review written by Alan Dale on this production. Mr. Dale is the dramatic critic of the New York American and has never before given unstinted praise to any production. Try and use it if you possibly can, as Mr. Dale's name has a real box-office value.

By ALAN DALE

"This much I'll say and you can flaunt it before my eyes evermore: a more remarkable, epochal, unforgettable, haunting and obsessional piece of eccentric, bizarre, cynical character acting than that contributed to "The Hunchback of Notre Dame" by Lon Chaney I have never seen on either stage or screen. If Victor Hugo could have taken one peep at this visualization of his own imagination, it would have given him a thousand sensational ideas.

You will dream of this "Quasimodo," you will thrill mentally at the recollection of this demoniac, cynical, leering, hideous monstrosity—the pivot around which revolves the tremendous episodes of a really marvelous picture. At times this "Quasimodo" is haroldlloydish, as he creeps along the cornices of Notre Dame, circles down its masonry, dropped from its heights, and viewed from aloft the turmoil and kaleidoscopic movement of Paris. This Quasimodo, intent upon his purpose—a dwarf of redoubtable character, a thwarted human being of hypertrophied intelligence, scum of the earth, but psychologically enormous—gave you the whole bagful of human emotions and contributed a screen characterization that will live forever. Everybody will speak of this astounding "Quasimodo," nobody can overlook him, he is as solid as Notre Dame itself.

You get the very marrow of Victor Hugo without the ineffable weariness of fishing for it yourself. The meat is all there, carefully prepared and screenically edible. Those quite ignorant of all appertaining to the hunchback can rectify their educational shortcomings by studying this film, and let me tell them that the study will be a profound pleasure. I am tired of mob scenes but those toward the end of this production give to mobs a new significance. They are so pulsatingly real, so clearly portrayed, and so realistically enacted that they seem not to be of the film, filmy. Then the finale—the cessation of "Quasimodo's" activities with the portentous Notre Dame bell, as he rings it for the last time, is the ne plus ultra of art.

Lon Chaney has stamped himself as an artist of purest ray serene. This bit of work cannot die. It is immortally fine. Patsy Ruth Miller was exquisite in the role of Esmeralda. Norman Kerry, Tully Marshall, beloved on stage and screen, and especially Ernest Torrence, were capital.

"The Hunchback of Notre Dame" is epoch making.

PATSY RUTH MILLER, one of the featured artists in drama at Strand Theatre.

Scene Cut No. 12

LAEMMLE'S "HUNCHBACK" FILM EPIC

Universal Has Created Work That Will Live For Years As Classic.

In producing "The Hunchback of Notre Dame," Carl Laemmle believed it would be, like the book, a work of creative art with the permanence of the ancient Cathedral itself and a picture for all days to come. He expected Victor Hugo's immortal classic to be the crowning achievement of the screen and in every way his anticipations have been realized.

"The Hunchback of Notre Dame" is a cinemagraphic masterpiece in the truest sense of the word. The sets, which include representations of the Cathedral of Notre Dame," the Court of Miracles, Place de Parvis, the Palais du Justice, the Bastile, and many streets of Paris of the period of Louis XI, are gems of mingled beauty, magnificence, quaintness, and are above all genuine replicas of a historic city whose greatness is thus conveyed forever on the silver sheet—the new art of the present, and of the future.

The screening of such an intricate story as this was a huge undertaking, especially when a physical production perfect to the last detail is in question. For so great a motion picture the industry and the public should be eternally grateful to Carl Laemmle.

But aside from the production itself, never before has such a remarkable individual performance been given as that of Lon Chaney in the stellar role of Quasimodo, the deformed bell-ringer of the Cathedral of Notre Dame. Mr. Chaney, known for years as "the man of a thousand faces," outdoes himself in its vivid impersonation. It would be inadequate to say that he gave a splendid performance. His "Quasimodo" is such a real recreation of the original that all we can say is—open a volume of Victor Hugo's "Notre Dame de Paris," read the minute description of the poor hunchback and see if you don't feel that no one could possibly be such as this character—then go see this production and find "Quasimodo" come to life. Mr. Chaney has realized the character not only physically, but psychologically. It is as though the living man was before us, and not an actor. Never did an actor more completely merge his identity in a role, or make his audience more fully lose sight of the individual.

Others in the cast are Patsy Ruth Miller, excellent in the role of Esmeralda; Ernest Torrence, as Clopin, King of the Underworld; Norman Kerry, as dashing Capt. Phoebus; Tully Marshall, as Louis XI; Nigel de Brulier, as Dom Claude; Brandon Hurst, as Jehan; Raymond Hatton, and a score of other, lack of space precluding mention of all. The advance notices stated there were seventy-five noted principals and a supporting cast of some 3091 extras, and after you see the picture you will agree that for once press-agents have stuck strictly to facts.

Probably no picture has ever been made that is 100 per cent. perfect, but here is one that is as close to perfection as anything that has ever been made, and this reviewer will go so far as to predict—that ever will be made.

In writing this review I have a copy of the criticism written by Don Allen of the New York World, following the world premier at the Astor Theatre in New York City, lying in front of me, and I feel that I hardly can do better than to quote what he has to say.

"That THE picture is here. We have seen scores of million dollar pictures and never before felt that one was worthy of the amount claimed to have been expended thereon, but in our estimation "The Hunchback of Notre Dame" is a bargain at any price. It's worth coming any distance, even from Australia, to see. If you would behold real screen ART by all means see this magnificent production. It is an unforgettable picture."

And Don Allen's words just about sum up our opinion.

FOLLOW-UP STORIES

Keep Hammering Just As Hard After Showing Starts!

CURRENT NOTES

For Use During The Run Of This Universal Production

Attention to some apparently insignificant detail is often the deciding factor in making a motion picture setting portray reality. The producers of "The Hunchback of Notre Dame" were not satisfied with the paving of their street scenes until tons of cobble stones had been hauled 38 miles by motor truck and placed by hand. Likewise, great care and preparation is represented in the scene in which "Quasimodo" pours molten lead on the heads of the mob storming the Cathedral. Water could have been used to effect the illusion, but a far more perfect result was obtained after extensive experimentation and research, but just what was used is a secret of the producer.

Carl Laemmle's stupendous production, "The Hunchback of Notre Dame," continues in such high favor at the ...... Theatre that it is selling out at every performance. All house records have gone by the boards. The tremendous surge of incidents in Hugo's story of the turbulent days of Paris provides dramatic material which inspired the producers to the greatest degree. The result is a pictured drama charged to the full with thrilling incidents.

The cast of "The Hunchback of Notre Dame," the Universal production which is now holding forth at the ...... Theatre, is of the first magnitude. Heading it is Lon Chaney, the greatest character actor on the screen today, and he is supported by Patsy Ruth Miller, Ernest Torrence, Gladys Brockwell, Norman Kerry, Winifred Bryson, Brandon Hurst, Nigel de Brulier, Kate Lester, Tully Marshall, Eulalie Jensen, Raymond Hatton and some 3091 other assisting players.

For years Lon Chaney toiled in studios for forty dollars a week, then came the "Miracle Man" and his salary jumped to $1000, gradually mounting until it was $2500 when he played the stellar role in "The Hunchback of Notre Dame." After the critics' reports of the world premiere at the Astor Theatre in New York, the star started receiving bids that ran all the way up to $4500, and he has not signed yet. But when newspaper men met him they found him the same hail fellow well met that he was when he received $40. The $1,500,000 production is now at the ...... Theatre.

The truth of the old maxim that every dog has his day was never better exemplified than at the Los Angeles public pound when dogs were being sought for the production that is now delighting theatregoers of this city at the ...... Theatre—"The Hunchback of Notre Dame." Twenty rag-a-muffin alley hounds which had been doomed to death at the pound were rescued and taken to Universal City. While prim Pekinese and beautiful coated collies were left to their fate, scorned mongrels walked around the scenes of the world's greatest production as "atmosphere players" of note.

"The Hunchback of Notre Dame," the Universal production which is now holding forth for a limited engagement, was made only after six months research work in Paris by Perley Poore Sheehan and a specially trained staff of investigators. For weeks at a time they browsed through libraries in private homes where extensive collections of Hugo's work and that of contemporary authors were available. The production itself was twelve months in the making and cost $1,500,000.

As an indication of the efforts of the big producers to make pictures that are suitable for all members of the family, it is interesting to note that when "The Hunchback of Notre Dame" was turned over to the censors by officials of the Universal Pictures Corporation that there was only one title changed and less than twelve feet of film ordered deleted. This is the production that is now holding forth at the ...... Theatre for a limited engagement. Lon Chaney is the star.

Lon Chaney made a special trip East during the first week of the New York showing of "The Hunchback of Notre Dame," just to appear at an American Legion benefit. He is an enthusiastic supporter of the ex-service man and at the special showing of the production at the Astor Theatre in New York he was forced to make a speech and was cheered for ten solid minutes. The big Universal production is now playing at the ...... Theatre.

Lon Chaney is the greatest character actor on the stage today for just one reason and that is that he works constantly studying types. When not engaged at the studio he prowls around the streets of Los Angeles, or whatever other city he happens to be in, following strange characters and making a note of their every move and gesture. This constant study explains his qualifications for his greatest role in "The Hunchback of Notre Dame," the Universal production now playing at the ...... Theatre.

Patsy Ruth Miller, the charming Esmeralda of Universal's "Hunchback of Notre Dame," which is now playing at the ...... Theatre, went on the stage for the perfectly good reason that she wanted to. She went to Hollywood right after graduation determined that she was going to break into pictures if she had to stay there for years. She was going to be a stenographer until that time, but by a lucky chance she was picked on her first visit to a studio for an extra role and did so well that she was kept busy continuously there. She is now a recognized star.

Ernest Torrence is noted as one of the greatest villains on the stage or screen today. He enjoys the distinction of having played on Broadway at the same time in the two greatest cinema successes of the age—"The Hunchback of Notre Dame" and "The Covered Wagon." The former production is now holding forth at the ...... Theatre. Lon Chaney is the star and he is supported by a brilliant cast, including such well-known artists as Patsy Ruth Miller, Gladys Brockwell, Tully Marshall, Nigel de Brulier, Brandon Hurst, J. Cossar, Norman Kerry and Kate Lester.

TENSE SCENE—In the Universal's super-production, "The Hunchback of Notre Dame," soon to be seen in this city. The film of the year.

Scene Cut No. 10

Universal Classic Takes Theatregoers By Storm

The production made by Universal of Victor Hugo's immortal story, "The Hunchback of Notre Dame," at the ...... Theatre, has met with high favor, exceeding any big production within ready memory and promising a permanence most gratifying to all who have the welfare of the screen at heart. In massiveness and thoroughness this production is a revelation and gives truth to the pronouncement by able critics that it eclipses anything previously offered.

Hugo's story was charged with a dramatic power such as he only could wield. The period of the fifteenth century in France was one wherein drama filled to overflowing the daily lives of its people. The extremes in station of the Parisian people were wide as the poles. And the author's love of the abnormal in character building, together with his marvelous knowledge of human nature, resulted in the creation of characters that clash with almost unbelievable intensity.

He made of "Quasimodo" a tremendous complex that while it was a dramatic triumph in shocking impressiveness was also clothed with a massive sympathy. If for nothing else, his story deserves true eminence through the drawing of this character. But, master-mind that he was, he made this character a protagonist of a seething love romance centered in the affection of an adventurous soldier in the army of Louis XI for a little Gypsy dancing girl reared among the thieves of the Parisian underworld.

Hugo pictured in writing a clashing conflict between the opposing forces of the underworld and those of the crown, and in transferring these to the screen there has resulted intensely thrilling drama that carries the spectator to the highest pitch of excitement. Due praise is merited by the director and producers for the big manner in which they have pictured with admirable fidelity and employment of the camera's full resources this master writer's drama. The enormous structures that were built to lend verity to the scenes have been acknowledged to be the last word in studio architecture.

HANDSOME—Norman Kerry and dainty Patsy Ruth Miller, in a scene from "The Hunchback of Notre Dame," coming here soon.

Scene Cut No. 6

"Hunchback of Notre Dame" Marks Zenith of Film Industry's Remarkable March

"The Hunchback of Notre Dame," now showing at the ...... Theatre, stands out as a mile-stone in the progress of moving picture entertainment.

One of the pioneers of the industry, who happened to be in this city on the opening night and who accepted a special invitation sent him by wire from Mr. Carl Laemmle, producer of the film, recalled the old days when anything over one reel was considered a feature, and when a little painted scenery was ample for a background for the actors, few in number, who cavorted through more or less conventional motions. The action, or "business" as it was called, was largely developed as the work went on.

The present masterpiece "The Hunchback of Notre Dame," presents such a contrast that it is hard to believe the strides which this form of entertainment had made in the few intervening years. Whole armies are seen from dizzy heights, and it is hard to believe that the scenes were not made at the ancient Cathedral of Notre Dame itself.

Every student of history knows the epoch-making events that centre around that famous building, builded on an island in the river at Paris, France. Every soldier who has been to Paris has seen its massive pile, and it will be hard to convince anyone who has been there that it is not the original building which is used in the film, and yet it is only one of the massive "sets" built for this wonder film.

And yet the enormity of the task in producing this moving picture production is almost forgotten in the development of the story and the masterfully skillful acting of Lon Chaney and his supporting cast, which includes Ernest Torrence, Patsy Ruth Miller, Norman Kerry and a host of others well known to devotees of the screen.

"The Hunchback of Notre Dame" made from the famous story by Victor Hugo, has again brought up the value of visual education through the films and shown how the most wonderful acting, together with most powerful dramatic action, can be blended with sincere fidelity to historical fact.

In Hollywood, where this wonder film was made and where the enormous sets were made, the school authorities were quick to see the possibilities of this replica of the facade of the famous Cathedral of Notre Dame at Paris, where so many historical events have taken place, and Mr. Carl Laemmle, producer of the film, graciously set aside suitable hours when teachers and their classes could visit this set and learn of its beauty at first hand.

CLEARS WAR MYSTERY AND LANDS A JOB

Red Letter Day in Life of Captain Waite When He Arrives at Studio.

It was a red-letter day in the life of Malcolm Waite, when he arrived at Universal City from Paris. First, he found his old pal, Norman Kerry, suddenly decided to become an actor, got a job in the biggest picture ever undertaken, and then cleared up a war mystery that has agitated the social set of New York, London and Paris for five years.

At the outbreak of the war Malcolm Waite was commissioned Captain of L Company of the 71st Regiment and sent with other units of the 27th Division to Spartanaburg, N. C. He scored high ratings as a company commander and was scheduled for France and a majority.

Then Captain Waite met the charming Mrs. Archibald White, of Paris and New York. It was generally understood in the social whirl that her favor depended largely upon the metal of an officer with troops. Captain Waite forgot the merry jingle of spur-chains on the ball-room floor and snapped L Company of the 71st into one of the most efficient organizations of the army. His prestige as an officer grew and he increased in the regard of the beautiful society girl, destined to become his wife.

Suddenly without explanation or warning Captain Waite was called to Washington, given an honorable discharge at the order of President Wilson and told that he was exempt from military service.

There was no explanation. He immediately boarded a train for Montreal and enlisted as a private with the Canadians where he was assigned to the tank corps and served with distinction until the armistice.

While Private Waite of the Canadians soldiered manfully and wondered what had happened to Captain Waite of the Americans, his family brought pressure to force the army intelligence section into an explanation.

From a friend in Washington Malcolm heard the story months later.

Captain Malcolm Waite, the message explained, was "busted" out of the American army because the young woman to whom he was engaged had once presided at a reception where Count von Bernstorff, the former German ambassador was a guest.

"The amazing thing about it," Waite said yesterday, "was that I had never seen von Bernstorff and that Mrs. White had never mentioned him to me."

Although his ambition to serve as a captain with the Americans was unrealized, Malcolm Waite immediately became a captain when he arrived at Universal City.

Through the influence of Norman Kerry and because he is a big strapping fellow and handsome, Waite was given a role as Captain of the Guards in "The Hunchback of Notre Dame," the Universal production which is now playing at the ...... Theatre.

Light Sufficient For City Used Making Picture

Sufficient light was on tap at Universal City during the filming of "The Hunchback of Notre Dame," the Universal production now playing at the ...... Theatre, to illuminate a city of over 100,000, and the current consumed during the production would supply an average small city for a year. Ten huge generator plants mounted on trucks were constantly employed on the grounds. A corps of 175 electricians manned these and the other equipment used in illuminating the vast areas in which the scenes were laid.

Difficulty was experienced for a time by Director Wallace Worsley and his chief cameraman, Robert Nehard, in keeping in touch with his electricians and other aides until a loud speaking device, which carried his voice a quarter of a mile in all directions, was installed.

FOLLOW-UP STORIES
Short Features Are Easy To Plant; Get These Over!

Famous Old Cathedral of Notre Dame Is Inseparably Linked With Art In History

Many Curious Facts Are Unearthed By The Investigators In Connection With Research Work For Big Film Production

One of the interesting aspects of the monster reproduction of the Cathedral of Notre Dame for the photoplay, "The Hunchback of Notre Dame," is the architectural dimensions of the famous old structure, according to Elmer Sheeley, art director of Universal City, who superintended the elaborate miniature of Victor Hugo's great romance, which is now playing at the ...... Theatre.

"Comparatively few people realize how the history of architecture is woven around Notre Dame as inseparably as religious history," states Mr. Heeley. "Notre Dame was the first of the great French Cathedrals in which Gothic principles of architecture were typically carried out. The choir was built in the year 1163, while the facade was built in the early part of the thirteenth century. Notre Dame is thus older than the Cathedral of Amiens, with which one naturally compares it. Therefore it is established that the Gothic architecture found its first real expression in the Cathedral of Paris.

"One of the things which caused us a great deal of trouble in reproducing the Cathedral at Universal City was the fact that the detail of the architecture has varied at different periods as a result of the 'restoration,' as deplored by Hugo. In the first edition of his famous novel he told us that 'if we examine one by one the traces of destruction imprinted on this ancient church, the work of time would be found to be the lesser portion—the worst destruction has been perpetuated by men—especially by men of art.'

"While admittedly the famous Notre Dame has suffered at the hands of the iconoclast, if we consider the vicissitudes through which Notre Dame has passed it is commendable that so much of the original structure has been preserved. Our research work proved that the most recent restoration has been carried out with a skill that is amply perceptible, and the workmanship might easily be likened to the label that is to be looking at an undefined ancient work.

"However, there are minute details of the art work that vary in portions of the cathedral which have been materially changed from the form dreamed by Hugo in the period of his novel. This made great care necessary that the sets be patterned exactly as described in the book, otherwise, while the production would have faithfully presented Notre Dame as today, for those who have studied Hugo closely it would have failed to carry the conviction that is so essential in a historical production.

"Lon Chaney, who played the stellar role in the production, is a close student of Hugo and was of great assistance in helping us check up these little details. The same care used on the Cathedral was exercised throughout the production, even down to the kinds of fastenings used on women's gowns of that period. No small measure of the great success achieved by the production can be traced to this care, full attention to the 'little things.'"

Hugo's Period Marked The Beginning of Modern Music

The development of music as we have come to know it, marks its progress from the 15th century, and an apt illustration of affairs musical may be apprehended as a sidelight in the production by Universal of Victor Hugo's "The Hunchback of Notre Dame," which comes to the ...... Theatre on ...... The scenes are those depicting the grand dance given at the home of a grande dame of the court, Mme de Bundefauriet.

The mere beginnings of a band are seen in the small group of musicians with its hautboy, viols and lutes. Of the music played in that period the advance compositions came from Netherlands' composers, who, as a result of the prosperity then enjoyed by the Netherlands, were encouraged in the fostering of the art. They sent teachers to all adjacent countries, and France, ever a lover of melody, received these tutors wholeheartedly.

The compositions were what might be termed stately, because of the demands of those in high stations for music in dignified tone. The dances were of the dignified variety, making much of minutes, measured steps and complete restraint of passionate expression. Thus it was a gradual development to the later popular manner. For there was a revulsion at that period to the heart music such as the troubadours indulged, because the traveling minstrel by then had virtually become disfavored.

Comparison between dancing of today and that period is interesting because of its utter reversal from complete restraint of the senses to answering inspiration to music of the older days. In the entire universe, to the slashing beat and threnetic air. When two or three centuries later the waltz was introduced into the French court there was an outcry against its naughtiness.

The troubadour, however, has his representation in the Hugo story in the person of Gringoire, a poet, as the minstrel when sang his verses has termed, but by way one of the few adherents of the older musical pursuit. And he sings his lute successfully as one of the jugglers and harmless artists of the production.

A COLD SHOULDER—Is all that Phoebus (Norman Kerry) receives from Esmeralda (Patsy Ruth Miller) in this scene from "The Hunchback."

Scene Cut No. 12

MAKING HIS LAST STAND, Chopin (Ernest Torrence) seeks to hold his ward, Esmeralda (Patsy Ruth Miller), from her lover.

Scene Cut No. 2

Esmeralda Was One of Author's Favorite Names

Beautiful Story About Victor Hugo Uncovered by Noted Photoplay Author.

A little known and beautiful story of the great French author, Victor Hugo is one of the treasures uncovered by Perley Poore Sheehan during several years residence in Paris during which he devoted all his leisure time to study of Hugo's life and work.

Sheehan personally supervises the spectacular productions in his adaptation of "The Hunchback of Notre Dame," the Universal production which is delighting local theatre patrons at the ...... Theatre. The story, as related by Mr. Sheehan, follows:

Hugo had an old friend in Spain, a famous architect named Count de Cerda, whose only daughter was a talented harpist. The Count was called "The Builder of Barcelona" because he rebuilt the old Spanish city. The family was rich and powerful, but met a series of reverses and lost all of the ancestral property.

With the de Cerda poverty stricken, the daughter, whose name was Claudde, had to use her talent as a harpist to earn a living for the family, instead of devoting it to charity as before.

Hugo was visiting the family in Barcelona when the matter was being discussed. It was decided the girl could not go on the stage carrying the noble old name of de Cerda. Therefore it was that Hugo said:

"Let the child go on this great adventure wearing the name of my heroine of 'The Hunchback' and I will give her a little goat with a silver bell and golden horns." Esmeralda decked the goat but took the name of Esmeralda and became, as they said at the great World's Fair at Chicago, the greatest harpist in all the world.

One who was Esmeralda's friend tells that one day while walking with her in Jackson Park near the facsimile of the old Spanish convent of La Rabida when suddenly she (Esmeralda) stopped with a cry and picked up something from the path.

"See," she cried, "I have again found the goat with the golden horns!"

The thing she had found was part of a stick pin of silver and gilt. Then, in a sudden nameless fright, the Spanish girl ran and threw the trinket into the lagoon, fearful that it would bring her evil fortune.

Patsy Ruth Miller plays the role of Esmeralda in the picture.

'Hunchback' Not New On Stage; Chaney Is Best

Veteran Thespian Discourses On Famous Actors Who Have Played in Classic.

One of the veterans of the stage who has long since retired from public life, recently was invited to attend a performance of "The Hunchback of Notre Dame," the Universal production which is playing here at the ...... Theatre. At the close of the performance he declared that Lon Chaney has accomplished the greatest piece of dramatic acting in the history of the theatre.

Recalling the impersonations of Victor Hugo's "Quasimodo, hunchback of Notre Dame," which have won a high place in theatrical history, the veteran cited the three-act stage version by Edward Kimball which was produced under the title of "Esmeralda." In this play Yates, one of the leading artists of his time, made an enormous hit in London. N. B. Clarke scored an equally great success at the old Bowery Theatre in New York City, which James Bennie Booth, Jr. duplicated at the National Theatre in Boston. Another notable performance of the role was that of J. E. Nagle at the famous old St. Charles Theatre in New Orleans.

During the making of the production at Universal City, Lon Chaney, the star remarked to an interviewer: "As actor, either on the stage or on the screen, gives the best that is in him when he tries to the life of it, the character that he is interpreting. He should study the story or script of the play until he gets himself into it; he should dream and take to him self the soul of the character; and likewise should have a sympathetic understanding of all the other characters. Though I have known Hugo for years, it was not until I began an intensive study of him for the character of 'Quasimodo' that I really felt the words that he had created.

"I have tried," said the critic, "have never ascribed to succeeded. No understudies the Quasimodo created by Victor Hugo; to express the form of the creature; the primal brute of him and the soul that struggled for voice in the blackness of his affliction. The camera demands infinitely more than the stage, in the way of detail, and that meant more and intensive study in preparation for the part.

"I was fascinated by the part and consider it the greatest role that I have had the good fortune to portray. The past has been called back as though by magic, and it has possessed all of us. The excellence is largely because of the excellence of Lon Chaney's work. . . . "

CAST LAUDS CHANEY IN BIG SCENE

Marvelous Ability of Actor Proven by Outburst of Praise From Colleagues.

Given a big part and the varied accessories of the theatre, it is not so difficult for an actor to play upon the emotions of his audience, but when he can move his fellow players to tears and cheers on a motion picture lot, with all the artifices of the trade of make-believe missing it, he has really accomplished something. Lon Chaney, star of the Universal production "The Hunchback of Notre Dame," which is now playing at the ...... Theatre, scored this honor during the filming of the Hugo masterpiece.

Two thousand "extras" were gathered in the huge area, before the towering replica of Notre Dame. From the shadows of the quaint mediaeval buildings they silently watched Quasimodo (Lon Chaney) going through the pillory ordeal. The executioners dragged and bound the misshapen figure to the revolving wheel. One of the guards raised his whip and the lash whistled through the air. Actual sobs broke from the audience of players. They were picture folks, part of the illusion themselves, but still as impressionable to really fine acting as laymen.

With the end of the scene came such an outburst as was never before heard on a motion picture lot. They applauded, they wept and cheered. Chaney, astounded, tried to speak, but couldn't. As he faced the cheering host—his own people—he actually wept. And he is not ashamed of it. Incidentally, the scene cost him a painful beating, for a lashing cannot be faked in a close-up, but the star says he was amply repaid for the pain that he endured.

Chaney, besides studying for months to secure the soul of the misshapen mountebank, had the aid of Victor Hugo's own sketches and the conceptions of all the distinguished French illustrators who had expressed the form of 'Quasimodo"—Brion, De Beaumont, Steinheil, De Rutred, and De Lemund. Chaney's make-up is the mystery of the theatrical world, for he always demanded and obtained absolute privacy when donning the trappings.

Chaney is five feet, nine inches tall, but when he issued from the dressing room and faced the cameras, he was a squat, distorted creature, not much more than four feet in stature, and, as the story describes the character—nearly as broad as he is tall. To preserve the great semblance throughout down to the finest detail, "still" photographs were taken at the end of each day's work and at the beginning of the following day's labors. In this manner the tiniest bit flaw in make-up was readily detected.

How well he succeeded in making his character a living, breathing personality is a matter of history. "The Hunchback of Notre Dame" is attracting capacity crowds in half a dozen cities from coast to coast, but it is the great production that is largely because of the excellence of Lon Chaney's work, whose name has been a sort of a dream reality. "I have felt as though I really were in the streets of ancient Paris, an illusion that has been shared by the most skeptical of the thousands of visitors."

Take the Special Story of Architecture, on this page, to the Art Critic, or Sunday Editor, of your paper and "Sell" it to him on its News Value.

Page Nine

FOLLOW-UP STORIES

Feature The Star Cast And The Great Love Interest!

TWO SPECIAL STORIES FOR THE WOMEN'S PAGE

Milady's Fashions Run In Cycles, Photodrama Proves It

Spit curls and short skirts in the court of King Louis XI, along about the year 1842, sounds a little bit incredible perhaps, notwithstanding the reputation of milady of Paris for first showing to the world new things of fashion. But nevertheless, history settles the matter which became of current interest when costuming for the characters in "The Hunchback of Notre Dame," the film classic now playing at the ...... Theatre, was occupying the attention of the Universal art staff.

Gladys Brockwell, who plays the part of Sister Gudule, and other feminine characters wore coiffures and gowns that are more generally associated with the Middle Ages, it is true, but had they appeared in the considered-to-be-modern short skirts and wearing spit curls, history would have vindicated them.

The story of the origination of the spit curl is none the less interesting than the fact that it actually was worn 500 years ago. It came into vogue soon after the hennin, the three-foot-high millinery masterpiece worn in the court scenes of "The Hunchback of Notre Dame," took Paris by storm as now styles do even at this day.

A queen of France, Isabel of Bavaria, it is recounted was baldheaded. A force of the hennin, or high peaked hat, worn in one of the other European countries, completely covered the head. Subtle Isabel, it is said, introduced this monstrosity of head gear in court circles to hide her own baldness. It was soon generally adopted and hair, for a time, was as completely covered by elaborate and uncomfortable hennins as ears have been in this era.

It was a court lady, whose tresses perhaps, had been her greatest charm, who had the temerity to allow just a whisp of hair to stray from beneath the front of her hennin, sort of proof that she at least was not wearing a cornucopia hat to hide a bald head. This visible look looked out of place to others perhaps and there may have been those who believed the lady had put her hat on hurriedly and that the visible whisp was an accident. She probably realized such to be the case and curling it as an indication that it belonged there, unwittingly invented the spit curl.

As to skirts, they have had their ups and downs so often that it is hard to tell just where and under what circumstances the abbreviated style originated. In fact, there are those who contend that the whole skirt was evolved from some sort of girdle and that it was short before it was ever long. There is historical record, however, that in the fifteenth century another Queen of France was proud of her shapely calves and shortened her skirts, and the court ladies followed suit.

Dainty Actress Qualifies As Social Expert

Winifred Bryson Says Fashions Move in Cycles, But Not Manners.

Ordinary every-day special formalities are products of evolution and many of our common expressions of speech and our salutations had their inception in life of another day, as Winifred Bryson, film actress supreme of historic parts, can tell. Miss Bryson is an authority on social customs, especially of the fifteenth century period, which "The Hunchback of Notre Dame," now playing at the ...... Theatre, portrays.

Social practice, Miss Bryson finds, changes slowly and almost reticently, a striking contrast to fashion in dress which follows for a single season the motive of one century or period, then often without apparent incentive, jumps to something entirely different and inspired by a different age. Etiquette, she says, changes only enough to somewhat synchronize itself with the world's advancement and unless they are wholly unharmonious with out time we cling to customs of conduct that date back to mediaeval times, change fashions of dress, modes of travel, and the rest of the world as it may.

Miss Bryson's familiarity with Parisian life in the day of Louis XI and her natural rich charm of manner make her especially fitted for "Fleur de Lys," the part she plays in "The Hunchback of Notre Dame."

Someone Found Cane That Spells Trouble To Owner

The taxicab driver who found an odd, twisted cane, carved with mystic African devices, in his cab had better return it to Perley Poore Sheehan. Otherwise his cab may skid into a telegraph pole, the bank foreclose his mortgage — or his mother-in-law come to visit him! The stick spells bad luck, with a capital "B"!

There is more truth than poetry about it, according to Perley Poore Sheehan, supervisor of the production of "The Hunchback of Notre Dame," in which Lon Chaney is starring at the ..... Theatre. And he doesn't say it because he wants the cane back, either. He hopes he'll never see it again.

Behind the loss of the cane, lies the story of a weird curse that rivals the legend of old King Tut's tomb.

The cane, presented to Sheehan some years ago by Sir Hugh MacDonald, then British envoy to Liberia, is known as a "magic stick," or "medicine stick," among the tribes on the West Coast of Africa. It carries a curse, bestowed on it by the African makers of witchcraft, against all who might carry it, save the rightful African priests.

"Through some political mixup it was taken from a voodoo man," says Sheehan, "and came into the possession of Sir Hugh. His admission that he was frankly afraid of the thing intrigued me. He gave it to me — and then my troubles began.

"It used to fall down in the middle of the night with a clatter and I'd wake in a cold sweat of fear. Often, when I knew I'd placed it in the corner of the room, I'd trip on it at night in the middle of my floor. Every time I was in the room with it, I felt a sinister influence.

"I believe, as Sir Conan Doyle does, in spirits—that is, I believe that there is some uncanny influence that we cannot fathom, which often manifests itself. Probably that cane is haunted by a poltergeist, or mischievous spirit.

"I know that objects long possessed by persons absorb the personalities of their owners. I would not care to carry the stick habitually carried by a criminal—his influence would be in it. So with the voodoo stick—a sinister influence clung to it.

"I hope the man who found it comes to no bad luck, but, seriously, I am afraid for him. As for myself—I never want to see the thing again."

Sheehan has a collection of several hundred sticks from all parts of the world. His most cherished is a recent gift; a magnificent rosewood cane with ivory handle, fashioned by Russell Powell, the well-known character actor and one of the cast of "The Hunchback of Notre Dame." Powell hand carved the stick, its manufacture consuming some five years.

"This cane, the gift of a friend," says Sheehan, "is just the opposite of the sinister talisman I lost. I consider that it is the best of good luck emblem."

Strange Gypsy Traits Bared In 'Hunchback'

Lovable But With Little Sense of Moral Responsibility, Hugo's Story Shows.

The intrusion of the gypsies into the population of France until they became an important element, dates from just prior to the period in which Victor Hugo placed his story, "The Hunchback of Notre Dame," the pictured production of which made by Universal is now the popular attraction at the ..... Theatre. The fact that the author made his heroine, Esmeralda, a gypsy is important in considering the time of which he writes, because he makes her the adopted ward of Clopin, the king of the Parisian beggars and thieves.

These nomads, arising from undetermined origin, though their English name is said to be a corruption of "Egyptian," were undoubtedly the off scouring of many nationalities, outlaws for any reason from escape from vassalage to conviction of crime. The gypsy of France at that period, called by the French "Bohemians" because the first band appearing there said they came from Bohemia, resorted to the time-honored pursuit of fortune-telling and palmistry. They were, too, in the poorly policed lands of that age, notorious for thievery. Their practice of stealing children for barter or rearing was also notable and won for them detestation.

Though Hugo does not state so, Esmeralda might well have been one of these stolen children. He gives her Spanish characteristics, which might go to prove the genesis of his conception of her. The freedom from social restrictions has been the dominant quality of the gypsy, and in the troublous times in mediaeval Europe this class flourished. This freedom also clothes them with considerable romance, for the mind of those subject to law and rule find glamour in that which, though it does not release them, frees others. Their more organized modern prototypes are the lowly hoboes afflicted with the nomadic spirit and often criminal in intent, though restricted to male membership.

The temperament of the gypsy makes love of music, especially the wild airs that suggest unrestraint, a paramount trait. Many of them were and are remarkable musicians. Esmeralda reveals that trait in her character through her ability as a dancer, and music has been utilized by gypsies not alone for their amusement but to capitalize it in their predations, either through obtaining money by fair donation or to mask their real thieving purpose. Thus they formed a large portion of that army of thieves and beggars ruled by Clopin and led by him in the great attack upon the forces of the crown when storming Notre Dame, which forms a memorable and thrilling scene in the pictured production.

Tully Marshall Has Best Role As Louis XI

Of the contributing personages whose presence is of major interest in the Universal production of Victor Hugo's "The Hunchback of Notre Dame," now at the ..... Theatre, that of Louis XI looms large and far beyond his immediate service as a dramatic agent in the minds of those who appreciate the prominent figures in history.

The period of Hugo's story is 1482, just a year before the physical dissolution of this monarch in whom was bound up so many mental characteristics that he was really a human chameleon and compound of an extreme diversity of virtues and vices, such as had no like in any figure in all history.

Through his twenty-one years of reign France was a scene of turbulence that seethed like the mythical pot of devil-dragon stew. He took up the scepter when France was a disorganized group of feudal states that were little more than separate kingdoms eternally consuming themselves with internecine strife. Never a heroic figure, he eventually winning the nickname of "The Universal Spider," yet he proved in numerous incidents his physical bravery. Nevertheless, he preferred guile and craft to boldness, and strategem to force. No loftiness or greatness of soul was natural to him.

He finally moulded France into a coherent kingdom through craft in statesmanship, treachery with friend and foe alike, force of arms, and subtle propaganda. As he so sounded the keynote of his court, so were ruled the lives of his people. Life was cheap, moral corruptions of all kinds and every agent of evil flourished. Because of this condition they were stern days, this period of cruelty.

Hugo, with his genius for thoroughness, was imbued with this spirit in writing "The Hunchback." That he was a man notoriously devoid of sense of humor aided in the imbiding. Hence his characters reflect this corruption. The cruelties inflicted upon the harmless Quasimodo are of the age. The power of Clopin, king of thieves and beggars so organized into an operative guild as to monopolize the pursuits of their calling, is true to the period and is its natural product. The dissolute members of the court and its military, of which Captain Phoebus is one, are tainted with the corruption.

Thus, as Tully Marshall acts Louis, the crafty arch-hypocrite, there is the ring of historical truth. He is the triumphant ruler, the wily monarch who prefers smooth deceits to frankness, coddling his achievements through craft. Therefore, though he appears but very little in the course of the action, yet his presence is of first import because he is the cause of the social turmoil and the breeder of its drama.

THIEVES HAD UNION IN DAY OF LOUIS XI

Picuresque Character That Ruled Parisian Underworld Depicted in Hugo Romance.

Students of sociological conditions find much in similarity in modern life with that of many ages. And when we read in the daily press of gang leaders who plan and superintend criminal acts, the expression can be fallen back upon, that things have always been the same.

True, different degrees have been obtained in the matter of thievery. There have been times when it flourished and attained its highest state of perfection. Such a time was in the reign of Louis XI in France during the period in which is situated Victor Hugo's "The Hunchback of Notre Dame." And the personage Clopin, prominent in the Universal production made from the story that is now showing at the .... Theatre, is no vagrant conception of the novelist, nor is it overdrawn in the power that this mediaeval king of thieves and beggars exerts in the action of the drama.

For in that period when social conditions of continental Europe, and France in particular, were in such a turmoil from reaction of more than a century of almost incessant warfare, society was pretty thoroughly disorganized. Through taxes imposed by the crafty and exacting Louis, the populace was in the throes of deepest poverty and the subject of every ramification of graft. The powerful nobles stole from the poor with impunity, and evil and corruption were the ruling spirits of all social life. Beggery was in the ascendancy, and the short step from beggary to thievery was easily bridged through the profusion of practitioners.

So numerous were they that it was most natural that a working guild be formed, both branches working in harmony, and equally as natural a consequence was it that chieftans or kings be chosen. Of such is Clopin in Hugo's story, a man whose rule over the predatory hordes gave him a power to be feared even by the forces of the law and crown. The clashes between his numerous cohorts and the crown were frequent, and it is said that victory rested often with the malefactors.

So when Clopin rallies his army of thieves and beggars to rescue his ward, Esmeralda, from the clutches of the King's forces, there ensues a battle of major calibre and one that furnished the makers of this production one of the most thrilling of scenes. Such an analytical writer as Hugo saw the value of Clopin and his subjects as a force for providing a great dramatic contention in building his wonderful story plot, for in this figure and what he represents is also that glamorous romance with which protestors against the law are ever invested.

Says Secret of Actor's Art Does Not Lie In Make-up

That the true secret of the actor's art lies not in the make-up box, but in the minds of the player and his audience, is the belief of Raymond Hatton, who is playing the role of Gringoire in "The Hunchback of Notre Dame," the Universal production which is now playing to capacity business at the .... Theatre.

"When one dons a costume for a part, he in a manner steps into a new life," says Hatton. "His actions and reactions, the entire mental attitude becomes different. This aspect of the thing should be realized by the actor, and made the most of. He should strive to completely submerge his conscious self into this sub-conscious thing that strives for expression.

"If one does this successfully, when the actor is seen on the screen, something of his mental spirit must get across to the receptive minds of the audience. It does not matter if that audience is Chinese or Russian, understanding not a word of English. The mind is universal, and the mental characterization properly done will gain an instant response. I think this is doubly true in the case of a picture laid in the mediaeval times, such as 'The Hunchback of Notre Dame.'"

Hatton's excellent performance of the effeminate poet in the Hugo classic would seem to prove his contention, as he is just the reverse type in real life. He is an enthusiastic horseman, golfer and swimmer.

Born in Red Oak, Iowa, he has spent the greater part of his life on the stage, as his parents were both performers. As he picturesquely phrases it, "my cradle was a theatrical trunk." He played several years in vaudeville and stock companies and then graduated into Broadway legitimate parts. He was early won over to pictures and has played a variety of parts, ranging from boys' roles to those of a man of 90.

Handsome Star Hates Harmless Guns and Swords

"Perfectly harmless — the blade slides right into the handle," the director informed Norman Kerry, who plays the part of Capt. Phoebus, in Universal's production, "The Hunchback of Notre Dame," which is now playing at the ...... Theatre. "It looks as if it's stabbing you, but it isn't," he supplemented, turning over the deceptive poinard to the villain.

Kerry examined it carefully, while the villain leered, and finally both bowed their approval.

The lights went on.

The camera cranks started grinding.

The villain sneaked in approved sneaky fashion—and stabbed.

There was a cry of pain from Kerry, and he danced briskly among the shrubs in agitated manner, at the same time trying to get both hands on the same spot on his back at once!

"He tried to murder me! Police. Help! he shouted.

"'S-funny!" remarked the director, "that's the first time that trick knife hasn't worked just right. It stuck in the handle the last half inch."

"Funny, be hanged," growled Kerry, and waltzed off to find a doctor.

It's a gay life at Hollywood, except when one is risking his life at the hand of a villain with trick knives, or leaping off three-story buildings.

FOLLOW-UP STORIES

Ask The Art Editor and Sunday Editor for Space

STORY IN FULL
(Not For Publication)

The spiritual background of the story is the Cathedral of Notre Dame (Cathedral of Our Lady) against which, as the story progresses, are hurled mighty opposing forces.

Quasimodo, the Hunchback of Notre Dame, has for master Jehan, brother of Dom Claude, the Archdeacon of the Church. Quasimodo worships Dom Claude with a spirit of reverent awe. Yet over the Hunchback Jehan exercises a control which many people attribute to Jehan's black magic, for Jehan is an alchemist whose dream of gold is the driving force which leagues him with Clopin, king of the thieves and beggars of mediæval Paris.

Supplying a romantic interest is the love which develops between Esmeralda, a gypsy girl whom Clopin has reared as his own, and Phoebus, a dashing young Captain of the King's Guard.

It is largely due to the reverence and awe in which Clopin's people regard Esmeralda that Clopin holds his sway over the thieves and beggars.

Opposing Esmeralda's and Phoebus' romance, however, is the base passion which thrills Jehan when he gazes upon the beautiful Esmeralda, as she dances in the Place du Parvis, the open space in front of the church.

He wants her. He determines to have her, even to the _____ _____ _____ _____ night, he has the innocent Quasimodo attempt to seize Esmeralda and carry her away.

The plan is frustrated by the timely arrival of Phoebus. Jehan deserts Quasimodo, who is captured. Esmeralda and Phoebus, looking deep into each others eyes, feel the awakening of their great love.

Quasimodo is presented for trial. Being deaf, he cannot hear the questions which an equally deaf judge puts to him.

The Hunchback's answers antagonize the court, and his sentence is therefore increased. Without knowledge of his punishment, Quasimodo is taken to the public pillory, where, amid the hoots and jeers of the populace, he is flogged upon his deformed and twisted back.

Bitterness pervades his soul, until Esmeralda, in pity for the poor and helpless creature, gives him a drink to cool his parched mouth. In that moment Esmeralda makes a friend. In that moment also awakens in Quasimodo the first awakening of love, and he becomes something akin to a man and much less of a creature.

Phoebus, through his attention to Esmeralda, has made an enemy of Clopin. Esmeralda, knowing that Clopin would not hesitate to kill her handsome Captain, decides that she will give herself to the Church. In this way Phoebus will be saved from Clopin's hatred, but at the expense of a great sacrifice by Esmeralda.

For a last farewell, Phoebus and Esmeralda meet in the garden of the Cathedral. Jehan who has watched them, sees in Phoebus an enemy whom he had best be rid of. While Phoebus and Esmeralda are locked in a fond embrace Jehan drives home the knife which barely misses Phoebus' heart.

Innocent Esmeralda is captured and at her trial protests that she is not guilty. The leering face of Jehan, at which she glimpsed in the garden, confronts her. She accuses him, but in turn is accused of being bewitched and is put to the torture to wring a confession from her lips. In agony the girl finally confesses and is thrown into a dungeon.

Esmeralda's absence from the Court of Miracles, the haunt of Clopin and the beggars, has thrown a pall over the place. Knowledge in those days did not spread quickly. A person could disappear, leaving no trace. So it was with Esmeralda as far as Clopin and the Court of Miracles were concerned.

Again Jehan confronts Esmeralda. In her cell, disguised in the robe of a monk, he pleads with her to be his. But Esmeralda denounces him, and in a wild passion, Jehan tells her that her handsome Phoebus is dead. With that knowledge, Esmeralda wished to die.

Phoebus is not dead. His soul is, however, for Jehan has brought to him the lie that Esmeralda has confessed that she attempted to stab him.

Comes then the day of Esmeralda's execution. Before the great Church of Notre Dame she is to stop for a space, to pray and do penance.

From the roof, Quasimodo looks down and sees the girl who succored him. It is the work of an instant for the Hunchback to do a death-defying slide down a rope in front of the Cathedral, snatch Esmeralda from her guards and carry her into the church, screaming "Sanctuary! Sanctuary!" For once inside the Cathedral, according to ancient law, any culprit was safe.

From now on Esmeralda becomes Quasimodo's guiding spirit. He worships her with as great a devotion as a dog bestows upon the master he worships. No sacrifice is too great for the Hunchback to make.

But Jehan has carried to Clopin the news that Esmeralda has been given Sanctuary, and also the fact that she will soon be given over to the authorities, for the law granting Sanctuary could be revoked at will.

This fans the flames of hatred in Clopin's heart against the aristocracy, whom he dreams of conquering. Jehan sees with satisfaction Clopin calling upon his people to follow him to Notre Dame, to tear the edifice down stone by stone if necessary, and rescue their beloved Esmeralda.

This is heard as well by the poet Gringoire, whom Esmeralda once saved from death at the hands of the beggars, and who, with poetic feeling, has seen and aided the romance between her and Phoebus.

To Phoebus Gringoire goes, bearing the news. New life flows in Phoebus' veins. Esmeralda is alive! It is the work of a few minutes, he is on his way to the Bastille to arouse the garrison.

Clopin's thousands of followers are deploying upon the Place du Parvis. Jehan sees their preparations for the attack on the Cathedral and himself secure for a moment, rushes toward the upper fastness of Notre Dame to take Esmeralda for his own.

But the mass on the Place has aroused Esmeralda, and she in turn rouses Quasimodo.

Now starts a monumental defense of the church by one deformed man and a girl against thousands, who even now are storming the doors of

TENSE SCENE, from "The Hunchback of Notre Dame," Universal's great super-feature production which comes to the Strand Theatre for an indefinite engagement in the near future.

Scene Cut No. 9

Picturesque Actor Gives Chaney Race For Honors

Few actors have had a more picturesque career than Brandon Hurst who plays the role of Jehan in "The Hunchback of Notre Dame," which is now playing at the _____ Theatre.

Born in London, Hurst went into the stage as soon as he graduated and saw active service in India. He declares that one of the most thrilling experiences of his life happened while he was stationed near Rawal Pindi in the Punjab, which Kipling immortalized.

Cholera was raging among the natives and Hurst, with few other men, was detailed to seek out cases of the deadly plague. During the march two of the soldiers shot a peacock. That night they disappeared and the next day Hurst, in beating about the bush, discovered the two men, stripped and bound back to back, lying in the burning sun.

Investigation showed that the natives had a superstition that the peacock was a sacred bird, and, enraged at the killing, had spirited the soldiers away and left them to a horrible fate. One of the men was already dead, but Hurst managed to rescue the other.

"Had the natives discovered me saving my comrade's life, he [or I] would have been up in short order," declared Hurst. "Believe me, that long trip through the jungle and back to camp with that man on my back was something I will never forget."

Hurst's work in the Universal production is declared to be one of the finest pieces of acting ever seen on the screen and he gives Lon Chaney, the star, a close race for first honors.

Fool Held Official Post During Reign of Louis XI

From time immemorial the fool has been the butt of punsters, scorned of the intelligent, and generally made ridiculous. As one poet has so aptly expressed it: "A fool's a fool, and there's no denying that!" However even as every dog has his day and the devil will have his due, so too has the fool had his moment of glory in history.

It was in Paris of old that the fools held sway of power for the nonce. During the reign of King XI the strange Festival of the Fools was celebrated in its palmiest glory. This was the one day of the year when full license was granted Parisians of every class. The result was that for the day the ancient city became a Babylon gone mad.

From early dawn the boulevards were thronged with people of every class—beggars who forgot to beg, thieves who forgot to ply their trade, and respectable shopkeepers who forgot to be respectable. Madness ran riot and buffoonery ruled. Music and song mingled with the hoarse shouts of the mob, and wine ran freely.

An interesting feature of the celebration was the serpentine dance which was executed at the height of the wild orgy. Marching in the form of an endless, weaving serpent, men, women and children swayed through the streets, chanting a weird sing-song.

The Festival of the Fools is one of the strange phrases of history revived in "The Hunchback of Notre Dame," the Universal production now playing at the _____ Theatre.

_____ _____ _____ power Jehan, and he throws Jehan into space, to crash a crumpled heap near Clopin, just as Clopin is meeting death through the streams of molten lead which Quasimodo had poured from the parapet.

Before the agony of this molten death, the cable falls back, meeting unprepared the sudden onslaught of Phoebus and his soldiers. There ensues a mighty battle, while in the Cathedral there is being enacted the great tragedy Quasimodo did not come out of

Special Story to Run With Announcement

Laemmle Yields On Local Plea

Manager _____ of the _____ Theatre, has just bagged the best theatrical plum of the year. Following his request for letters from patrons desiring to see the Universal production "The Hunchback of Notre Dame," he was literally swamped with mail, each pledging patronage and support. These letters Manager _____ sent on to Carl Laemmle, president of Universal, and so impressed that official that he agreed to waive his plans for road-showing the production here, which meant it would not be seen until next year, and agreed to let it out on a rental basis to the _____ Theatre.

The Universal chief, in a letter to Manager _____, expresses his opinion that the theatre-goers of this city owe a vote of thanks for the tenacity and enterprise of the local exhibitor.

There probably has never been a production more in demand among theatre-goers and exhibitors alike than the picturization of the Victor Hugo classic. It opened in New York at the start of a new theatrical season with eight strong musical comedies and dramatic shows having their premieres on the same date, and with thirty-eight other big attractions housed in nearby theatres along the great "White Way." Tickets were priced at ten dollars each for the opening night and they were sold out days in advance. Lon Chaney, star of the production, who was in attendance at this premiere was given one of the greatest ovations ever tendered an actor. He was carried on the shoulders of members of the audience to the stage and forced to make a speech.

his fight with Jehan unscathed. Three times had Jehan plunged his knife into the bell-ringer's back.

And now even as Phoebus and his men put the mob to route, and while Gringoire guides Phoebus toward the upper portion of Notre Dame, Quasimodo lies dying.

There is one flash of happiness on his face as he sees Phoebus and Esmeralda wrapped in each other's arms

NIGEL DE BRULIER AS DON CLAUDE THE PRIEST

THE AMBASSADOR
Los Angeles

July 24th, 1923.

Mr. Carl Laemmle,
Universal City, Calif.

Dear Mr. Laemmle:

    I take great pleasure in extending to you my most sincere congratulations on your wonderful production of "THE HUNCHBACK OF NOTRE DAME" taken from the novel written by Victor Hugo.

    To my mind it is the last word in dramatic power and colorful portrayal that has been produced on the screen. The scenes, from beginning to end, are magnificent. There is nothing to mar the historical accuracy as exhibited in the play. Scenes descriptive of Parisian life in the reign of Louis XI are such that no one conversant in history can raise any objection. Of course, the novel written by Victor Hugo is of such a nature as to prejudice a great many minds against the historic Church of that period, which is the Catholic Church. The most fastidious of Catholics cannot take the lease exception to any scene and it overturns the bitter taste that a reading of THE HUNCHBACK OF NOTRE DAME leaves in one's mouth.

    You deserve the approval of all our fellow co-religionists in presenting to the world the HUNCHBACK OF NOTRE DAME as it was produced on the screen this afternoon. I hope that the work will bring you increased mental and financial satisfaction.

    I am,

        Yours sincerely,

signed *John H. Clifford*

Rector Church of the Nativity
5624 So Vermont
Los Angeles.

CARL LAEMMLE

Founder of Universal City

Tells Why

"The Hunchback of Notre Dame"

Was Selected to be Made
The *Crowning Achievement*
of the Screen

CARL LAEMMLE

 HAVE repeatedly been asked why I selected "The Hunchback of Notre Dame" for such a massive production, but I do not think that anyone coming fresh from its showing will ask the question. He will have the answer in his own emotions. Hugo's eternal classic was selected because it is the creation of a giant among authors; because it is established in the appreciation of the wide world and as a work of creative art, has the permanence of the ancient cathedral itself.

A romance established in the hearts of millions that will endure for centuries and the book will pass its spell from generation to generation—never old, but always with the freshness and fire of the author's flesh and blood expression. Such a book should make a picture with the same time-defying quality. With the aid of a staff of skilled editorial minds, all the world's literature was debated to select the ideal story — the story of human conflict, absorbing action and with the spectacular element that furnishes high pictorial value.

All along I had in mind Victor Hugo's romance and I was gratified when the majority, reporting individually, named "The Hunchback of Notre Dame" as the ideal story. To tell the truth, I was so carried away with the large possibilities of it that I would have produced it whatever the verdict of the others.

I feel that there has been put into the production all the beauty, color and charm of the book—all of its massive character and as it stands, it is not a production only for today. It is, like the storied cathedral, for all days to come.

VICTOR HUGO

PROGRAMME

CARL LAEMMLE *Presents*
LON CHANEY in
"The Hunchback of Notre Dame"
VICTOR HUGO'S
Mighty Epic of a Mighty Epoch!
A UNIVERSAL PRODUCTION

WALLACE WORSLEY	Director
PERLEY POORE SHEEHAN	Adapter
EDWARD T. LOWE, JR.	Scenarist
ROBERT NEWHARD AND TONY KORUMAN	Photographers
Quasimodo	LON CHANEY
Clopin	ERNEST TORRENCE
Esmeralda	PATSY RUTH MILLER
Phoebus	NORMAN KERRY
Mme. de Gondelaurier	KATE LESTER
Jehan	BRANDON HURST
Gringoire	RAYMOND HATTON
Louis XI	TULLY MARSHALL
Dom Claude	NIGEL DE BRULIER
Monsieur Neufchatel	HARRY L. VAN METER
Godule	GLADYS BROCKWELL
Marie	EULALIE JENSEN
Fleur de Lys	WINIFRED BRYSON

and TWENTY-EIGHT HUNDRED ADDITIONAL ARTISTS

Scenes, Medieval Paris. *Time*, The Reign of Louis XI, A. D., 1482

Projection under the supervision of Precision Machine Company

Music score arranged by Dr. Hugo Riesenfeld

WALLACE WORSLEY

THE spiritual background of the story is the Cathedral de Notre Dame (Cathedral of Our Lady) against which, as the story progresses, are hurled mighty opposing forces.

Quasimodo, the Hunchback of Notre Dame, has for a master, Jehan, brother of Dom Claude, the Arch-Deacon of the Church. Quasimodo worships Dom Claude with a spirit of reverent awe. Yet over the Hunchback Jehan exercises a control which many people attribute to Jehan's black-magic, for Jehan is an alchemist whose dream of gold is the driving force which leagues him with Clopin, King of the thieves and beggars of medieval Paris.

Supplying a romantic interest is the love which develops between Esmeralda, a Gypsy girl whom Clopin has reared as his own, and Phoebus—a dashing young Captain of the King's Guard.

It is largely due to the reverence and awe in which Clopin's people regard Esmeralda that Clopin holds his sway over the thieves and beggars.

Opposing Esmeralda's and Phoebus' romance, however, is the base passion which thrills Jehan when he gazes upon the beautiful Esmeralda as she dances in the Place du Parvis, the open space in front of the church.

He wants her. He determines to have her, even to the extent that upon a certain night, he has the innocent Quasimodo attempt to seize Esmeralda and carry her away.

The plan is frustrated by the timely arrival of Phoebus. Jehan deserts Quasimodo, who is captured. Esmeralda and Phoebus, looking deep into each others eyes, feel the awakening of their great love.

Quasimodo is presented for trial. Being deaf, he cannot hear the questions which an equally deaf judge puts to him.

The Hunchback's answers antagonize the court and his sentence is therefore increased. Without knowledge of his punishment, Quasimodo is taken to the public pillory, where amid the hoots and jeers of the populace, he is flogged upon his deformed and twisted back.

Bitterness pervades his soul, until Esmeralda, in pity for the poor and helpless creature, gives him a drink to cool his parched mouth.

A UNIVERSAL PRODUCTION

In that moment Esmeralda makes a friend. In that moment also awakens in Quasimodo the first awakening of love and he becomes something nearer a man and much less of a mere creature.

Phoebus, through his attention to Esmeralda, has made an enemy of Clopin. Esmeralda, knowing that Clopin would not hesitate at killing her handsome Captain, decides that she will give herself to the Church. In this way Phoebus will be saved from Clopin's hatred, but at the expense of a great sacrifice by Esmeralda.

For a last farewell, Phoebus and Esmeralda meet in the garden of the Cathedral. Jehan, who has watched them, sees in Phoebus an enemy whom he had best be rid of. While Phoebus and Esmeralda are locked in a fond embrace, Jehan drives home the knife which barely misses Phoebus' heart.

Innocent, Esmeralda is captured and at her trial protests that she is not guilty. The leering face of Jehan, at which she glimpsed in the garden, confronts her. She accuses him, but in turn is accused of being bewitched and is put to a terrific torture to wring a confession from her lips. In agony, the girl finally confesses and is thrown in a dungeon.

Esmeralda's absence from the Court of Miracles, the haunt of Clopin and the beggars, has thrown a pall over the place. Knowledge in those days did not spread quickly. A person could disappear, leaving no trace. So it was with Esmeralda as far as Clopin and the Court of Miracles were concerned.

Again Jehan confronts Esmeralda. In her cell, disguised in the robes of a monk, he pleads with her to be his. But Esmeralda denounces him and in a wild passion, Jehan tells her that her handsome Phoebus is dead. With that knowledge, Esmeralda wishes to die.

Phoebus is not dead. His soul is, however, for Jehan has brought to him the lie that Esmeralda has confessed that she attempted to stab him.

Comes then the day of Esmeralda's execution. Before the great Church of Notre Dame she is to stop for a space, to pray and do penance.

From the roof, Quasimodo looks down and sees the girl who succored him. It is but the work of an instant for the Hunchback to do a death-defying slide down a rope in front of the Cathedral, snatch Esmeralda from her guards and carry her into the Church, screaming—"Sanctuary! Sanctuary!" for once inside the Cathedral, according to ancient law, any culprit was safe.

From now on Esmeralda becomes Quasimodo's guiding spirit. He worships her with as great a devotion as a dog bestows upon the master he worships. No sacrifice is too great for the Hunchback to make.

But Jehan has carried to Clopin the news that Esmeralda has been given Sanctuary, and also the fact that she will soon be given over to the authorities, for the law granting Sanctuary could be revoked at will.

The HUNCHBACK of NOTRE DAME

This fans the flame of hatred in Clopin's heart against the aristocracy, whom he dreams of conquering. Jehan sees with satisfaction Clopin calling upon his people to follow him to Notre Dame, to tear the edifice down stone by stone if necessary, and rescue their beloved Esmeralda.

This is heard as well by the poet Gringoire, whom Esmeralda once saved from death at the hands of the beggars, and who, with poetic feeling, has seen bud and die, the romance between her and Phoebus.

To Phoebus Gringoire goes, bearing the news. New life flows in Phoebus' veins. Esmeralda is alive! It is but the work of a few minutes until he is on his way to the Bastille, to arouse the garrison.

Clopin's thousands of followers are deploying upon the Place du Parvis. Jehan sees their preparations for the attack on the Cathedral and himself secure for the moment, rushes toward the upper fastness of Notre Dame to take Esmeralda for his own.

But the noise on the Place has aroused Esmeralda and she in turn arouses Quasimodo.

Now starts a monumental defense, the defense of the Church by one deformed man and a girl against thousands, who even now are storming the doors of the building, while Phoebus and his soldiers are pouring from the Bastille.

Then comes Jehan. Deaf, Quasimodo does not hear Esmeralda scream and it seems that Jehan would accomplish his evil purpose.

Quasimodo, turning to seek his helper, sees her in the arms of the man who has been his master. Sees her screaming for help, the girl whom he loves. Jehan and Quasimodo fight, but Quasimodo's great strength soon overpowers Jehan, and Quasimodo throws Jehan hurtling into space to crash in a mangled heap near Clopin, just as Clopin is meeting his death by the molten lead which Quasimodo pours from the parapet.

Before the agony of this molten death, the rabble falls back, meeting unprepared the sudden onslaught of Phoebus and his soldiers. There ensues a mighty battle, while in the Cathedral there is being enacted a great tragedy.

Quasimodo did not come out of the fight with Jehan unwounded.

Three times did Jehan drive his knife into the Hunchback's breast.

And now, even as Phoebus and his men put the crowd in the Place to rout, and even while Gringoire guides Phoebus toward the upper portion of Notre Dame, Quasimodo is dying.

There is one flash of happiness on his face as he sees Phoebus take in his arm and crush to his breast the Love that could never have been his. Then, with his strength fast waning, Quasimodo drags himself toward the bell-tower, to ring for a last time his beloved bells which have been the voice of his soul.

And there, ringing his own death-knell, Dom Claude finds the poor Hunchback.

A UNIVERSAL PRODUCTION

ESMERALDA DANCING IN THE STREET

QUASIMODO WARNS THE SHOPKEEPER NOT TO TRIFLE WITH HIM.

ESMERALDA BELIEVING PHOEBUS IS DEAD IS COMFORTED BY MARIE

CLOPIN AND THE RABBLE ENTERING THE GAUNDELAURIER HOME TO STEAL ESMERALDA

The HUNCHBACK of NOTRE DAME

A UNIVERSAL PRODUCTION

Esmeralda rescues Gringoire

The Hunchback rings the bell for the last time

Clopin locks Esmeralda in her room to prevent her meeting Phoebus

Mons. Neufchatel

Dom Claude and Esmeralda come to the aid of Quasimodo in his hour of greatest trial

The HUNCHBACK of NOTRE DAME

Items of Interest About The Crowning Achievement of the Screen

Universal's Production of

"The Hunchback of Notre Dame"

with LON CHANEY

Presented by CARL LAEMMLE

The average working day for the twenty-eight hundred artists was twelve hours.

Six months were spent in preparation.

One year was spent in actual production.

One million, two hundred and fifty thousand dollars. ($1,250,000) was spent.

In point of money spent—the most expensive picture ever made.

In point of entertainment value received, the most in-expensive picture ever made.

The average working day for the two hundred technical and executive directors was fourteen hours.

The total personnel engaged numbered over four thousand.

Wallace Worsley, the director, required ten assistant directors and twenty-eight field captains.

10 Camera Men
10 Assistant Camera Men
105 Electricians
20 Sculptors
750 Carpenters, Masons, Property Men, Costumers.
550 Arcs and 50 Electric Suns for Night Scenes.

A UNIVERSAL PRODUCTION

The Cathedral of Notre Dame (Our Lady) is an exact replica in every infinite detail of the Cathedral as it looked in 1482, an extraordinary feat and an archeologic, historic and technical triumph.

Lon Chaney, the star, required three hours and a half each day to make up for "Quasimodo."

The sets were insured by Lloyd's for half a million.

Its dimensions are 225 feet in height and 150 feet in width. The total area used for the construction of the Cathedral is 6,000 square feet.

One scene, the Grand Ball of Louis XI, was rehearsed by 2,000 people for forty-eight hours.

Meals were served "on the lot" by experts loaned by the U. S. A. Quartermaster Corps.

More than 5,000 costumes were specially made.

A building 125 feet long with 18 windows was designed to store and pass out the costumes.

In addition to the Cathedral, other historical "sets" include exact reproductions of the Court of Miracles, Place du Parvis, Palais du Justice, Interior of the Bastille, Seven Noble Mansions, 35 Statues, and eight unnamed streets, each 200 feet long.

We wish to call your attention to the cast used in "The Hunchback of Notre Dame." All are so well known that additional comment is unnecessary.

1850 extras were checked in, dressed and made up, and on the set in 31 minutes. The same number were served box lunches and and hot coffee in eight minutes.

The cobblestones used in the street scenes of this production were hauled 38 miles by truck and placed by hand.

The immense crowds were directed by means of a radio amplification device which permitted unit control by the director, for the first time in motion picture production.

Every foot of "The Hunchback of Notre Dame" was made at Universal City, California.

Mr. Chaney did not use any doubles in any of his hazardous scenes.

The length of the Place du Parvis was 448 feet.

The HUNCHBACK of NOTRE DAME

PRINCIPAL PLAYERS

Lon Chaney: Born in Colorado, and, from a dancing comedian, developed to the greatest character actor of the screen beginning with the Universal productions—"Fires of Rebellion," "Broadway Love," "Anything Once," "A Broadway Scandal," "That Devil Bateese," "The Wicked Darling" and "Paid In Advance." A success in "The Miracle Man," now followed by the greatest artistic achievement of his career," "The Hunchback of Notre Dame."

Patsy Ruth Miller: Pronounced by visiting French authorities on Victor Hugo and his works to be the ideal "Esmeralda" for any production of the cathedral romance. A natural emotional actress and a charming girl. Fans may recall her as the little "Shireen" in "Omar the Tentmaker." Exotic parts are her specialty and that's the reason she had her golden chance in "The Hunchback of Notre Dame."

Norman Kerry: Plays soldier roles convincingly, because he was educated at St. John's Military Academy, Annapolis, Md. Devoted to horseback riding and fencing—and romantic poetry! He fitted perfectly into the "Merry-Go-Round," and, in "The Hunchback of Notre Dame" he completely realizes the creation of the great French master.

Ernest Torrence: The best actor of vividly sinister roles on screen or stage. Born in Edinburgh and educated for music; a gold medal student of the London Academy. Played lovers' parts in romantic stage comedies and was a London favorite. Then a long line of successes in musical comedy and the screen, where, though thousands shuddered at him, they nevertheless loved him. This is so because his characterizations are always to the life, and in Clopin, king of thieves, in "The Hunchback of Notre Dame," he says, he has contributed his best work to the great classic. And, by the same token, his work is classic.

Raymond Hatton: Born in Red Oak, Iowa, and began his stage career, portraying character roles. Now, after an unbroken series of fine screen delineations, he is rated as one of the six greatest character actors on the Screen. He has brown hair and blue

A UNIVERSAL PRODUCTION

eyes; and, to make a perfect picture as Gringoire, the poet in "The Hunchback of Notre Dame," he let his hair grow to the medieval length.

Tully Marshall: A native son of California and an alumnus of Santa Clara College. Stage career of 36 years as actor, manager and producer, and an impressive list of screen achievements. He is a deep student of psychology, and, in assuming a role, devotes himself to study, so as to get into the soul of the character. This fact gives particular significance to his portrayal of Louis XI in "The Hunchback of Notre Dame."

Nigel de Brulier: Gifted actor from the beginning; member of Henry Irving's company; student of history and occultism. Played the symbolic character of Tchernoff, in "The Four Horsemen;" John the Baptist, in Nazimova's "Salome" and the gentle Pir Kahn, in Kipling's "Without Benefit of Clergy." Some one has said that he was created for the atmosphere of "Notre Dame."

Winifred Bryson has come into popularity through her beauty and winning personality and the roles she assumed have been those of aristocratic misses or the simpler but not less attractive girls of humbler station. She has rich charm of manner and as the medieval beauty, Fleur de Lys, in "The Hunchback of Notre Dame" she was never shown to better advantage. She has been an admirer of Hugo from her school days.

Brandon Hurst: Player of many parts on stage and screen and a dramatist of established reputation. "Jehan, the role in which it was my good fortune to be cast," he says, "is a big, malign creation—of the stature of the cathedral itself. I feel that its portrayal is a peak event in my varied experience."

Harry L. Van Meter is from Missouri, having been born at Malta Ben. Physical culture instructor, then actor in stock with Blanche Bates, Henry Kolker and Orrin Johnson. Years of varied work for the screen. Wore armor with less effort than any man in "The Hunchback of Notre Dame." For which he was indebted to his early physical culture work.

Gladys Brockwell: Born in Brooklyn. Stage career since childhood; for a time with Willard Mack. Many emotional successes, including "The Soul of Satan." Highest dramatic point reached as Godule in "The Hunchback of Notre Dame," characterized as one of the most effective bits of tragic acting ever given to the screen.

Eulalie Jensen: Born in St. Louis; stage career with Bernhardt, in tour of the United States. Has played in stock, in comic opera and in notable productions for the last ten years. She is equally at home in melodrama or comedy, and her Marie in "The Hunchback of Notre Dame" is a characteristic contribution.

Kate Lester: "The grand dame of the screen." Born in England; educated at Normal College, New York; stage career with Richard Mansfield, Julia Marlowe, John Drew and Mrs. Fiske. With principal film companies; one of the best known faces on the screen. By breeding and experience eminently fitted for the proud patrician role in "The Hunchback of Notre Dame."

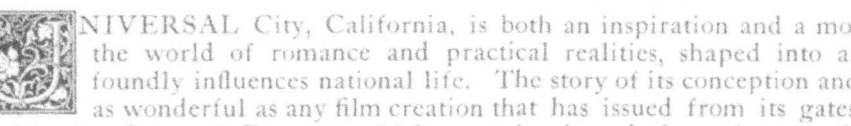

UNIVERSAL CITY

Only City in all the World Built for and Devoted Exclusively to the Elevation of the Screen.

An Eternal Monument to the Vision of Carl Laemmle, Pioneer Picture Producer, Prophet of the Picture World, Who Built a City Out of Dreams, Inspiration and Courage.

UNIVERSAL City, California, is both an inspiration and a monument. Here is the world of romance and practical realities, shaped into a power that profoundly influences national life. The story of its conception and its completion is as wonderful as any film creation that has issued from its gates to entertain the world—the Gates of Dreams, which vaguely shaped themselves in the fancy of Carl Laemmle as the inspiration of the enchanted city came to him at a time when the industry was young.

With the vision of a seer, he was far in advance of his time; but he beheld clearly what the future had in store, and Universal City was built, not only for the demands of the present but to meet the conditions of a broader glorious future. And so it is today one of the marvels of a giant industry and always the city of the future, for the very spirit that animates it is progressive, constructive, and for all time. Universal! Aptly named.

Figures dealing with average construction and mechanical accomplishment are dull and mean when compared with the wonder of this city of cities. The Magic Carpet and the Wonderful Lamp of Arabian fancy are overshadowed by the limitless breadth and depth of the creation here possible. In Universal City time and space have been eliminated. At a wish, so to speak, we are swept back into the Middle Ages or to the dim dawn of time.

Universal City! City of Enchantment, with its Gates of Dreams, through which come shapes to delight us children of a larger growth. City of the Universe on the highway of the Stars!

Universal Pictures—Past, Present *and* Future

"THE Hunchback of Notre Dame" marks a new epoch in the history of the motion picture. It is a new milestone of progress in the development of Art. From this vantage point of accomplishment the Universal Pictures Corporation, which created it, takes pleasure in calling attention to a few of the pictures which have made it great and to a few coming productions which you will greatly enjoy.

With these past successes Universal is glad to have you associate its name in pleasant memory. It may surprise you to know that the first big five-reel success ever made in the United States was made by Universal. It was called "Traffic in Souls" and started the late George Loane Tucker on his screen career. Far ahead of its time Universal made a great costume picture with Anna Pavlowa. More recently you recall "The Storm," "The Flirt," Reginald Denny in Jack London's "The Abysmal Brute," "Trifling with Honor," "Human Hearts" and "Merry Go Round" with Mary Philbin and Norman Kerry, which like "The Hunchback" was so astoundingly real that the company had to make affidavit that it was made in its entirety at Universal City, California. So much for the glorious past.

May we call your attention to a few of the successes Universal has now in production? You will want to see Mrs. Frances Hodgson Burnett's greatest story, "A Lady of Quality." As a play it made the fame and happiness of Julia Arthur, and as a picture it is going to do the same for beautiful Virginia Valli. Whether you saw Rita Weiman's play, "The Acquittal," or not, you must see this gripping drama in moving pictures with Claire Windsor and Norman Kerry. Reginald Denny's fame has been so well established that his forthcoming picture, "There He Goes," by Byron Morgan, will be certain to interest you. And after seeing Mary Philbin in "Merry Go Round," you will be on the qui-vive of expectancy for her next picture. Universal has purchased for her Owen Kildare's singularly beautiful novel, "My Mamie Rose."

Little Baby Peggy's spectacular success in two reelers has prompted Universal to make her a five-reel attraction star and already three pictures are in prospect for her. One is a picturization of Frances Hodgson Burnett's delightful story "Editha's Burglar," which Augustus Thomas chose as the subject matter for his first play. "A Chapter in Her Life," picturized by Lois Weber from Clara Louise Burnham's book "Jewel," is a picture of unique charm. For vital, soul-stirring drama, "Thundering Dawn," with J. Warren Kerrigan and Anna Q. Nilsson, provides a vivid contrast to it. Admirers of Priscilla Dean will have three treats in store for them in the William A. Brady stage success "Drifting," also "White Tiger," and "The Storm Daughter," all fitting sequels to "Outside the Law" and "The Virgin of Stamboul." Following "A Lady of Quality," Virginia Valli has in prospect Owen Davis's play, "Up the Ladder," still a popular attraction in Chicago. Hobart Henley, whose success with "The Flirt" and other great productions is so well known, is working on a huge production of Booth Tarkington's novel, "The Turmoil." And among the twenty super-productions which Universal is making this year, none will be more unique or more spectacular than the production which it will give to the famous anonymously written novel, "Damned."

Great speculation has torn the literary world as to the identity of the author. We are pleased to let you know her name. This is the first announcement that Miss Ethel Smith Dorrance wrote "Damned."

"LOVE THEME" (Domenico Savino)

from the picture "The Hunchback of Notre Dame"

Andantino Moderato

By permission G. Schirmer, Inc.

CARL LAEMMLE Offers
The HUNCHBACK of NOTRE DAME
By VICTOR HUGO
With LON CHANEY
DIRECTED BY WM WORSLEY
The FESTIVAL OF FOOLS
Morgan
A UNIVERSAL PRODUCTION

```
                                PICTURE  NO:
                                STORY BY:    VICTOR HUGO
                                ADAPTED BY:  PERLEY POORE SHEEHAN
                                SCENARIO BY: EDWARD T. LOWE, JR.
                                DIRECTED BY: WALLACE WORSLEY.
```

MAIN TITLE (1)........ THE HUNCHBACK
OF
NOTRE DAME

An adaptation of Victor Hugo's great classic,
by
Perley Poore Sheehan.

Scenario by Edward T. Lowe, Jr.

. . . . .

SUBTITLE (2)   FADE IN ON: Chappel sheet cover (2)

The Cathedral Church of Notre Dame de Paris.

FADE OUT.

1.   EXT. LONG SHOT OF MEDIEVAL NOTRE DAME FADE IN. ON
The scene fades in on long shot, showing Notre Dame de
Paris as it was in the period of the story. This shot
should contain all that is valuable in the way of at-
mosphere in the art drawing, with a lighting that ac-
centuates the mysticism and awe that Notre Dame inspires.
After a fairly short introductory scene of this nature,
~~LAP DISSOLVE THE SCENE INTO:~~

SUBTITLE (3)   A LEGACY OF THE AGES TO ALL NATIONS. . .
                  A MONUMENT OF HUMAN FAITH. . . . .
                  A TEMPLE TO THE UNIVERSAL GOD . . . . . .

LAP DISSOLVE OUT AND INTO:

EXT. LONG SHOT OF MEDIEVAL NOTRE DAME
~~FADE IN ON THE ABOVE~~
Continue the same artistic treatment of the view for a few feet. It is not necessary - - nor is it advisable at this point - - to show any action. Concentrate rather on the subject, Notre Dame. After a few feet of this, ~~DISSOLVE ONE AND TWO:~~

SUBTITLE (4)   THE ONE HAVEN OF REFUGE IN A BRUTAL AGE,
                THE MOTHER OF A SUFFERING HUMANITY,
                A SANCTUARY WHERE THE PERSECUTED COULD
                ALWAYS FIND PROTECTION. . . . .

~~LAP DISSOLVE INTO:~~

3. EXT. SUPER LONG SHOT OF MEDIEVAL NOTRE DAME
    ~~THE SAME AS IN THE PREVIOUS TREATMENT.~~
    Showing what is really a view of Paris rather than of Notre Dame. The Cathedral occupies the picture center and should be so lighted that the eyes focus to it naturally. In this scene can be incorporated a sense of movement, though it is not necessary. After a few feet of this view, CUT IN:

SUBTITLE (5)   FROM TIME IMMEMORIAL,
                THE HEART OF THE WORLD,
                THE HEART OF FRANCE,
                THE HEART OF PARIS.

BACK: Continue the super long shot for a few feet and then FADE OUT, with the light dwelling on Notre Dame in such a way as to accentuate the thought incorporated in the title. The prologue ends as THE SCENE FADES OUT.

. . . .

INT. BELFRY OF NOTRE DAME MEDIUM FULL SHOT ~~LAP DISSOLVE IN ON THE BELFRY~~
showing the bells of the tower, two of which are in action. Shoot this through a soft edge vignette aperture, and pay strict attention to the lighting, incorporating here, as well as everywhere else possible, the intangible suggestion of something ethereal. Hold for a few seconds on a view of the inanimate thing which are Quasimodo's soul, and then ~~LAP DISSOLVE INTO:~~ Bells stop ringing

7. EXT. MEDIUM SHOT AT PARAPET OF GALLERY AFTERNOON
    This shot is a bit larger than the medium close-up from which we dissolved into the tower. The view incorporates more of the tower shutters, thus identifying the source of sound which Quasimodo has heard. He is still looking up toward the bells, with awakening reverence and spiritual aspiration on his face. Make it clearly evident here that these bells are his soul - a part of him, loved by him. Now, as Quasimodo holds this position, CUT IN:

SUBTITLE (7)   DIN. . . . HALF HEARD. . . THE BELLS OF
                NOTRE DAME HAD SPOKEN THE VOICE OF
                HIS SIMPLE SOUL. . . . THE ONLY VOICE
                HE COULD HEAR.

8. EXT. CLOSER SHOT AT PARAPET AFTERNOON
    Quasimodo, as in above scene, is still looking up toward the tower, this closer shot serving to accentuate the sense of infinite pity which we must feel for him - a pity that is to grow into love, a love that is to grow into an understanding of the great tragedy of the creature. Now the tolling of the bells ceases, as becomes evident in Quasimodo's shifting of his interest to the street level below. As he shifts his gaze downward and leans further out over the parapet, the better to see, the Hunchback's expression loses all sense of spirituality. He is the abysmal brute. He scorns and hates all humanity. He grinds his teeth. He grotesquely spits. Continuing this for a few feet. CUT TO:

SUBTITLE (6)   FADE IN:
                TEN YEARS BEFORE COLUMBUS STARTED TO
                AMERICA, THESE BELLS RANG THE HOLY
                PRAYERS OF NOTRE DAME, A CHURCH
                WHOSE FAMILIAR OF THAT DAY WAS KNOWN
                AS QUASIMODO.
                FADE OUT.

4. EXT. MEDIUM SHOT OF MEDIEVAL NOTRE DAME AFTERNOON FADE IN.
    The scene fades in on a medium shot, shooting upward from below the gallery which joins the two towers of Notre Dame. This view, however, includes only a portion of the left tower, with Quasimodo, the Hunchback of Notre Dame occupying a position near one of the stone chimeras. Like the stone image, he also leans with his elbows on the parapet, his chin in his hands, his gaze outward, over all Paris. There is no movement on the part of Quasimodo; so far as we know at this point, he might well be one of the chimeras himself, and it is this effect that this scene is intended to give. It is a definite planting, without calling specific attention to it, of the fact that Quasimodo is as much a part of Notre Dame as is the stone image at his side. This scene should not be too long, and is more of a connecting link between the last long shot of the prologue and the closeup which is now to follow as we LAP DISSOLVE INTO:

5. EXT. MEDIEVAL NOTRE DAME MEDIUM C.U. AFTERNOON
    The scene LAP DISSOLVES IN ON THE ABOVE. The view now concentrates on Quasimodo and the chimera, emphasising the Hunchback's far-away, all-embracing, yet unseeing expression. In spite of the Hunchback's ugliness, there must be that about him which will arouse a feeling of sympathy and speculation. For several seconds this position is held. Then gradually it becomes evident that Quasimodo's reverie has been broken, for there comes a transition in his expression - a softening - a reaction to reverence, awe and spiritual aspiration as he slowly turns and looks up toward the tower of Notre Dame, the shutters of which form a portion of the background for this view. Now, as he listens, LAP DISSOLVE INTO:

9. EXT. LONG SHOT PLACE DU PARVIS. LATE AFTERNOON
    This angle is from the parapet of the Cathedral, shooting downward into the open space in front of Notre Dame - the Place du Parvis. In the left b.g. can be seen a portion of the Seine, supposedly a bridge covered with tall houses. In the b.g. are a number of city dwellings of the rich - medieval palaces with only a yard or two of open spaces separating them. The building nearest the camera to the left is the Gondelaurier mansion. This fronts immediately on the street with the suggestion of a very narrow garden at one side of it. The building is of stone, four-stories high with a deep slate roof and a small turret on the riverside. This building will be described in greater detail in subsequent scenes. To the right, in b.g., for as much as will come in range of the camera, are other residences of less impressive architecture and crowded close together-these being the residences of ordinary bourgeoise. The open square, which is about an acre in extent, is garlanded with evergreen wreathes and banners, suspended from a series of temporary masts. In the back center of the Place are two platforms about five feet high and placed fairly close together. Surmounting one of these platforms is a gibbet, consisting of a crossbeam on two uprights. From the cross-beam are suspended two chains about a yard apart and dangling a length of three feet or so, from which criminals may be hung. To the left of this, on the other platform, is the "wheel" or pillory, where criminals are otherwise punished. Both the gibbet and pillory will also be described in greater detail further on. This shot shows that the Place du Parvis is already swarming with the populace - mostly of the poorer and more dissolute elements. There is a drunken and boisterous revelry, evident even in a long shot. Hold this shot long enough to indicate that people are continuing to arrive. In this shot also there should be registered the fact that the nobility are at home in the houses in the b.g., the windows of which are open and decorated to some extent by hanging tapestries. From these windows the nobility look down upon the populace. There is no movement of carriages or other vehicles in this shot, but a small party of horsemen canter across the b.g., causing the pedestrians to scamper to left and right. Apart from the decorations, it may be seen that there are a series of booths, or temporary stalls somewhat loosely constructed and arranged about the periphery of the Place, where sweetmeats, sausages, etc., are sold, likewise where various fakirs and small side-shows are established.
    CUT TO:

76

10. EXT. LATE ENCEPLACE DU PARVIS LATE AFTERNOON
The angle of this shot is from the Gondelaurier house, shooting toward Notre Dame. As a b.g. to this long shot, we have the full facade of Notre Dame, the camera being at a sufficient elevation to command a complete view of the decorations. At regular intervals around the Place and somewhat in advance of the decorative masts, there are shorter posts each surrounded by a fire-basket. These fire-baskets are a loose mesh of flat wrought-iron and are about two feet in circumference and raised eight feet above the ground. The baskets have been filled with a prepared mass of hemp and resin, for lighting purposes. There is just enough action in this scene to show that this is a period of general revelry and license. In the f.g., two women of the middle class - of thirty or forty years of age, and fairly good-looking, very desirous of appearing to be "perfect ladies" - are accosted by two drunken and poorly dressed hoodlums. One of them tries to steal a kiss from the younger lady and receives a stout box on the ears from the elder woman. The other hoodlum laughs uproariously as his companion falls back. This gives the key to the general feeling of license and good humor afloat. CUT TO:

SUBTITLE (8)   THE FESTIVAL OF FOOLS...THE ONE DAY
               OF THE YEAR WHEN FULL LIBERTY WAS
               GRANTED TO PARISIANS OF EVERY CLASS.

B.JR: In this action, which follows the title, the movement is rather slow in order to show various bits of action in the crowd. In contrast to the slow movement of the camera, however, we have a fairly swift sequence of action in the crowd. We see a group of four dancers - two men and two women - prancing along arm in arm and frightfully disguised. One is a dwarf with a Turk's turban on his head. The other man is dressed as Satan in the classical conception of him with horns and forked tail. One of the women is extremely fat, with her mouth and eyes grotesquely magnified. The second woman is apparently naked except for her cloak, but wears a large skull of death's head for a mask. In the next succeeding action we see a jet black negro, swallowing a sword while a group of interested beholders crowd about. We see a fat clown riding a small burro. He is assailed by a group of young street wenches who surround him. He tries to kiss them all. Two soldiers in armor, partly drunk, bump into a civilian burgher and laugh at him when he protests. One of the soldiers kicks the burgher and sends him sprawling. Before this action can be followed up, there is a general movement in the crowd to indicate a more important movement. The camera now stops, and as the crowd presses back to form a lane, CUT TO:

11. EXT. PLACE DU PARVIS.SHOT ACROSS PARVIS. LATE AFTERNOON
This shot is from the direction of left-hand corner of Notre Dame, shooting in the general direction of the bridge near the Gondelaurier home. This shot shows a lane has been formed near the Gondelaurier house, and is still in process of formation by the simple manner of a bunch of cross-bowmen on foot and in light armor, jostling back the people roughly on either side. In command of this movement is a mounted Captain, Monsieur Neufchatel, who rides his horse back and forth, and gradually forward, urging his men to do their work thoroughly. The soldiers are rough. The people are docile. In the f.g. is seen a hideous fake cripple - a supposedly legless man in a barrow on small wheels which he propels along with his hands on the pavement each hand holding an iron stirrup. He joins the general movement to get out of the way, but resents being jostled by the soldier nearest him.   CUT TO:

12. EXT. PLACE DU PARVIS. C.U.   LATE AFTERNOON
In this c.u. the legless man, subsequently referred to as the "cul-de-jatte," is seen as he headed out of the line of march, but with his head turned toward the soldier in sneering resentment. The soldier gives him a brutish grin and pokes him out of the way with a violent shove of his pike-staff. The cul-de-jatte lets out an explosive curse and hastily rolls into the mob. Any other faces visible in this shot are laughing at the incident.   CUT TO:

13. EXT. PLACE DU PARVIS SHOT ACROSS PARVIS LATE AFTERNOON
This is a continuation of SCENE 11. While the people are jostled back on either side of the lane by the soldiers and they progress out of range of camera off right foreground, a group of four heralds are seen riding abreast down the lane, lifting their trumpets to their lips, sounding the royal salute. Back of the mounted heralds is a group of mounted horsemen, not more than twenty in number, behind whom is seen a cumbersome carriage of the epoch, drawn by four horses. The carriage is flanked by a squad of horsemen.   CUT TO:

14. EXT. PLACE DU PARVIS MOVING INSERT C.U. OF CARRIAGE LATE AFTERNOON.
The carriage is open on both sides. In the back of it there is a bench covered by a draped cloth, spotted with fleur-de-lys. In front of the bench there is what is equivalent to a small table, also covered with a draped cloth. On this table is a large Bible, closed. On a stool at the side of this table is seated a white-haired priest who is in familiar conversation with King Louis, who is seated on the higher bench. King Louis is the figure of a man who doesn't care for this kind of publicity, but is watchful and discerning.
CUT IN:

SUBTITLE (9)   "HIS MAJESTY, KING LOUIS XI."

BACK: King Louis is in almost pitiable contrast to the royal pomp of his entry. He is a small and wizened figure, pale and shifty, shabbily dressed. He draws his gray fur-trimmed cloak about him. An old gray hat is pulled well down over his face. The front of his hat is decorated by a single leaden figure of a Saint. While he shiftily talks to the monk and watches the populace, he nervously fingers the beads of a rosary. CUT TO:

15. EXT. GALLERY OF NOTRE DAME C.U. QUASIMODO LATE AFTERNOON
Quasimodo, looking down into the Parvis, is witnessing the royal entry. To him the King is the world - organised society - and the spectacle merely increases his feeling of savage contempt. He puts out a hand to a bit of ancient statuary at his side and as if without any great effort, crunches off a fragment of it. For a moment he holds this fragment as if he would hurl it at the King below, but his impulse is fading without any loss of bitterness as we
CUT TO:

16. EXT. PLACE DU PARVIS MOVING INSERT C.U. OF CARRIAGE LATE AFTERNOON.
Louis is still fingering the beads of his rosary while he shiftily talks to the monk and watches the populace. He is still shifting his eyes over the crowd as he speaks:

SUBTITLE (10)   "WE LIVE OUT IT IS HISTORY. IT SAVORS OF DISRESPECT TO BOTH GOD AND KING."

B.U.: The monk placates Louis with an inclination of his head and a suave assurance that everything is alright.
CUT TO:

17. EXT. PLACE DU PARVIS LONG SHOT LATE AFTERNOON
The crowd is closing in the lane as Louis' procession progresses slowly across the Parvis. Just for a short scene of this and then CUT TO:

18. INT. UPPER CORRIDOR OF NOTRE DAME MED. SHOT LATE AFTERNOON
This is a narrow corridor of Gothic masonry, simple and unadorned. Upstage is an entrance which gives onto a circular stone staircase. Along the right-hand side is a series of three or four plain doorways, leading into as many cells. These doors match up with the door of Jehan's cell, subsequently described. (CONTINUED NEXT PAGE.)

18.   (CONTINUED.)
Coming toward the camera is Dom Claude, the Archdeacon of Notre Dame. While he walks meditatively, there is a certain animation about him that shows him to be of a human and gracious nature. He progresses down scene to a MEDIUM C.U. position, near the door of Jehan's cell. He stops, glances at the door, glances up. CUT IN:

SUBTITLE (11)   DOM CLAUDE? THE SAINTLY ARCH DEACON OF NOTRE DAME.

BACK: Dom Claude's face is animated. It registers both tenderness and devotion to duty. His brother is a source of anxiety to him but he has faith in God and man. He will speak to his brother and try to win him from his evil ways. As he turns to the door into Jehan's cell, CUT TO:

SUBTITLE (12)   SINCE THE DAYS OF CAIN AND ABEL, SONS OF THE SAME MOTHER HAVE DIFFERED AS DAY FROM NIGHT. THERE HAD ALSO LONG DWELT IN NOTRE DAME THE ARCH DEACON'S EVIL BROTHER, JEHAN.

19.   INT. JEHAN'S CELL IN NOTRE DAME. FULL SHOT AFTERNOON
The full shot discloses a stone cell of necessary proportions. A narrow window, the only one of this room, is in the center of the upstage wall. A little to left of center is a heavy Gothic table, littered with manuscript scrolls and large tomes. Placed on the extreme left of the table is a wrought iron standard, with cross bar, from each end of which are suspended flat oil lamps, like saucers with a little beak. This will serve to give lighting values to the face of Jehan, who is seated at the table. In the right wall is a low arched door, wider in width than normal, and framing this, a simple Gothic design. Beyond this door, in the corner, is a large stone fireplace, about half-way up in which has been built a masonry shelf. On this shelf burns a charcoal fire. There is a bellows to actuate the fire, and also various chemical retorts, the apparatus of a medieval alchemist. On a little iron tripod
(CONTINUED NEXT PAGE.)

19. (CONTINUED)
over the fire there is a retort, in which is a bubbling liquid of fire. In a conspicuous position on the upstage wall is a skin of an owl, arranged in such a way as to give the impression of a crucifix.
Seated at the table is Jehan, a man of forty or so, with a lean and evil face; a man whom we dislike and hate from the start. He is leaning over the table, poring over the pages of a large volume, with the flickering light of the oil lamps heightening the evil lines of his face. The door on right opens and Dom Claude steps into the room - kindly, smiling expectant. Jehan turns, looking up with an expression of guilty surprise toward Dom Claude, who has stopped for just an instant to glance toward the fire-place where the retort is bubbling. Dom Claude now turns and as he crosses, there is an ever increasing expression of righteous indignation on his face. As he reaches Jehan,
CUT TO:

20. INT. JEHAN'S CELL CLOSER SHOT AT TABLE AFTERNOON
Jehan does not rise, but hunches forward looking up at Dom Claude with fawning hypocrisy. As if slowly confirming his worst fears, Dom Claude's eyes sweep to the owl stretched in the semblance of a crucifix, this being in view on back wall. The sight of this perversion of a sacred emblem is what moves Claude to open denunciation of his brother. He now looks down at Jehan, while Jehan smiles placatingly under his gaze. Dom Claude sternly speaks:

SUBTITLE (13)   "IS IT POSSIBLE THAT YOU SHOULD PERSIST
                 IN THIS DEVIL'S MAGIC, IN SPITE OF ALL
                 MY PLEADING?"

BACK: Jehan reflects a moment as he fingers a cobblestone lying on his table. He shortly expects to make this stone into gold, but he keeps the secret to himself. Thought of what the stone may become, however, gives him courage to speak to his brother:

81

23. (CONTINUED.)
ACT: Clopin's meditations are momentarily interrupted by a drunken woman of ragged habit, who stumbles into the scene drinking from a bottle. She laughs and thrusts the bottle toward Clopin, who turns on her with a slow movement. She retreats before his glowering look. This action has been observed by Dom Claude, who has appeared now within the open door of the Cathedral from within. As Dom Claude looks with benevolence at the scene outside. CUT TO:

24. INT. PLACE DU PARVIS. M.C.U. DOM CLAUDE LATE AFTERNOON
As Dom Claude, with a touch of gentle protest and consternation, sees the action about to take place between Clopin and the drunken woman. CUT TO:

25. EXT. PLACE DU PARVIS. MED. CLOSE STEPS NOTRE DAME LATE AFTERNOON
The drunken woman has recovered from her rebuff and has again started to offer Clopin a drink from her bottle. Simultaneous with her movement, Clopin seizes up a short crutch, which has been lying at his side, and swings it to give her a blow. The crutch is seized from behind by Dom Claude. Clopin, with a fierce snarl, turns to see who it is that has interfered with him. During this action, the drunken woman ambles out of scene. This leaves the scene to Dom Claude and Clopin. There is a static moment of suspended action while Clopin and Dom Claude hold the crutch and confront each other. Then Clopin's defiance quails under the steady gaze of Dom Claude, whereupon Dom Claude relinquishes his hold on Clopin's crutch, straightens up with great mildness and dignity. This action has been observed by Jehan, who also emerges from the left door of the Cathedral. Jehan makes his entry like a man in haste, but he stops sharply with acute interest as he sees the action of Dom Claude and Clopin. CUT TO:

26. EXT. STEPS OF NOTRE DAME. C.U. OF JEHAN LATE AFTERNOON
In this c.u. we see Jehan look at his brother with contempt, mingled with hatred. There is also a contempt but a brightening of interest as he looks at Clopin. He permits himself a bitter, sardonic smile as he witnesses Clopin's defeat. Jehan draws back slightly as if to avoid a possible interview with his brother. Just for a flash, CUT TO:

27. EXT. PORCH OF NOTRE DAME. MED. LONG SHOT LATE AFTERNOON
This shot is from the door of the left entrance to the Cathedral, shooting toward the Parvis. In the f.g. is Jehan, standing with his back almost to camera. He is closely observing the action between Dom Claude and Clopin, upscene. The b.g. of this shot is the Parvis with its multiple movement suggested, this shot being essentially a MEDIUM CLOSE SHOT of Clopin and Dom Claude. As Dom Claude, with dignity retires from the scene, exiting f.g. left, along the porch of the Cathedral, Clopin snarls down and around in evil humor to his former position. Jehan still smiling bitterly, and with the air of one who approaches an old acquaintance, goes upscene to Clopin and touches Clopin on the shoulder. Clopin whirls, as if he would strike the person who has taken this liberty. He is only slightly mollified when he sees the mocking face of Jehan. CUT TO:

28. EXT. STEPS OF NOTRE DAME. C.U. JEHAN & CLOPIN LATE AFTERNOON
This shot shows Clopin on the right and Jehan standing on the left, just having touched Clopin on the shoulder. Jehan speaks a sneering title:

SUBTITLE (18) "EVEN YOU, FRIEND CLOPIN, MUST YIELD TO THE POWER OF MY REVEREND BROTHER."

(CONTINUED.)

28 (CONTINUED.)

BACK: Jehan [struck through] a step or two so that his head is almost on a level with that of Clopin who is now seated [struck through] on the top step of the Cathedral porch. In the conversation which follows, they may thus carry on a conversation without having the appearance of doing so. Both are watchful. They are speaking of a possibility which obviously they have discussed before. They do not look at each other while they talk, except perhaps from the corners of their eyes. They are plotters and potential colleagues. Clopin, after a moment of savage reflection and goaded on by the crafty Jehan, retorts:

SUBTITLE (19) "WHEN I HAVE THE SAY-SO, THERE'LL BE NEITHER KING NOR CLERGY......"

BACK: As Clopin says this much of his sentence he stops, looking up at Jehan with a grim expectancy as if to see whether or not Jehan is still in full accord with a treason that has already been discussed between them. Jehan gives Clopin a quick look of cunning interest as Clopin concludes his sentence with the words:

SUBTITLE (20) "..............EXCEPT ME."

BACK: Clopin savagely taps himself on the breast with his right fist while his left fondles the handle of a knife which he partly draws out of concealment from his ragged sash. Jehan is cunning and calculating. He has a thought in the back of his head which he only partly expresses when he says:

SUBTITLE (21) "GOLD'S THE STUFF THAT MAKES KINGS AND KEEPS THEM ON THEIR THRONES."

BACK: Clopin responds to this thought with a glint of savage joy and menace as he says:

SUBTITLE (22) "GOLD.........AND STEEL."

(CONTINUED.)

28   (CONTINUED.)
            BACK: As Clopin finishes this, he draws out his big pointed
            knife from his sash and presents it, point upward, toward
            Jehan. Jehan looking out over the Parvis has a quick movement
            of caution and warning. Now, as Clopin returns the blade to
            his sash, CUT TO: *then the [?] look up*

noon shot
28*   *Shot of Place showing the crowd as*
      people call each other attention etc
      point upward OK

                    From Top of church
29.   EXT. PLACE DU PARVIS. LONG SHOT DOWN TO PARVIS LATE AFTERNOON
            This view is from above, shooting down into the Parvis.
            Jehan's movement of caution in the previous scene has been
            partly occasioned by the sudden ~~stir of~~ interest in the
            people, who as the word is passed from one to another, all
            look up toward the facade of the Cathedral - a sea of faces
            and pointing hands indicating a tense excitement as they see:
            CUT TO:

→ 28*1 *Shot on Quas[imodo] as he jumps up on railing*
                                                          30

                              People all pointing upward as in (29)
                    Double exposure from fourth floor
30.   EXT. FACADE OF NOTRE DAME SHOT FROM ABOVE. LATE AFTERNOON
            This shot places the camera at a point in space in front of
            Notre Dame, shooting downward, giving an unusual perspective.
            In fairly closeup position, that is at the gallery parapet,
            is Quasimodo, sitting on a water spout which projects over
            the dizzy space below. There is nothing below him but empty
            space. For a moment of so we see him sitting there, uncon-
            scious of danger. Now he suddenly swings himself around
            under the water spout and flings himself through space.
        →   CUT TO: *Quas jumps from railing to gargoyle in center*

30*   *Quas swings from first gargoyle to other second gargoyle* OK
OK 30*1 *Double exposure shot of above scene (20x)* OK

→ *Shot*#2 *Still with double + miniature. Quas jumps from second*
         gargoyle to capital and down column.

Hill

31. EXT. FACADE OF NOTRE DAME. MED. C.U. LATE AFTERNOON
This view shows a narrow ledge and a masonry corner of the facade of Notre Dame. Quasimodo is just landing on the ledge and clutching the corner of the tower with his outstretched arms and flattened hands. He holds this perilous position for a moment or so with his back to camera, then turns to look down and back at the people below with his face partly to camera. He sullenly grins, completely indifferent to his own danger. He makes a ferocious face at the people below and at imminent risk of breaking his neck, releases the hold of one of his hands, puts his thumb to his nose and twiddles his fingers. CUT TO:

Shot — Close up of crowd

Side Immature cross [illegible] with dummy

32. EXT. NOTRE DAME MED. SHOT LATE AFTERNOON
This shot is far enough away to show Quasimodo, a minute figure, clinging as described to the masonry of the Cathedral, about halfway down. The people are at once jubilant and apprehensive. They laugh and cheer and point as Quasimodo continues his descent, the direction of which is such that his entry into the following scene will be near the right-hand side of the left portal to the Cathedral. As Quasimodo continues his descent, leaping and clinging to whatever offers handhold. CUT TO:

Gallery of saints

33. EXT. PORCH OF NOTRE DAME. MED. SHOT CLOPIN & JEHAN LATE AFTERNOON
This shot includes a portion of the masonry of the Left Centre door. Clopin and Jehan have continued their [illegible] discussion while Quasimodo [illegible] descending the facade of the Cathedral. There is still a degree of caution in their interchange, but they have come to a better understanding. Now Quasimodo comes into the scene down above and his arrival fits in with the logic of the events that has taken place between Jehan and Clopin. (CONTINUED.)

33. (CONTINUED.)
Clopin is frankly looking up at Quasimodo as the [illegible]
[illegible]. Jehan carries on his discussion with Clopin by saying:

SUBTITLE (23) "HE DOES MY BIDDING. HE KNOWS THE SECRETS OF NOTRE DAME. COMES THE DAY OF UPRISING AND WE'LL USE THIS HALF-APE, HALF-DEVIL TO SEIZE THE CATHEDRAL'S TREASURE."

BACK: As Jehan finishes the title, Clopin throws a sharp glance at Quasimodo [illegible]. CUT TO:

Longer Shot on Centre door as Feas [illegible] with picture Jehan leaves Clopin signals hand to follow.

34. EXT. PLACE DU PARVIS BASEMENT OF A HOUSE NEAR NOTRE DAME MEDIUM SHOT LATE AFTERNOON
The location will be known as Sister Gudule's cell. In the foundation of one of the houses there is a low arched aperture with heavy iron bars on a level with the basement. This aperture is about four and a half feet wide and only about two feet high. The cell of the floor within is several feet below the street level. To the right of the arched aperture is a sunken and narrow stone doorway on the cell level, reached by three narrow and very steep steps. Ordinarily the door is closed - a plain wooden door of heavy construction. This part of the set should be dank and aged. In this general shot the action is merely that of the shifting crowd, when into scene comes Esmeralda, followed by her three musicians as later described, and the woman Marie with the performing goat. Marie, thirty or thereabout, has traces of beauty and a dissipated look, but she is devoted to Esmeralda - a gypsy chaperone. Esmeralda walks lightly at the head of the little troupe. As she advances, there is a movement toward her of the people who hail her appearance with joy, shouting: .CONTINUED.

34. (CONTINUED)

SUBTITLE (24)   "ESMERALDA! ESMERALDA!"

  BACK: As the crowd surges in ahead of Esmeralda, she
  smiles sweetly at those about her. With her progress
  blocked, she pauses. CUT TO:

35. EXT. PLACE DU PARVIS C.U. ESMERALDA LATE AFTERNOON
  While Esmeralda smiles and is conscious of the friendly
  greetings about her, there should be a strong suggestion
  of her mystery and mysticism. She is a girl who sees
  visions and is touched with wonder. Yet she smiles.
  On this dawning smile, CUT IN:

SUBTITLE (25) A DANGER IN THE PARIS STREETS....
       A CHILD OF MYSTERY EVEN TO THOSE
       WHO KNEW HER BEST................

*Note: Esmeralda where opportunity
for closeup will manifest some affection*

  BACK: Esmeralda, sweetly smiling, undergoes now a sudden
  transition to surprise and dismay culminating in a wide-
  eyed gentle horror. She has just heard a shriek of denunciation intended for herself. She casts her frightened
  eyes in the direction of Sister Gudule's cell. CUT TO:

36. EXT. PLACE DU PARVIS. C.U. WINDOW OF CELL LATE AFTERNOON
  Sister Gudule is seen at the barred window, clutching the
  bars with her long-nailed and skinny hands, her face showing demonical frenzy as she shouts: (CONTINUED.)

36. (CONTINUED.)

SUBTITLE (26)   "CURSED GYPSY! THOU DAUGHTER OF SATAN! AWAY! AWAY! MAY HELL TAKE THEE AND ALL THY KIND!"

BACK: Sister Gudule is in a state of frenzy - a woman of forty perhaps, but prematurely aged, with wild, unkept hair. She is gray, thin, exalted. Just for a flash of this, then CUT TO:

37.   EXT. PLACE DU PARVIS. MED. GROUP SHOT NEAR CELL LATE AFTERNOON
Esmeralda is shrinking in dismay, still wide-eyed but obviously feeling nothing but pity for the demented woman, and anxious to be on her way. Others of the populace, including two women of the people, are now crowding closer to Sister Gudule's window. One of these women is an habitué of Paris and knows the story of Sister Gudule; the other woman is a stranger in quest of enlightenment. As Esmeralda starts out of scene, and these two women come up closer to Gudule's window, ~~CUT TO:~~ and start talking.

[handwritten note: Scene # / med. shot]

→ *Another flash of Gudule shaking her fist and cursing Esmeralda as Esmeralda leaves scene*

→ *Inside cell as Gudule turns from cursing Esmeralda and her eye see the shrine/her face softens she walks toward shrine*

→ *Shot on shrine as she comes in and kneels.*

38.   EXT. PLACE DU PARVIS MED. C.U. TWO WOMEN LATE AFTERNOON
There is exaggerated concern and interest on their faces as the one explains to the other.

SUBTITLE (27)   "THEY CALL HER SISTER GUDULE. YEARS AGO, ~~SHE WAS RICH AND BEAUTIFUL. THE GYPSIES STOLE~~ HER ONLY CHILD. AND NOW........."

BACK: As the woman completes her title with a gesture toward Gudule. ~~CUT TO:~~ *lap to.*

39. INT. GUDULE'S CELL MEDIUM SHOT
We pick up Sister Gudule as she turns from window. As she sees baby's shoe, her face softens to spiritual quality as she prays. FADE OUT.

SUBTITLE (28)   EACH YEAR ON THE "FESTIVAL OF FOOLS" THE VAGABONDS CHOSE THE UGLIEST MAN IN PARIS TO BE THEIR EMPEROR FOR THE NIGHT.

40. EXT. PLACE DU PARVIS DOWN SHOT NIGHT FADE IN
The scene fades in with the Parvis viewed from above, shooting downward at an angle of about forty-five degrees from the Cathedral toward the back and right of the Parvis. It is now full night and the entire Parvis is lit up by the fire-baskets previously mentioned and the illuminated booths. This light is sufficient to show that the Parvis is densely crowded with merry makers. There is a long serpentine dance with alternate men and women. There are rather denser crowds about the booths. Just within the range of the camera toward the f.g. there is a clear space in the light of one of the fire-baskets which will be the place where Esmeralda will be picked up subsequently. In this shot it is vaguely seen that a white goat is dancing on its hind legs in the midst of three musicians seated Turk fashion on the edge of the carpet. Esmeralda is there, but is not dancing. The center of the aperture picks up the entrance of the Hunchback's "royal" procession as he comes into the Parvis on his litter. This procession is headed by a dancing group of musicians beating on drums and playing flageolets. The "King" is on his litter. He is surrounded by numerous torch bearers. The advent of this procession again starts a general movement in the crowd in that direction. The procession advances toward the center of the Parvis and as it reaches this central position and loses its processional nature as the paraders cluster around in a group, we start a downward movement of the camera toward this central point. This movement of the camera is a gradual progression until the scene is consumated in a medium closeup of the Hunchback. (CONTINUED.)

40. CONTINUED.
The incidental action of this descent of the camera to the closeup is that the crowd is beginning to desert this center of interest for another to the right, that is to say, where Esmeralda is about to begin her dance. As the camera approaches the Hunchback, we see that Quasimodo is still unaware of this desertion of his erstwhile followers. At first he is still filled with a stupid satisfaction. He takes his role of Emperor of the Fools, seriously. The tinsel crown hangs over one ear. He carries the sceptre in the classical position. His cape is drawn high about his shoulders. Now in the closeup we see a gradual but swift transformation in his face as he awakens to the fact that his part of the show is over. He is filled with amazement, then fury. He expresses this in a gaping protest just as he rudely dropped out of the scene.   CUT TO:

41.- EXT. PLACE DU PARVIS. LARGER SHOT TOWARD ESMERALDA'S LOCATION. NIGHT
This shot is from Quasimodo's location in Medium f.g. toward the action at Esmeralda's carpet. Quasimodo has been dropped by those who carried his litter and he now sits in dumb fury in the ruins of this. The last of the litter bearers escape and are rushing toward Esmeralda's carpet except for the poet, Gringoire. Gringoire is a type of the ragged and starving but witty and devil-may-care poet of the Paris streets. He is dressed in shabby black tights and doublet. At his belt there hangs an ink horn, a small roll of parchment, and a saggy, empty purse. He wears a rakish torn felt hat with a quill stuck through the felt. This quill he may use as a pen. He stands there now with his feet apart and a look of philosophical amusement on his lean face as he contemplates the fallen King. CUT TO:

42. EXT. PLACE DU PARVIS CLOSER SHOT GRINGOIRE & QUASIMODO NIGHT

This places Quasimodo in immadiate f.g. with Gringoire back of him. Gringoire faces the camera. He speaks:

SUBTITLE (29) "CHEER UP, O MY ABYSMAL BRUTE!
A FEW MORE SHOCKS LIKE THAT AND
MAYHAP THOU WILT BECOME AN ANGEL."

BACK: As Quasimodo gets to his feet, scraping his crown from his head and his mantle from his shoulders, he makes a swing at the smiling poet who scampers away with great agility. Quasimodo, now left utterly deserted, stands like a gorilla with his clubbed sceptre in one of his hands and gazes off toward the rival center of interest. CUT TO:

43. EXT. PLACE DU PARVIS. MED SHOT ESMERALDA'S CARPET. NIGHT

This scene is strongly illuminated by a flaming fire-basket which is out of scene. There are other fire-baskets receding into the b.g. The interest is concentrated on the worn carpet about eight feet square about which the crowd is pressing. On the side of the carpet nearest the source of light are seated the three gypsy musicians previously mentioned, and Marie. One of these plays a drum held between his knees. He has a single light drun stick held in his right hand, but he also drums with the fingers of his left hand. He is a lean and swarthy gypsy type with a clean chin and a stringy black mustache. At his right is a very fat and flabby flageolet player who clowns his music and unshaven. At this second player's right is a grotesque bony musician, who plays a small pipe by blowing into it through one nostril. He is constantly gulping for wind and takes his music very seriously. At this third player's right and somewhat in the shadow is Marie, whose part it is to take care of the goat and also serves as the duenna for Esmeralda. The goat has finished its antics and is now being helf by Marie, who turns to look into the shadowy b.g. expectantly. As we come into the scene, the musicians finish their piece and also turn slightly. From the shadows there emerges the gaunt and wicked figure of Clopin, King of the Underworld. Clopin turns with sullen satisfaction and speaks to someone over his shoulder. The crowd begins to shout:

(CONTINUED.) Change this action. Marie finishes dance passes tambourine [illegible] Clopin sees this and makes beggar call [illegible] Esmeralda etc.

43 (CONTINUED.)

SUBTITLE (30)   "ESMERALDA! ESMERALDA!"

BACK: As the action continues, Clopin - always with his
air of cunning watchfulness and greed - draws partly aside
to admit the entry of Esmeralda. She emerges from the
shadows just back of Clopin, steps forward to a position
just back of and between Marie and the musicians. There
she pauses for a moment in the full light with an expression
on her face of rapt and mysterious concentration. She
seems to disregard the plaudits of the crowd which increase
at sight of her. Clopin with a final glance at her of bitter
and sardonic satisfaction, withdraws somewhat further back
into the shadows. In contrast to the dirty and ragged company
about her, she is clean, simply but exquisitely dressed,
innocent and like a creature from another world. There is
nothing tawdry about her. She ~~walks no sandals~~. Her hair
is unconfined. Her gauzy dress falls to a little lower
than her knees. Her legs are bare, ~~but on her feet is a
pair of Moorish slippers~~. Even in this brief shot it should
be indicated in the attitude of her companions that she is
regarded as a superior being. She is looked up to by them
with both love and reverence, and almost painful anxiety
to please her, to obey her every whim. The shadowy Clopin
takes all this in with a grim and satisfied calculation.
CUT TO:

44.   EXT. PLACE DU PARVIS C.U. ESMERALDA NIGHT
This c.u. limited to Esmeralda's head and torso, should
emphasize the qualities indicated in the longer shot. She
is youth, beauty, innocence and most of all, mystery. She
does not smile. She gazes into space like a dreamer, an
artist, who sees a vision of a higher plane and will express
this vision in terms of art. CUT IN:

SUBTITLE (31)   BOUGHT FROM THE GYPSIES IN BABYHOOD
                 BY THE KING OF THE PARIS UNDERWORLD
                 AND REARED AS HIS OWN, ESMERALDA
                 EXERTED AN UNCONSCIOUS SPELL THAT
                 GAVE CLOPIN A CONSTANTLY GROWING POWER.

Note: Clopin watches Esmeralda with a certain amount of affection. added subtitle's own thought

BACK: In the conclusion of the scene, Esmeralda comes out
of her (CONTINUED.)

44.   (CONTINUED.)
abstraction long enough to drop her eyes and smile slightly
toward the musicians - a cue for them to commence - then
resumes her rapt expression. As she then starts out of
scene to take up her dance. CUT TO:

S.i.t.H.(31's) Esmeralda had found a way even to Clopin's savage and uncouth heart.

45.   EXT. PLACE DU PARVIS MED. C.U. CLOPIN NIGHT.
Clopin has a saturnine smile as he follows the movement of
Esmeralda into her dance. But his expression changes
almost instantly to one of slumbering and watchful ferocity
as he glances over the immediate crowd to see that this
treasure of his is safe. CUT TO:

46.   EXT. PLACE DU PARVIS MED. SHOT AT MUSICIANS NIGHT
This c.u. shows Marie and the three musicians, all of them
with their eyes raised ~~to the camera focus of interest~~, which
is Esmeralda. The expressions of all - even of the
musicians while they busily devote themselves to their
music - signify a continued and concentrated fascination
and adoration in harmony with the thought expressed in the
title. ~~For a flash of this, then~~ CUT TO:

Change

47.   EXT. PLACE DU PARVIS MED SHOT AT CARPET NIGHT
This shot is in the general direction of Clopin, placing
the musicians on the right, upscene. The crowd to the
left and elsewhere within the range of the camera are held
back from crowding in too close by three beggars who have
apparently volunteered their services for the occasion.
(CONTINUED.)

47. (CONTINUED.)
They are followers of Clopin who exchanges a glance with at least one of them before retiring from view. One of these beggars is the apparently legless man. Another beggar besides having a bandage over one eye has a wooden arm terminating in an iron hook. The third beggar is seemingly a blind man with a heavy shade over his eyes and a sign pendant about his neck inscribed with the word AVEUGLE. These beggars should be striking and unforgetable types, sinister, ragged, insolent, and in a way, terrible. They figure later on. All of this intensifies the impression of sheer beauty and innocence presented by Esmeralda as she moves into her dance. This dance so far as possible should be light, swift, graceful, and highly individual. It should reveal as much as possible of Esmeralda's physical charm but should in no sense be pornographic. It isn't the dance that interests Clopin. He exits while the dance is under way. While Esmeralda dances, there is a movement back of the legless beggar. Two or three of the spectators are rudely shoved aside. They would protest, but they see who the assailant is, and respectfully make room for him with manifest fear. It is Quasimodo. The Hunchback is still in a disgruntled mood. After shouldering and wallowing a place for himself on the edge of the carpet, Quasimodo settles down lower and lower - with most of his attention all the time on Esmeralda, until he is lying flat on his belly. Now as he brings his gnarled hands up to support his chin, CUT TO:

48. EXT. PLACE DU PARVIS C.U. QUASIMODO. EDGE OF CARPET NIGHT
This is the c.u. of an abysmal brute looking up with still unawakened dreams and passions at an angel. His face is horrible, yet again filled with that dawning speculation, tinged again with anger and unreasoning jealousy. Hold this last expression as we CUT TO: curiosity

49. EXT. PLACE DU PARVIS MED. SHOT OF ESMERALDA NIGHT
This shot is from the direction of Quasimodo's gaze. It might be novel to shoot upward toward Esmeralda as she dances down into fairly close f.g. with Quasimodo's head and shoulders showing in extreme c.u. At any rate, Esmeralda, seeing Quasimodo's gaze, falters in her dance and holds the position as forgetfulness of everything except the Hunchback subsides away from her. He horrifies and hypnotizes her. She backs away in horror and fear. CUT TO:

50. EXT. PLACE DU PARVIS C.U. QUASIMODO. EDGE OF CARPET NIGHT
On Quasimodo's face is a look half-scowl, half-sneer, a savage resentment of the girl's attitude toward him. This softens to a suspicion of grief as the scene FADES OUT.

SUBTITLE (32) THE ANCIENT PRISON FORTRESS OF THE BASTILLE, FAVORITE LODGING PLACE OF KING LOUIS.

51. EXT. LONG SHOT OF THE BASTILLE. NIGHT FADE IN
The scene fades in on a long shot of the Bastille by moonlight...

52. INT. LOUIS' ROOM IN BASTILLE. MED. SHOT
This is a large circular room, on the top floor of one of
the towers of the Bastille. The floor is covered with the
straw matting, while the rafters of the ceiling are decorated
with fleur de lys, cut out of metal, the spaces between being richly decorated. The walls are dimly painted in the
same motif. There is one long and pointed window, latticed
with brass wire and iron bars. The window swings inward and
is seen to be of stained glass, exhibiting the Arms of the
King and Queen. Through this window can be discerned the
dim and distant towers of Notre Dame. (At least a mile
away.) There is one door, on the left, arched and the
inside of it upholstered with cloth. There is one very
magnificent folding arm-chair, richly upholstered in leather
and silk, studded with a thousand golden nails. Near the chair,
center, is a large table, covered with figured cloth. On
the table, various manuscript-scrolls, quills, sand-box and
a large silver mug for ink. To one side a chauffrette, something like a portable oven, and near this is a prie-dieu, or
prayer-desk, plainly draped. Seated at the table is King
Louis, his chin in his hand, his eyes on the floor. He is
Pensive, almost bitter. He still wears his plain peaked cap
and his plain black cloak, with a narrow border of squirrel
fur. His legs are encased in woolen hose and low shoes with
round toes. Back of him is a chamberlain, more elaborately
dressed, with a complicated hat of the period and a cloak,
reaching to the ground, somewhat resembling the robes now
worn by judges. The light is furnished by a large hanging
brass lamp with a number of bars and smoking flames around
the edge of the reservoir. In the shadows to the left of the
chamberlain who stands back from his Majesty, is an old white-
haired monk, the same seen in the processional, who lurks
there in the double capacity of confessor and door tender.
As we pick up the action, everone in the room is absolutely
motionless. The others are looking at the King with an air
of absorbed attention. The King himself is as if fascinated
by a spectacle which only he can see. CUT TO:

53. INT. LOUIS' ROOM IN BASTILLE. C.U. LOUIS NIGHT
The closeup registers the pity and haunting quality of Louis'
face as he beholds his vision. LAP DISSOLVE INTO:

54.   LONGER SHOT ROOM IN BASTILLE NIGHT
            This shot permits the vision to be seen. This vision is
            as per picture A-14. LAP DISSOLVE BACK TO:

55.   INT. LOUIS' ROOM IN BASTILLE. C.U. LOUIS NIGHT
            In this c.u. we show the King giving a slight start as he
            comes out of his reverie. CUT TO:

SUBTITLE (33)   "WHERE IS THAT YOUNG SCAPEGRACE, PHOEBUS DE
                        CHATEAUPERS?"

56.   INT. LOUIS' ROOM IN BASTILLE. MED SHOT NIGHT
            In this shot we pick up our other characters as they were
            in scene #52. At the King's question, there is a slight
            start of activity, and the Chamberlain and the old Monk
            both respond to indicate that Phoebus has been waiting out-
            side. The Monk opens the door, and Phoebus de Chateaupers
            come in. He makes a gallant entrance. He is in semi-
            military attire, but is very dandified. At the spectacle
            of the King seated there with his back still turned, Phoebus
            is somewhat at a loss as to how to proceed. The Monk with
            a grim look, occupies himself in closing the door. The
            Chamberlain has leaned toward His Majesty, and in response
            to Louis' whispered request, hands to his Majesty, a rolled
            manuscript. During this action, Phoebus is on tenter hooks
            anxious to speak or act but not knowing exactly what to do.
            Then Phoebus sweeps around and drops to one knee, bowing
            low before His Majesty, and remains thus with head down as
            (CONTINUED.)

56. (CONTINUED.)
Louis gives him a wry smile. The King leaves him in this position for a moment or so, then as he rolls the manuscript the King speaks again:

SUBTITLE (34) "NO DOUBT THERE IS REASON ENOUGH THAT YOU HANG YOUR HEAD IN SHAME."

BACK: At this Phoebus straightens up abruptly. He remains on one knee, but he makes a gesture of protest. He is about to burst into self defences when he detects the King's sly smile. The King now thrusts the rolled manuscript at him with a playful semblance of hitting him with it and speaks the final title:

SUBTITLE (35) "A PLAGUE ON YOU FOR A PRESUMPTUOUS STRIPLING! HERE'S YOUR CAPTAIN'S COMMISSION YOU'VE BEEN PESTERING ME FOR."

BACK: Phoebus' reaction to this is acute. He makes a move as if to seize the royal hand and kiss it, but Louis gets to his feet and summons Phoebus to do likewise. Even as Phoebus bows and thanks his King, he is considerably taller and infinely better dressed than his Majesty. King Louis dismisses him with a gesture and starts to stroll toward one of the windows as Phoebus starts to back from the room. This takes them slightly upstage. When they are several feet apart, and just as Phoebus, profiting by the fact that the King's back is turned, is turning up his nose at the chamberlain, Louis suddenly turns and stops Phoebus' action by lifting his finger. This brings Phoebus back toward the King. As he crosses toward Louis, CUT TO:

57. INT. LOUIS' ROOM IN THE BASTILLE. MED. CLOSE NIGHT
Shoot this in the direction of the door. This places Louis on the right, in immediate f.g. Phoebus is coming down to him. Louis turns slightly so as to face Phoebus as he reaches a point on the left opposite his Majesty. There is an immediate reversion to seriousness and suspense as Louis meditates his words and Phoebus awaits breathlessly. Louis speaks with an air of deep thought:

SUBTITLE (36) "THERE IS A MURMURING OF TREASON ABROAD IN THIS OUR CITY OF PARIS."

BACK: Phoebus is mystified and somewhat alarmed but is all attention as Louis unsmilingly studies him for a few seconds. CUT TO:

58. INT. LOUIS' ROOM IN THE BASTILLE. C.U. LOUIS NIGHT
Louis is the religious zealot, overlaid with cunning. His eyes are shifty as his brain works. He speaks:

SUBTITLE (37) "DO MY PEOPLE THINK TO WIN HEAVEN BY STRIFE AND POLITICS?"

BACK: Louis completes the title. There is a partial sneer on his face. Then as his mood breaks, CUT TO:

SUBTITLE (40)   MADAME DE GONDELAURIER HAD NOT RECENTLY
                REOPENED HER TOWN HOUSE ON THE PLACE DU
                PARVIS.

59.   INT. LOUIS' ROOM IN BASTILLE. MED CLOSE FOR TWO NIGHT
      Phoebus is eager to assure his Majesty of his own loyalty,
      but stops his speech and gesture as Louis speaks again:

SUBTITLE: (38) "MAYHAPS A WATCHFUL EYE WILL HELP THEE TO
                BECOME SOME DAY OUR GOVERNOR THEREOF...."

      BACK: Phoebus is bedazzled with joy, but his Majesty
      checks any outburst with a commanding gesture and com-
      pletes his title as he continues:

SUBTITLE (39)   ".........IF EVER THOU CANST LEARN TO
                LET THE WENCHES ALONE."

      BACK: Phoebus' reaction to this is to blushingly and
      seriously protest until the King's face relaxes into
      a slow smile, whereupon Phoebus in a spontaneous out-
      burst, declares that with such a prospect he'll never
      so much again as look at a girl as long as he lives.
      His florid declarations are smilingly dismissed and the
      King once more turns away from him as Phoebus starts to
      exit, backing away. CUT TO:

61.   INT. MADAME DE GONDELAURIER'S SALON. AFTERNOON FADE IN
      The scene fades in on what is about a long shot. The room
      is large, probably forty feet long by twenty-five feet. At
      the center of the upstage wall is a dais, raised two or three
      steps from the floor, on which is a massive Gothic chair
      under a rich canopy. On either side of this are French doors,
      opening into a corridor or hallway, giving egress to other
      portions of the house. The period calls for rather severe
      Gothic furnishings, but should none the less indicate wealth
      and a love of detail. There are three windows down r. thru
      which can be seen the Parvis of houses adjoining. Between
      these windows is an elaborate fireplace. On the left, an
      arched entrance to the main hall, and arched entrance which
      will be described in due course. This large salon opens
      through another arched doorway, into what is called the
      "Petit Salon" which necessarily is a part of the same set.
      The Petit Salon gives access to the Place du Parvis de Notre Dame
      thru two French windows, each having its own wrought iron
      balcony overhanging the street. Between these windows
      also, is a decorative fireplace somewhat smaller than that
      of the larger salon. There are a number of Gothic chairs
      and benches about, with additional accommodations in the
      form of double chairs or "courting seats," between the window
      on the right. The walls when not covered with tapestry,
      are wainscoted with shallow Gothic panels. The rafters of
      the room are painted with heraldic emblems. Now to pick
      up the action. CUT TO:

60.   INT. LOUIS' ROOM IN THE BASTILLE. MED. SHOT
      Phoebus is backing toward the door which the Monk opens.
      M. Neufchatel's manner relaxes somewhat and he smiles at
      Phoebus. Together they exeunt, swaggering. The Priest
      closes the door. Louis, once more pensive, comes down to-
      ward his table as the chamberlain presents further manu-
      scripts for his perusal as the scene FADES OUT.

62.   INT. MADAME DE GONDELAURIER'S SALON AFTERNOON MED.SHOT
      Madame de Gondelaurier, a woman of the Grande Dame type, is
      giving exquisite instructions to two servants about her.
      A word as to the placing of the chairs....and then Madame
      turns, starting down scene. Through the arch largeness
      Petit Salon, where just within the doorway, she stops. For
      a second she looks down scene toward the direction of
      Fleur de lys and Phoebus. Then, as she starts toward
      them, CUT TO:

63.   INT. DE GONDELAURIER' PETIT SALON MED FULL SHOT AFTERNOON
      This scene is shot from such a position as to show, on
      the left, the two windows which open onto the little iron
      balconies. On the right is the door from the Salon proper.
      The upstage wall is practically covered with a medieval
      tapestry. In the upper right-hand corner (approximately)
      sitting/standing in the doorway, a rather aged and harmless type
      of duenna, whose particular duty is to chaperone Fleur de
      lys. In fairly close f.g. near the first window toward
      camera are Fleur de lys and Phoebus. He is in Captain's
      light armor. Fleur de lys is young, pretty, coquettish,
      somewhat of a flirt, and well pleased that Phoebus has
      found her at least pleasing. Her back is almost to the
      door, through which her mother has appeared, and as
      she works on her tapestry, Phoebus, with the manner of a
      gallant saying "pretty things" to a pretty girl, is lean-
      ing slightly over her chair in a bending position. Madame
      de Gondelaurier smiles upon this pretty picture for a space
      then, not wishing to interrupt, crosses to the center
      window, adjusting the curtains and opening the French win-
      dows wider, peering through the casement toward the Place
      du Parvis. Phoebus, a daredevil in matters of the heart as
      well as the sword, espies a curl peeping out from under
      Fleur de lys' conical head-dress, and toys with it, the
      while whispering a compliment, which to Fleur de lys'
      coy disapproval, as she draws away.

SUBTITLE (41)   "FIE! I GOOD PREVARICATOR. THOU
                WOULDST SAY AS MUCH TO ANY WOMAN."

      BACK: As Fleur de lys says this, she glances in the
      direction of her mother. Phoebus laughs and does not deny
      the allegation. It is at this moment that Madame de Gon-
      delaurier turns to observe them, and seeing that they have
      broken from their former "close" position, calls to them
      to come and observe the pretty sight in the Parvis. Fleur
      de lys rises, and starts toward the window. Meanwhile,
      Madame has again directed her gaze into the Parvis and
      Phoebus, seeing this, makes a playful grab at Fleur de lys
      as she passes, while she, with pretended shyness, flashes
      a coy smile and runs to the window. Phoebus follows.
      CUT TO:

64.   INT. DE GONDELAURIER PETIT SALON   MED CLOSE AFTERNOON
      This shot is from the interior of the room, shooting
      thru the French window onto the balcony and beyond,
      toward the Place du Parvis, with Notre Dame the b.g. for
      the picture. Fleur de lys enters, and as she does so,
      Madame de Gondelaurier withdraws from her position on
      the balcony, with the obvious purpose of throwing Fleur
      de lys and Phoebus into intimate contact in that confined
      space. Fleur de lys, being as much of her mother's mind
      as that lady herself, senses the opportunity and steps
      onto the balcony. Phoebus, entering at the same moment,
      is smiled upon by Madame, who with the complacent authority
      of kinship, guides his place to a place near Fleur de lys.
      With this accomplished, she smiles and exits.   CUT TO:

65.   EXT. BALCONY OF DE GONDELAURIER HOME MED. CLOSE AFTERNOON
      This c.u. shows Fleur de lys and Phoebus on the balcony,
      with their interest at the moment centered upon each other,
      instead of toward the activity in the Parvis. Fleur de lys
      turns from Phoebus coyly, while Phoebus, taking advantage
      of the moment, slips his arm about her waist. What Fleur
      de lys sees in the Parvis is now her excuse for apparently
      not noticing Phoebus' act and she exclaims, "Oh, Phoebus...
      see!"   However, Phoebus, laughing, sees nothing at the
      moment but her, and pulls her slightly closer to him.
      CUT TO:

66.   INT. DE GONDELAURIER PETIT SALON MED SHOT MADAME DE
      MORTEMER. AFTERNOON
      The old lady's apparent interest is on the beads which she
      is stringing by means of a copper wire. However, at odd
      intervals we can presume that she keeps the young ones
      under observation, especially as she lifts her eyes at
      this moment from her work for a flash of satisfied approv-
      al toward the action at the window. Then, with a little
      sigh of vicarious joy - wishing that she were young again,
      she returns her attention to her work. This scene is
      short. CUT TO:

67. EXT. BALCONY OF DE GONDELAURIER HOME   MED. C.U. AFTERNOON
~~Now, as Phoebus persists in not looking toward the Parvis, but instead, insists on drawing~~ Fleur de lys closer to ~~him, that~~ young lady, ~~with an apparent manner of annoyance (but secretly pleased)~~ exclaims more insistently:

SUBTITLE   (42)   "PHOEBUS ! SEE...THE CUTE LITTLE GOAT!"

BACK: ~~The title serves two purposes. It again identifies Phoebus by name, and it also tells us even before we show it, that Esmeralda is again to be seen. Phoebus turns, directing his attention toward the Parvis, and Fleur de lys, taking advantage of her seeming interest at that place as if unconsciously, snuggles closer in his embracing arm.~~   CUT TO:

Phoebus turns and sees med shot also close up of goat and smiles

med shot   *Esmeralda & goat*

68. EXT. PLACE DU PARVIS   LONG SHOT TOWARD DE ~~GONDELAURIER~~ HOME AFTERNOON-
~~This shot is from a point about the center of the Place du Parvis, toward the Gondelaurier home,~~ showing the balcony on which ~~Phoebus and Fleur de lys~~ are standing. Now, in fairly close ~~f.g. is this activity~~. On the carpet is Esmeralda's goat, doing a prancing turn. Seated on the edge of the carpet, legs crossed under her, is Marie, who accompanies Esmeralda and the three musicians. Now the value to get over here is this: Fleur de lys has said, "Oh, Phoebus! See the cute little goat." Phoebus has been reluctant in turning, and this action should be cut so that just as he is turning, the goat ceases its antics, is hauled to port by the ~~old man~~, and Esmeralda, who has been beating a little tattoo on the tambourine in her hands, tosses it to Marie and herself occupies the center of the carpet, so that as Phoebus looks down into the Parvis, it is Esmeralda he sees, and not the goat. Esmeralda swings into her light and fantastic Gypsy dance, to the approval of the crowd which has gathered about the carpet.
CUT TO:

close shot on goat & man
close shot on Esmeralda dancing

69.   EXT. BALCONY OF DE GONDELAURIER HOME. MED. C.U AFTERNOON
Fleur de lys is looking toward the Parvis - as is also
Phoebus. The expression on his face is that of a man
who has suddenly discovered a **new** interest. Fleur de
lys now turns toward him, and she, being a woman, senses
this change of interest. True, he still has his arm
about her, but - she frowns ever so slightly and directs
her gaze again toward the Parvis.   CUT TO:

** *Shot of Neufchatel being announced by servant [?] footman and greeting Madame. She indicates Phoebus is on balcony. He starts out.*

[Retire?] toward place

70.   INT. PETIT SALON OF DE GONDELAURIER HOME MED. CLOSE AT
WINDOW.   AFTERNOON
This medium shot is from the inside of the Petit Salon,
thru the window to the balcony, where Fleur de lys and
Phoebus are still standing. Even with his back to the
camera, it becomes apparent that Phoebus' interest is
becoming more and more centered on the dancer in the
Parvis, and especially does this become noticeable to
us and to Fleur de lys as Phoebus removes his arm from
Fleur de lys' waist and leans farther over the iron railing. She turns to him, with a flash of jealous pique.
But this is interrupted, obviously by the appearance of
someone past the camera, for Fleur de lys, a bit startled
by the interruption, turns quickly. Monsieur de Neufchatel
enters. He has presumably been directed to this point,
and now, coming to a standstill, raises his chin, and to
call the attention of Phoebus, speaks:

SUBTITLE   (43)   "HAS MY CAPTAIN FORGOTTEN HIS COMPANY
OF THE GUARDS?   THEY AWAIT HIM AT THE
BARRACKS."

BACK: Fleur de lys at once registers interest, and tugs
at Phoebus' sleeve. Phoebus is reluctant to take his gaze
from the scene in the Parvis. Fleur de lys insists:
"Phoebus!" He turns, sees that the messenger, whom he has
really not heard, is his friend and springs to greet him.
This scene is characterized by its lack of formality on
Phoebus' part, but a contrasting "correctness" on the part
of Neufchatel, now on his Majesty's business. The expression
on Fleur de lys' face shows that she is reluctant to have
Phoebus go, yet inwardly relieved that something has served
to turn his interest from the girl in the Parvis. Phoebus
turns to her. "Mademoiselle!" And with the word, he takes
her hand, carries it to his lips for a fleeting caress
(more of a formality than a token of love) as he speaks:
(CONTINUED.)

They exit toward doors, Neufchatel in lead to open door for Phoebus. Fleur de Lys remains looking after them. Cut in different angle of her to eliminate the doors.

70. (CONTINUED.)
    SUBTITLE (44)   "A CE SOIR!"

    BACK: With this as his good-bye, Phoebus turns to Neufchatel, who, with a low bow to Fleur de lys, joins Phoebus and exits with him, the two of them talking in a smiling manner as they hurry out of scene. Fleur de lys looks after Phoebus with a little toss of her head, satisfied - yet regretful of an opportunity lost and pleased with the thought of the evening to come, smiles after Phoebus and starts toward her tapestry, to resume where interrupted.

71. INT. BELL RINGER'S ROOM MED. CLOSE AFTERNOON
    This room is the same as described in the final scenes - where Quasimodo rings his death knell. Only two cables suspended from aloft, one of them larger than the other. On the larger cable Quasimodo is engaged in a revelry of gymnastic movements, as he rings the great Bourbon, the biggest bell of all, of Notre Dame. As the cable rises and falls in response to his efforts, Quasimodo is as often upside down as otherwise. Just a short scene of this, then CUT TO:

72. INT. BELFRY OF NOTRE DAME MED. CLOSE AFTERNOON
    In this belfry as described later on in detail there are but two bells, one very large and the other only slightly smaller. The biggest of these bells swings ponderously but rapidly back and forth in time with Quasimodo's movements. CUT TO:

73. INT. BELL RINGER'S ROOM OF NOTRE DAME MED. CLOSE AFTERNOON
    Quasimodo, clinging to the biggest cable with both hands, turns a complete somersault as the big cable comes down with his weight. As he starts to turn a reverse somersault,

74. EXT. PLACE DU PARVIS MED. SHOT AT AFTERNOON
    This shot shows a medium view of the activity around the carpet on which Esmeralda dances to the tapestry of the crowd. Gringoire is visible, on the left, munching chestnuts, but without interest in them. All his interest is for Esmeralda. Now, appears Monsieur Neufchatel, followed by Phoebus. Monsieur progresses, but Phoebus, for a closer look at Esmeralda, reins in his horse. As he does so, CUT TO:

75. EXT. PLACE DU PARVIS MED. C.U. PHOEBUS. AFTERNOON
    Phoebus, just reining in his mount, looks toward Esmeralda. Phoebus is a D'Artagnan, romantic and handsome. His heart begins to flame. CUT TO:

103

76.   EXT. PLACE DU PARVIS. MED. SHOT ESMERALDA   AFTERNOON
Shoot this thru a soft edge vignette effect and play for
lighting on Esmeralda which will give her an ethereal beauty,
glorified in a halo of back lighting. Now, in turning in
the dance, she becomes aware of the eyes of Phoebus upon
her. She does not stop abruptly, slowly palpitates to a
standstill, looking toward Phoebus with something of the
same expression there was in Phoebus' expression when he first
glimpsed her. CUT TO:

76 * C.U. Esmeralda

SUBTITLE (45)   TO ESMERALDA, THIS DASHING CAPTAIN OF THE
                    GUARD HAD BECOME THE PRINCE CHARMING OF
                    HER DREAMS.

BACK: Now as Esmeralda further registers her innocent and
rather demure adoration of Phoebus, ~~CUT TO:~~ *as Phoebus throws her a kiss (77) she tosses back her head and laughs and then suddenly whirls into a wild rhapsodic dance*

77. *75* EXT. PLACE DU PARVIS C.U. OF PHOEBUS AFTERNOON.
This closeup of Phoebus should be shot in the same mood as
the one of Esmeralda.... a glorified picture of handsome
and romantic youth, reacting to the beauty of "The Girl."
Hold this for a few seconds, ~~and~~ then ~~CUT TO:~~ *he throws her a kiss*

77 * Closed shot on Esmeralda as she starts coming out of CU...

77 ** Shot on Gringoire as he notices the foregoing and looking between Phoebus and Esmeralda ~~takes out paper and~~ with a knowing smile starts to write

78 79-80 ok EXT. PLACE DU PARVIS. MED LONG SHOT   AFTERNOON
This shot is from in back of Esmeralda, toward Phoebus.
Incorporate in the general activity, the fact that Gringoire
is taking the scene in with a romantic understanding, while
some of the others, with a flash of comprehension, titter
among themselves as they see Esmeralda, held spellbound as
she looks toward Phoebus. Now, upscene, at the extreme left,
Monsieur de Neufchatel rides into scene and reins his
horse with a sort of gruff impatience. CUT TO:

79. EXT. PLACE DU PARVIS. MED. C.U OF MONSIEUR DE NEUFCHATEL
    AFTERNOON
    Monsieur is reining in his horse, with his expression of
    gruff impatience. With definite emphasis, he calls to
    Phoebus:

SUBTITLE (46)   "HAST FORGOTTEN WHAT HIS MAJESTY SAID
                ABOUT THE WENCHES?"

    BACK: For just a flash as he calls this.   CUT TO:

80. EXT. PLACE DU PARVIS MED. C.U. PHOEBUS. AFTERNOON
    Monsieur de Neufchatel's words drift to Phoebus' ears thru
    the spell which holds him. He is loath to leave. Mechan-
    ically, he spurs his horse, moving out of scene, yet turn-
    ing to gaze lingeringly.   CUT TO:

81. EXT. PLACE DU PARVIS. C.U. ESMERALDA. AFTERNOON.
    Esmeralda looks after Phoebus, held, like him, in the thrall
    of love at first sight. To her, all things have ceased,
    except her fascination, a beautiful realization of love.
    Hold this for a few seconds and then CUT TO:

82. ~~†81~~ EXT. PLACE DU PARVIS. MED. LONG SHOT   AFTERNOON
This ~~shot is~~ some distance from Esmeralda and is from the
general direction of the street which would carry Phoebus
toward ~~the Bastille~~. Upscene, Esmeralda still gazes after
Phoebus. In immediate f.g. approaches Neufchatel, jogging
along slowly, waiting for Phoebus to catch up with him.
Now he turns, calling again, but Phoebus, looking back
toward Esmeralda, rises slightly in his saddle and throws
her a kiss. Then, touching his horse with the spurs,
Phoebus turns, catches up with Neufchatel and comes toward
camera, as we CUT TO:

Esmeralda breaks through crowd to watch Phoebus go while other gypsies start to collect money for the dance

82 * *Reverse shot on Phoebus and Jehan as Phoebus turns [?] saddle and again throws Esmeralda a kiss, over gallery off.*

83.   EXT. PLACE DU PARVIS. ~~MED~~ Close SHOT Esmeralda AFTERNOON.
~~This shot shows Gringoire on the left. He is taking in the
scene with complete understanding, while~~ Esmeralda, now
~~completely turned from her original position when she first
glimpsed Phoebus,~~ is reacting to the kiss he has thrown her.
Her beauty is intensified by the wonderful smile which
idealizes her face. It is possible?......Possible? Then,
with sudden abandon, Esmeralda swings into a rhapsodic
dance. CUT TO:

83 * *Med shot*

84.   EXT. PLACE DU PARVIS. MED. C.U. GRINGOIRE AFTERNOON
~~Gringoire's~~ face etherializes as he forgets his last chest-
nut and lets it fall. He has observed all, and with the
understanding of a poet, philosopher and romanticist,
Gringoire responds. With sudden inspiration, he takes the
scroll of parchment from his belt, uncaps his inkhorn and
from the perforations in his hat, takes the feather that
serves him as both plume and quill. It becomes obvious that
Esmeralda has inspired Gringoire's poetic fire. He thinks,
then with poetic inspiration starts to write. In the b.g.
of Gringoire's closeup, there is a suggested movement of
Jehan and Quasimodo, following him like a respectful dog,
approaching thru the crowd. ~~This movement need not be
sharply defined, but only suggestive.~~ Now as Gringoire
inspects with a critical eye, what he has written. CUT TO:

85. EXT. PLACE DU PARVIS C.U. OF PARCHMENT. AFTERNOON.
The view shows a c.u. of a much used parchment on which is written in French of the period, the following:

   Angels, you fair daughters of Eve,
   Who gild the road to hell itself
   Or lead the way to Paradise.

After time for the translation to be read, CUT TO:
(FRENCH)
   "Elles sont des anges, ces jolies dames,
   Qui dorent les routes de l'enfer même,
   Ou celle de paradis."

86. EXT. PLACE DU PARVIS. MED. C.U. AT GRINGOIRE. AFTERNOON
~~Gringoire studies his parchment with a delicious appreciation. He is rather jarred in this poetic mood by the arrival of~~ Jehan and Quasimodo on his left. Quasimodo from behind Jehan merely looks at Esmeralda with a sullen sort of fascination. Jehan rolls his eyes slightly to left and right to make sure that his expression is not observed and then lets himself go into a spasm of lecherous desire. Gringoire turns and perceives the effect of Esmeralda on both Quasimodo and Jehan. Once more he smiles at his manuscript with a knowledge that he has put down a great truth. CUT TO:

87. EXT. PLACE DU PARVIS. LARGER SHOT AFTERNOON
Esmeralda is still in the thrall of her suddenly discovered love. She dances with happy abandon to the music furnished by the three musicians, who look at her in the idolatrous manner as before described. In the b.g. Jehan watches Esmeralda with his thoughts clearly depicted on his face. Gringoire rolls his manuscript and replaces it in his belt, resuming the munching of his chestnuts while Quasimodo in his manner of sullen fascination, likewise watches Esmeralda. FADES OUT.

SUBTITLE (47) JEHAN, DARING THE DEADLY VENGEANCE OF CLOPIN, HAD LONG LISTENED TO THE PROMPTING OF A DARK DESIRE.

88. EXT. FIRST PARIS STREET LOCATION MED. SHOT NIGHT FADE IN.
~~This, like the other Paris street, is a narrow, torturous and illy lighted lane; it curves sharply to the right, giving indication that it intercepts some other street from the Place du Parvis.~~ Coming toward the camera is Jehan with quickened steps, craft, alert, and expectant, his idea being to intercept Esmeralda at the Carrefour de Notre Dame. Following him a few paces behind, is Quasimodo glancing now and then at Jehan, now and then toward the rear. This scene is comparatively short, and as Jehan and Quasimodo come toward camera. CUT TO:

89. EXT. SECOND PARIS STREET LOCATION MED. SHOT NIGHT
This street is another narrow and torturous lane which leads to the Carrefour de Notre Dame. In contrast to the previous scene, there is a street light of the type to be described, in f.g. which serves to illuminate Esmeralda as she comes toward f.g. Esmeralda is not running, nor is she taking her time. Rather, she is hurrying along the deserted illy-lighted street with the manner of a person anxious to get a lonesome and dangerous journey finished. With Esmeralda's direction established. CUT TO:

101

90. EXT. THIRD PARIS STREET LOCATION MED. SHOT NIGHT
This shot is near the intersection of the street with the Carrefour de Notre Dame and shows Gringoire scampering toward f.g. pursued by a large cur dog. It is evident from Gringoire's action that he has stolen the sausage which he holds flopping in his hands and the dog has been sent to chase him. Gringoire on inspiration, breaks off a goodly sized chunk of the sausage and throws it to the dog, which grabs it and decamps, leaving Gringoire highly pleased. As he progresses toward camera, CUT TO:

91. EXT. FOURTH PARIS STREET MED. SHOT NIGHT
Coming toward camera at a rollicking gallop is Phoebus and the horsemen. In fairly close f.g. Phoebus reins in, as do the others, and turns in his saddle for a cheery good-night to his comrades who hail him with familiar and good-natured pleasantries as they turn their horses in the direction of intersection street on right. They gallop off in that direction, Phoebus remaining at his location as they pass him. With this action in progress we CUT TO:

92. EXT. CARREFOUR DE NOTRE DAME MED SHOT NIGHT
This view is toward the Second Paris Street location, but entrance to the intersection of Phoebus and his men further than this. From the First Paris Street is produced on the right, at the level of the second floor, cut into the wall of the corner building, is a niche about six feet high, two feet wide and one foot deep, sufficient to contain a figure of the Virgin, done in primitive and formal sculpture. The lower portion of the niche is screened by a rather elaborate blanket or small balcony of forged iron, intended to contain inflammable material for the purpose of lighting. There is a sense of slow flame in this basket with a sufficient glow to light up the immediate neighborhood. It is in this lighting that the principle action now takes place. Coming toward the camera, some distance upscene is Esmeralda, still hurrying in her timid manner. (CONTINUED.)

91.- (CONTINUED.)
Now, in f.g. at the point where the Third Street terminates, Gringoire enters scene in a dash, turning upscene toward the corner and glimpses Esmeralda, he is suddenly set upon by the three beggars previously described and is dragged backward toward the middle of a concealed entrance on the left f.g. From this location, the action in the Carrefour cannot be seen. CUT TO:

93. INT. CARREFOUR DE NOTRE DAME. MED. CLOSE AT LOW ANGLE. NIGHT
THE beggar grabs Gringoire by the legs. The one with the iron hook grabs for his sausage and gets it, while the "blind" man grips Gringoire about the waist. Gringoire lets out a stream of fear. CUT TO:

SUBTITLE (48) "HELP! MURDER! THIEVES! MURDER UPON!"

BACK: Only for an instant, however, can Gringoire scream. The "blind" man claps a hand over Gringoire's mouth and the poet is dragged into the darkness of the low arched entrance. This should all be done very quickly. CUT TO:

94.- EXT. FOURTH PARIS STREET MED SHOT NIGHT
Phoebus comes toward camera. For our own information, he has been separated from his comrades by the space of just about a minute. As he hears Gringoire's scream, he reins in, instantly places the direction of the cry and then, spurs out of the scene toward foreground. CUT TO:

95. EXT. FIFTH PARIS STREET. FULL SHOT NIGHT
Some distance upscene can be seen Phoebus' comrades. They too rein in, hesitating for a few seconds in an uncertain manner, and then, hazarding a guess at the location of the cry for help, turn their mounts about and start toward f.g. at a gallop. A short flash of this and then   CUT TO:

96. EXT. CARREFOUR DE NOTRE DAME. MED. SHOT NIGHT
Except for Esmeralda, the place is deserted. She is standing uncertainly at the point where she stopped in fear at Gringoire's scream for help, remaining rooted to the spot while she witnesses his disappearance. As she stands thus, CUT TO:

97. EXT. FIRST PARIS STREET MED CLOSE NIGHT
This view is at the spot where the first Paris street intercepts and terminates in the Carrefour de Notre Dame. Hurrying toward the f.g. comes Jehan and Quasimodo. Make it obvious from Jehan's manner that he is hurrying. Suddenly now in close f.g. Jehan stops, as does Quasimodo, who is directly behind him. As Jehan sees Esmeralda, he lays a heavy hand on Quasimodo's shoulder and in fierce excitement, gestures to Quasimodo to seize the girl. Quasimodo, himself in a tremor of excitement, looks quickly in the direction of Esmeralda and then at his master, to make sure of Jehan's intent. Then, as Jehan emphasizes his wishes with a shove, Quasimodo springs forward toward camera.   CUT TO:

98. EXT. CARREFOUR DE NOTRE DAME MED. SHOT NIGHT
This is shooting in the direction of where the First Paris Street intersects and shows Jehan in the b.g. In close up to Esmeralda. As she hears the movement of Quasimodo springing toward her she swiftly turns and then is petrified with horror. She shrinks and throws up her hands
(CONTINUED.)

98. (CONTINUED.)
as Quasimodo seizes her. In an instant she is struggling in his grasp. Quasimodo has his first movement of turning to carry the struggling girl back toward Jehan, when still holding Esmeralda, he looks out of scene past camera with a look of startled ferocity.   CUT TO:

99. EXT. CARREFOUR DE NOTRE DAME FULL SHOT NIGHT
Upscene is the action as described. Phoebus rides into scene from f.g. and reins in his horse on his haunches in such close proximity to Quasimodo and the girl that Quasimodo is forced to throw up a hand to seize the bridle. During this melee,   CUT TO:

100 EXT. FIRST PARIS STREET   C.U. OF JEHAN   NIGHT
Jehan flashes consternation, then fear and caution as he takes in the situation and turns to flee. As he sees that reinforcements are coming he definitely registers rage and disappointment and flees upscene. On this action, CUT TO:

101 EXT. CARREFOUR DE NOTRE DAME   MED. FULL SHOT   NIGHT
Some distance upscene the melee of Quasimodo, horse, Phoebus and Esmeralda has resulted in Phoebus now drawing Esmeralda up in front of him while still battling off Quasimodo, the Hunchback being unaware of Jehan's flight and the arrival of the horsemen, who now dash into the scene from over foreground. On this action, CUT TO:

102 EXT. CARREFOUR DE NOTRE DAME   MED. FULL SHOT   NIGHT
This view is the reverse of the normal angle. In fairly close foreground are Phoebus and Esmeralda on horse. Esmeralda is still in the throes of her recent alarm. Not so, Phoebus. He flashes a quick smile of appreciation at Esmeralda as he draws her tender body close to his own, then flashes a look of angry command as he turns to the horsemen who have by this time surrounded Quasimodo. Phoebus indicates Quasimodo and barks the order:

INSERT TITLE (49)   "TIE ME UP THIS VARLET. TOMORROW, HE'LL BE WHIPPED."

BACK: As Phoebus completes the order several of the horsemen who have already tumbled from their mounts handle Quasimodo roughly and begin to tie him.   CUT TO:

103 EXT. CARREFOUR DE NOTRE DAME   MED. CU. NEAR ARCH   NIGHT
This view is such that it shows the arch in foreground left and at the same time, the action upscene, where Esmeralda can be seen with Phoebus on horse. The soldiers are tying Quasimodo. The one-armed vagabond appears cautiously in close foreground from the direction of the arch and registers surprise and fright as he sees that the center of the trouble is Esmeralda. He takes merely one glance, faces camera for a second registering continued consternation and fright, and starts to duck into the low arched doorway to inform his fellows what has happened, as we CUT TO:

104 EXT. CARREFOUR DE NOTRE DAME.   MED. FULL SHOT IN DIRECTION OF FIRST STREET UPSCENE   NIGHT
Skirting the activity of the soldiers who have tied up Quasimodo comes Phoebus, with Esmeralda. She is lost in happy contentment, forgetful of everything, except the one fact that she is in Phoebus' arms. Quasimodo by this time, has been bound and is now in position between two of the mounted soldiers, and his hands tied in back of him but with his feet free to trudge along between as they start. Phoebus slows up for two or three seconds to glance at this activity.   CUT TO:

105 EXT. CARREFOUR NOTRE DAME   C.U. FOR TWO
We pick up Phoebus and Esmeralda as they turn to look into each other's eyes. Phoebus speaks:

SUBTITLE (50)   "SO TENDER A DOVE SHOULD BE SAFE IN HER NEST AT SUCH AN HOUR. BUT FEAR NO MORE."

As Esmeralda droops her eyes under Phoebus' gaze, then coyly looks up at him and speaks:

SUBTITLE (51)   "I have no more cause for fear any, Captain."

Esmeralda looks at Phoebus with a tell-tale glance of trusting innocence and again drops her eyes. Phoebus looks at her with kindling admiration and increasing desire not unmixed with tenderness. As he starts to turn his horse, CUT TO:

106 EXT. CARREFOUR DE NOTRE DAME. MED. FULL SHOT IN DIRECTION
OF FIRST STREET UPSCENE   NIGHT.
As Phoebus turns his mount, still embracing Esmeralda, he
takes general direction from which Gringoire appeared in
earlier scene. At the same time, the soldiers with Quasimodo
between them, start in the same general direction, but take
another street as is shown in next scene. CUT TO:

Take out

107 EXT. CARREFOUR DE NOTRE DAME SHOT FROM SECOND PARIS STREET
NIGHT.
This view toward the point where the streets intersect, shows
on the left the niche with the image of the Virgin, upscene.
Coming toward f.g. is Phoebus, with Esmeralda held upon his
horse in front of him. They are in a world apart, especially
so Esmeralda, to whom the emotions of love are new and something to be enjoyed to the utmost. Upscene, Phoebus' soldiers
cross the street, with Quasimodo silhouetted for a moment in
the night from the niche, and then disappear into an inter-
secting street in upscene, as Phoebus and Esmeralda continue
toward f.g.   CUT TO:

Fade Out

108 EXT. CARREFOUR DE NOTRE DAME MED. CLOSE AT LOW ARCH. NIGHT.
The idea is that the three miscreants have simply kept themselves concealed until the soldiers are out of sight. Now,
the one in the little wheeled box appears first from the
gloom, looking in all directions, and signals the other two
that the coast is clear. These two now appear with Gringoire,
stripped and vanquished, in his "medieval B.V.D.'s" a pitiful
spectacle, yet still trying to win his captors with his sense
of humor. They start out of scene, left as we CUT TO:

Gringoire begins with beggars

109 EXT. CARREFOUR DE NOTRE DAME LONG SHOT FROM SECOND PARIS
STREET NIGHT.
This view gets the niche with the Virgin on the left.
Going upscene dimly lighted by the glow from the niche,
are the vagabonds, led by the one in the little cart.
Gringoire, perforce allows himself to be dragged upscene,
a pathetic silhouette, upon which, CUT TO:

Take out
Fade In

110 EXT. A PARIS STREET MED SHOT AT WINE CELLAR NIGHT
This is a dingy exterior with a sunken door and two sunken
windows somewhat lower than the level of the street. The
windows are curtained but dimly lighted. Over the door is
a crudely painted sign bearing a picture of an apple and
a naked woman and the words "La pomme d'Eve." At the opening of the het, Phoebus has brought his horse to a halt
in front of this door and is inviting Esmeralda to come
into the place with him. His intentions are amorous without being brutally so. Esmeralda has her misgivings but a
perfect faith in the gallant captain. As she coyly assents
and Phoebus swings down from his horse ready to lift Esmeralda down after him, CUT TO:

SUBTITLE (52)   FOR PHOEBUS DE CHATEAUPERS IT WAS BUT
ONE MORE ADVENTURE. BUT FOR ESMERALDA
IT WAS THE REALIZATION OF A DREAM.

111 EXT. A PARIS STREET CU AT DOOR TO WINE CELLAR NIGHT
The horse is tethered to a ring at the side of the door.
Phoebus with one arm reassuringly about Esmeralda, smiles
down at her as he starts to knock. As he does so, the door
opens. The effect is of a flood of light coming from the
interior, but no one is seen by Phoebus and Esmeralda. As
they start to enter, CUT TO:

112 INT. LA POMME D'EVE FULL SHOT NIGHT
The view is toward the door, upscene. Half way down scene
from either side are two broken walls intruding on the
range of camera from left and right. These protruding
walls are in the sense of casement pillars supporting the
weight of the house above. The entire interior, especially
that part in the foreground, suggests a combination of
living room and public wine room. There is very little
furniture. The place is lighted by a cluster of candles
in a hoop against one of the walls, with a suggestion of
other candles elsewhere. In that part of the room nearest
the camera there is a bare table of antique workmanship
with a stool and a chair at the side of it. To the left
is the suggestion of a fireplace. To the right there is a
box-like couch serving as a bed. As we pick up the action,
an old woman is just turning from the door by which Phoebus
and Esmeralda have entered and is ushering them down scene
into her sitting room, that part of the room in the foreground. Phoebus is still the gallant, Esmeralda is still
obeying him at the promptings of faith and love. As they
start toward camera, QUICK FADE OUT.

113 INT. SPIDER WEB EFFECT. CU. QUICK FADE IN.
Quick fade in on a spider web, peculiarly lighted, showing
a butterfly fluttering dangerously near. It heads for the
web now, and as it struggles to release itself from the
net, QUICK FADE OUT.

114 & 116 in one

114 INT. POMME D'EVE. MED. CLOSE IN F.G. ROOM   NIGHT
QUICK FADE IN.
As the scene fades in, Esmeralda is seated at the table
in a chair, Phoebus has drawn up his stool close to her
side and is seated in it, talking to her gallantly. On
the table is a bottle and two glasses. The old woman now
takes this bottle and pours it into another, which has
been partially uncorked. It is the innocent, nervous
rather ~~than not~~ ~~with~~ ~~of~~ ~~much~~ attitude of this
~~Esmeralda~~. The knowing old woman should indicate the sad
foreboding ending. With the departure of the old woman,
Phoebus becomes more ardent. Esmeralda is entirely innocent.
She is pleased, but she has the air of living a happy dream.
She speaks: *never saw any wildest dreams of your hope to touch such life as yours.*

(CONTINUED NEXT PAGE)

114 (CONTINUED)
SUBTITLE (53) "THEN IT IS TRUE, WHAT THE FORTUNE
TELLER TOLD ME........"

Author says think, what did she tell you!

115 INT. LA POMME D'EVE CU OF ESMERALDA NIGHT
This should be one of the most exquisite closeups of
Esmeralda obtainable--dreamy, poetic, rapt. She is looking
into space, lost in happy thoughts. She speaks:

INSERT TITLE (54) "........THAT I SHOULD BE WOOED BY A NOBLE
CAPTAIN OF THE GUARDS."

OK

BACK. As she completes the title, she lifts her eyes in
the direction of Phoebus with a melting look of adoration.
On this CUT TO:

Phoebus says "She was right about as you were letter never before"

116 INT. LA POMME D'EVE CU FOR TWO NIGHT.
Phoebus is listening to Esmeralda with intense interest.
While Esmeralda's eyes are raised to his, his hand comes
to her shoulder as if for a closer embrace, but he brushes
down her flimsy gown, partly exposing her shoulder and
breast. This reveals a thin gold chain. To this chain is
suspended a jewel like a piece of amber or jade on which
is engraved a Gothic monogram. While Phoebus' action in
stripping the girl's shoulder was wholly amorous, Esmeralda
was unaware of any evil intention upon his part. Phoebus
now lets his hand strain down the chain closer to the girl's
breast and is as if stopped by the amulet. This causes a
momentary diversion of interest upon his part. He takes
the amulet between his fingers and brings it to his lips.
His movement is observed by Esmeralda with a quickening
interest. He asks her what the amulet is and she replies,
speaking:

Esm looks at his action and then turn then and innocently notes #OK yeah genult too

INSERT TITLE (55) "THEY SAY THIS AMULET WAS PUT ABOUT MY
NECK BY MY MOTHER. I NEVER KNEW HER.
MAYBE SHE IS DEAD. BUT I KNOW THAT SO
LONG AS I WEAR IT NO HARM CAN BEFALL ME."

116   (CONTINUED)
BACK. As Esmeralda completes this title and looks at Phoebus with a most perfect innocence, Phoebus slowly withdraws his hand. His whole attitude indicated that he has been vanquished by her trustfulness and this illusion to a mother possibly dead. He pushes back his stool. He rises. He bows with a somewhat florid but sincere courtesy and speaks:

INSERT TITLE (55)   "IF MADEMOISELLE WILL PERMIT ME
                  I SHALL SEE HER SAFELY ON HER WAY."

BACK. Esmeralda is brought to a realization of actualities by Phoebus' remark. She gives him a bright, quick smile and as she gets to her feet, while Phoebus still bows, the scene FADES OUT.

SUBTITLE (57)   THE COURT OF MIRACLES - THE CITY OF THE
                  THIEVES - A HIDEOUS BLOT ON THE FACE OF
                  PARIS - A SINK FROM WHENCE ESCAPED EVERY
                  MORNING, AND TO WHICH RETURNED TO STAGNATE
                  EVERY NIGHT, THAT STREAM OF VICE, MENDICITY,
                  AND VAGRANCY WHICH EVER FLOWS THROUGH THE
                  STREETS OF A CAPITOL.

117   LONG SHOT THROUGH ARCH COUR DE MIRACLES NIGHT
The arch makes a sombre frame to what lies beyond. Even this arch should convey a sense of squalor and age, rags hanging like stalactites to the left and a dead and deformed tree to the right. In the immediate f.g. under the arch, the pavement is broken, slimy with filth, holding a stagnant puddle fed by an open sewer which drains the courtyard seen through the arch. We hold this preliminary shot long enough to give a strong impression of ramshackled buildings and mob movement through the arch, fitfully lighted by the flames of torches and bonfires. LAP DISSOLVE THE SCENE THRU THE ARCH OUT LEAVING THE F.G. A FRAME OF THE ARCH. INTO THE BACK BLACK PREVIOUSLY FILLED WITH THE PICTURE IN THE COURT. THE FOLLOWING TITLE DISSOLVES IN:

SUBTITLE: (58)   THE COURT OF MIRACLES, SO-CALLED BECAUSE
                 HERE THE BLIND SAW AGAIN . . . .

118   MED. SHOT COUR DE MIRACLES NIGHT
Showing a blind man entering a group of one or two other people. He opens his eyes, showing that now he can see.
CUT TO

SUBTITLE (59)   . . . . BECAUSE HERE THE LAME WALKED . . . .

119   MED. SHOT COUR DE MIRACLES NIGHT MED SHOT ANOTHER LOCATION
This action picks up a distorted cripple as he comes to
another group and unwinds himself, showing that he is
perfectly well built, and physically fit. With this
established, CUT TO

SUBTITLE: (60)   . . . . AND ~~BEGGARS~~ BECAME ARISTOCRATS.

120   MED. SHOT COUR DE MIRACLES NIGHT
We pick up the King of the Gypsies surrounded by some of
his followers. He is in a pompously braggart mood. He is
seated behind a table while those about him, fawn on him
with profound respect. CUT TO.

SUBTITLE: (61)   IT WAS HERE THAT CLOPIN, KING OF THE
UNDERWORLD, REIGNED SUPREME.

121   EXT. COUR DE MIRACLES MED. SHOT NIGHT
The courtyard while wholly surrounded by the ramshackle,
tumble-down, high-gabled buildings previously alluded to,
conveys the impression of a veritable rabbit warren with
passages and subterranean outlets in all directions. To
the left are the low windows and the sunken floor of
Clopin's personal haunt. From the windows of this and
here and there elsewhere about the court comes glimmers
of light indicating that other houses are likewise occupied.
But all the buildings give an impression of sinister darkness.
Over these houses is the moonlit sky, with the towers of
Notre Dame vaguely silhouetted against them, say, a
quarter of a mile away. The moonlight, however, does not
to any noticeable degree effect the appearance of the court,
which is a place of deep shadows and flaring light. Wherever
the light is strong there is a movement of chaotic revelry,
drunkenness, brawling, primitive and brutal love.
(Continued)

121   (Continued)
There are any number of stray dogs and cats about, also
children. Everything is sordid and horrible; an ante-room
of the Inferno. On the right, near center, is a rough
platform of planks on trestles, the design generally filled
in and strengthened with wine - casks, stools, benches, a
gypsy camp-fire with a big cauldron over it, Clopin's so-
called "throne." In front of this and to the right so as
to form an integral part of the general design is a stout
frame of two posts with a cross-beam at the top, about eight
feet tall, later to be used as a gibbet. The rope hangs
from this and is not being used as a swing by ~~a number of~~ the
riotous and vicious children. On the "throne" sits Clopin,
in his characteristic attitude, with one leg stretched out
in front of him, the other partly bent under him. There is
a suggestion of action as Clopin regulates the dispute
between two old beggars, a man and a woman, who have
evidently appealed to the "throne." Clopin gives a decision,
whereupon the female beggar with a ferocious grin of triumph,
seizes the old man and drags him away. This shot, purely
atmospheric, should be at least fifteen feet, exclusive of
the title and should not interfere in any way with the main
action which now begins with the arrival in the scene of the
three beggars with Gringoire. The legless beggar in his
wheeled trough is in the lead. While still under the arch,
he kicks himself free of his wheeled trough and reveals
himself an able-bodied man with two perfectly good legs.
He is actuated by speed and excitement. He is immediately
followed by his two companion beggars who are escorting the
tremulous and half-naked Gringoire. The beggar with the
wooden arm wrenches this free, showing that he has two good
arms and he now uses the wooden arm as a club. The blind
beggar simultaneously snatches his bandages away and reveals
a pair of flashing sharp eyes. Non-descripts now swarm
in the general trail of Gringoire's captors, eager to be on
this new excitement. While the general drift is still through
the arch, the leading beggar springs toward Clopin's throne
with the hand uplifted. As he reaches the proximity of
Clopin, CUT TO

122   EXT. COUR DE MIRACLES MED. SHOT CLOPIN'S THRONE NIGHT
We pick up Clopin as he gets the news that the beggar brings.
His movement is slow, as full understanding of it comes to
him. Clopin's eyes are held hypnotically on the prisoner.
By this time, Gringoire's other two captors have brought
him up to a position before the "throne." Now the first
beggar, somewhat to the left of Clopin, screams his denunciation of Gringoire, as he speaks:

SUBTITLE: (62)   ~~"THIS IS THE VERMIN ~~~~~~~~~~ THE
~~KING~~ ~~~~~~~~~~ THAT CARRIED?
OUR LEADER!"~~

Just for a short flash as this is spoken, to give an
impression of Clopin's dreadful reaction, and then CUT TO

123   EXT. COUR DE MIRACLES C.U. OF CLOPIN NIGHT
Clopin now begins a slow brushing movement with his hand
across his lips as his face reveals an intensifying purpose
for a murderous revenge. His expression becomes almost
mystically satanic, insane but calculating. The brushing
movement of the hand across his mouth is now a mere nervous
twitching like the tail of a tiger about to spring. He
shouts:

SUBTITLE: (63)   "WHO ARE YOU?"

For just a short flash as Clopin speaks this, then
CUT TO.

124   EXT. COUR DE MIRACLES C.U. OF GRINGOIRE NIGHT
This is more of a profile closeup of Gringoire than it is
a full face shot. He is looking up at Clopin, at first with
a paralyzed horror; then by a mental effort, he masters
himself. In his best manner, trying to make a good impression,
he speaks:

SUBTITLE: (64)   "MERELY A POET, YOUR MAJESTY . . . BY
NAME GRINGOIRE."

As Gringoire speaks this, CUT TO.

125 EXT. COUR DE MIRACLES LARGER SHOT FOR GROUP NIGHT
This reply causes a shout of savage laughter from the sluggish women and outlandish men who have drawn near. Gringoire is rudely buffetted about, while Clopin, mystically satanic, calculates what the penalty shall be. One of the men in the mob about Gringoire touches him with the point of a knife. Gringoire jumps about, to the mocking amusement of the crowd. They are like a band of apaches around a prisoner. CUT TO

126 EXT. COUR DE MIRACLES C.U. OF CLOPIN NIGHT
Clopin's face does not relax to amusement. He is calculatingly tense as he glares toward Gringoire. Now, addressing those about him, but without turning his head to any particular person, he bellows:

SUBTITLE: (65) "AND WHAT SHALL BE DONE WITH POET GRINGOIRE?"

For a flash as Clopin finishes this question, then CUT TO.

127 EXT. COUR DE MIRACLES MED. GROUP SHOT NIGHT
Gringoire's knees knock together in fear as he sees the threatening faces about him. The Cul-de-jatte, near Clopin, screams:

SUBTITLE: (66) "HANG HIM! HANG HIM! THAT'S WHAT THE BOURGEOIS DO TO US!"

As the crowd takes up the cry, Clopin gives Gringoire a ferocious grin and jerks his hand in a command to go ahead. Simultaneous with this action, Gringoire shudders and shrinks and looks about him in a pitiful search for sympathy. There is no sympathy. As the crowd closed in to seize Gringoire, CUT TO

128 EXT. COUR DE MIRACLES MED. SHOT AT GIBBET NIGHT
We pick up the action with the crowd dragging Gringoire over to be hung. In spite of his fears, Gringoire cannot convince himself that this is serious. He tries to joke with his captors as they work to foreground. Their only reply is buffets and jeers. Gringoire is now under the gibbet. He takes note of it for the first time with a spasm of acute fright, but still he attempts to treat the matter as a joke. One ruffian sticks a keg under the gibbet and to this Gringoire is hoisted. Meantime another ruffian has bounded to the cross-beam of the gibbet and is arranging the chain that hangs therefrom, looping the chain up. Now another member of the mob about Gringoire tosses to the man on the cross-beam a ragged sash five or six feet long. One end of the sash is tied to the chain. Numbers of vagrants battle for the honor of tying the other end of the sash about Gringoire's neck. During these operations, Gringoire balances himself precariously on his shaky keg. His hands are free. Involuntarily he embraces a fat horror of a woman who laughs in his face. As a general background to this action there is a grotesque dance of crippled and such about the victim. In the midst of this action Clopin enters from foreground. He stalks pensively, bitterly, his arms folded on his chest. He contemplates the preparations for hanging Gringoire with sour abstraction, then shoots out a hand to stop the action. CUT TO

129 Continued
BACK: In quick succession, Gringoire is examined by the fat old horror of a woman whom he has involuntarily embraced, and a tall thin woman, and then a fairly good looking girl. Gringoire's reaction to all of these is characteristic. The fat old woman is willing enough to take him for a husband, but Gringoire intimates by an action of his own that he would rather hang. The crowd roars with hoots and jeers. The tall thin woman also is inclined to favor him, but Gringoire has his eyes on the fairly good looking girl. She is left practically alone with him as she shoves the others out of the way, but after a careful examination of Gringoire's good points and bad, she winks at Clopin and pantomimes "string him up!" Again the crowd is shouting "Hang him!" At this Clopin gives a signal. All those in the immediate proximity of Gringoire draw back except the ruffians who put the cask in place on which Gringoire stands. This fellow now seizes Gringoire from behind and hangs him while kicking the cask away. Gringoire makes frantic efforts to free himself and to keep the cask in place. Once or twice he is almost "standing on air" as the ruffian heaves down on him. It is a tense situation. Such faces as are seen apart from Gringoire's register nothing but a straining and delighted interest. It is obvious that in a moment or two Gringoire will be definitely hung. A suggestion even may be put across that Gringoire has been strangled as a chance of expression is seen on all faces as Clopin swiftly turns and the ruffian who has been hanging on Gringoire steps swiftly away from him. Just a flash of all this as Gringoire hangs limp-
THEN CUT TO

129 EXT. COUR DE MIRACLES C.U. AT GIBBET NIGHT
This angle should give us a medium closeup of Gringoire and Clopin, as Clopin makes the gesture which stops the action. Clopin has just raised his hand in command. Gringoire has just begun to swoon and sag. Clopin speaks:

SUBTITLE: (67)   "HOLD! MAYBE OUR POET GRINGOIRE IS WILLING TO BE MARRIED!"

Gringoire recovers. He recovers with an expression of "Who? Me? be willing to be married?"- He recovers a measure of his wit. He smiles and pantomimes his delight at the proposal. Clopin, unrelentingly grim, turns slightly and yells:

SUBTITLE (68)   "HEY! FEMALES . . . ANY OF YOU WANT A HUSBAND!"

130 EXT. COUR DE MIRACLES LONGER SHOT NIGHT
This shot is from in back of Gringoire, a reverse angle to the preceding scene. We cut in on the action of the previous scene with the rushing entrance of Esmeralda. Her eyes are distended with sympathy and horror. She pauses for only the fraction of a second as she cries out for the people to stop, to save the victim. But she is the first to reach Gringoire. She has her arms about him. There is an instant response to her cries. They are cutting Gringoire down. As he sinks in a crumpled heap with Esmeralda receiving his head in her arms, as she kneels to support him, CUT TO

131 EXT. COUR DE MIRACLES C.U. GRINGOIRE & ESMERALDA NIGHT
Esmeralda shielding Gringoire's fainting head in her arms, blazes a look of indignation at those about her. She speaks:

SUBTITLE (69) "HAVE YE SO LITTLE MISERY THAT YE MUST CREATE MORE?"

As she evidently searches the faces in front of her, looking up, and comes around to that of Clopin, she concentrates on him her angry indignation. During this action, Gringoire opens his eyes and sees he is in her arms. A seraphic smile gradually spreads over his face. CUT IN.

SUBTITLE: (70) (THIS IS ON THE PARCHMENT SCROLL AND IS SIMPLY ANOTHER OF THE APHORISMS WRITTEN BY GRINGOIRE).

"LE PARADIS EST ICI-BAS . . . ."
Les Poemes de Gringoire.

LAP DISSOLVE THIS INTO THE TRANSLATION:

"NOR MUST WE DIE TO FIND WHAT HEAVEN IS."
The Poems of Gringoire.

Leave this for the shortest possible space to permit reading and then CUT TO

BACK: Gringoire is still looking up into Esmeralda's face. He is in heaven for the moment. She, however, is looking defiantly toward the direction of Clopin. Then Esmeralda bids Gringoire come with her. Now, aided by the fickle crowd, and Esmeralda, he rises. They move through the crowd toward the haunt. CUT TO

132 EXT. COUR DE MIRACLES MED. FULL SHOT NIGHT
Just a short scene of Esmeralda, supporting Gringoire, moving toward the haunt, on left, followed by Marie. The crowd is yelling and cheering. Clopin, prominently silhouetted against the light, is a solitary figure of plotting rage. The revelry continues. the scene FADES OUT.

SUBTITLE: (70) ONCE AGAIN THE PLACE DU PARVIS HAD
RESUMED ITS CHARACTER AS A SCENE FOR
TRAGIC ATONEMENT.

133 EXT. PLACE DU PARVIS   LONG SHOT   AFTERNOON   FADE IN
The scene fades in on a long shot toward Notre Dame, stripped
of its decorations, with the point of central activity at
the pillory. A curious, good-natured and expectant crowd is
gathering at this location, coming from all directions. There
is a leisurely attitude in their movement until they near
the central activity. At this point there is jostling as the
spectators strive for choice locations. Upon this general
activity.   LAP DISSOLVE INTO:

134 EXT. PLACE DU PARVIS   MED. SHOT AT THE PILLORY   AFTERNOON
Gathered about now there is a mob, of ever increasing proportions, of people who have come to witness the price of
"justice" there to be exacted. "Character" types should
predominate. Upon the parts of all there is an attitude of
jollification. The fact that someone is to suffer doesn't
bother them in the least. Jokes are cracked. People laugh.
Interest centers at the moment on the man under the wheel --
the pillory keeper - who with a critical eye is greasing
the windlass underneath the structure with a chunk of ham
fat   CUT TO.

135 EXT. PLACE DU PARVIS   MED. C.U. OF JOKERS   AFTERNOON
This closeup shows two burghers talking. One of them is fat
and inclined to be jocular. He is enjoying life in general.
His companion is cadaverous and saturnine. The fat burgher
speaks to his companion:

SUBTITLE: (71)   "HOW'D YOU LIKE TO BE TIED UP THERE?".

His companion looks at the pillory out of the corner of his
eyes and to the other's amusement, unsmilingly speaks:

135   Continued

SUBTITLE   (72)   "'TIS ONLY BY THE GRACE OF GOD THAT I'M NOT."

           The fat burgher laughs and enjoys the ripple of laughter that his companion remarks have created. The principal point of interest in this scene, however, is the young mother, with a yelling brat, which she is trying to quiet, pointing to the pillory with remarks on the order of "Baby, see the pretty wheel", as she bounces the squealing infant up and down. The idea to be gotten over in these scenes is that punishment of the kind to be shown is looked upon more as a popular spectacle than something terrible.   CUT TO.

136   EXT. PLACE DU PARVIS. C.U. OF CHARACTER.   AFTERNOON.
           This character, a man, has a weird face, with one eye, perhaps partly crossed, and a heavy black stubble of beard over his face. He is gazing with a fascinated interest at the wheel, dropping his eyes now to glimpse the activity underneath the structure. He sees.

           Changed.

137   EXT. PLACE DU PARVIS   C.U. UNDER PILLORY.   AFTERNOON
           The action shows the pillory-keeper, feeling the eyes of the crowd upon him, giving great attention to the ponderous mechanism of the windlass. He is about to try the handles of the windlass, when two very rough and dirty gamins of the streets rush thru the scene, the one behind chasing the one in front, who is the possessor of an apple. The one in front ducks into the pillory-keeper, almost upsetting him. The apple is dropped and the pillory-keeper with a backhand swipe, knocks the first gamin and then the second, out of the scene. He picks up the apple, stuffing it in the breast of his blouse, and then, picking up where he left off, gives a few turns to the windlass handles.   CUT TO

138   EXT. PLACE DU PARVIS   C.U. OF PILLORY.   AFTERNOON.
           A general murmur of interest goes up. "See - - it turns!" "Look, Baby - - see the pretty wheel." Comments of a various nature are passed. Shoot this scene toward the weird character as described in previous closeup. Then, as his eyes are glued on the moving wheel.   CUT TO:

139   EXT. PLACE DU PARVIS. C.U. OF CHARACTER.   AFTERNOON.
           The weird character's eyes dilate slightly as he watches the revolving wheel with tense interest. Otherwise, his expression scarcely changes. He is fascinated by the instrument of pain and we can imagine that he is looking forward to the moment when it will exact "justice". From this character, make a swinging panorama shot to show, now, on his right, a couple - - two young lovers, greatly interested in the proceeding, yet not so greatly but that the youth takes this opportunity to snatch a kiss from the girl, who with a delighted laugh, paradoxically slaps his face. Now there is a general murmur; a turning of interest. The information spreads, necks are craned. "They" are coming.   CUT TO.

140   EXT. PLACE DU PARVIS. MED. SHOT AT PILLORY.   AFTERNOON
           This scene should shoot in the general direction of the bridge which would be the most direct route to the Place du Parvis. As the scene opens, however, the foreground is a mass of people. With the murmur of "Here they come," there is a general straining of necks and a jostling of elbows, mingled with oaths and curses, as the crowd parts, making a lane, which gives a glimpse through it, of the oncoming "procession". With this movement established.   CUT TO.

141   EXT. PLACE DU PARVIS. RUNNING INSERT. MED. SHOT AFTERNOON.
           The action, is at a stand-still as the scene opens. Coming toward the camera is the procession from the Palaise de Justice. Heading the procession are two archers, on horseback. Two files of soldiers make a broad lane, in which is the procession proper. Behind the horsemen are some supernumeraries of the Court, on foot. These same people will later be identified in the Court scene at the Palais de Justice when Esmeralda is tried. Central in this group is Monsieur de Torteru. He is a large fellow, vain and dull, of wonderful physique and in a way, handsome. At least he thinks he is handsome. He is looked upon with great respect by his associates and Monsieur le Torteru feels his importance and shows it. All are very familiar and chatty. There is no adherence to strict formality. They are on public view and are enjoying it immensely. Behind this group is a fairly large four-wheeled cart, drawn by a splendid Normandy carthorse. The animal is led by a jailer, simply dressed in hooded cloak and tights. Three other jailers, all wearing similar costumes, carrying staves, and with heavy sheathknives in their belts, are in the cart with Quasimodo. One of these carries an hourglass at least a foot high, which he holds under his arm. These jailers in the cart also treat the occasion as a picnic, grinning at the crowd, waving at pretty girls, jesting and laughing. Behind the cart follows a squad of more cross-bowmen, on foot. Back of them, a sergeant, on horseback. Then follows the rabble, a hooting, jeering mob of gamins, grown-ups and children. It is as if they were en route to a festival of some kind. The three jailers standing in the cart feel their importance, for they are in the public eyes more than the others. But there is no great sense of discipline anywhere. Tied in the cart is Quasimodo. After a general establishing scene of this activity,   CUT IN:

SUBTITLE: (73)   HERE WHERE HE HAD BEEN CARRIED IN TRIUMPH, A CREATURE OF MAN-MADE "GLORY", QUASIMODO RODE AGAIN, THE VICTIM OF MAN-MADE "JUSTICE".

142 EXT. PLACE DU PARVIS. RUNNING INSERT. AFTERNOON C.U.
This closeup shows Quasimodo and the manner in which he is fastened in the cart. His hands are tied behind him and about his neck is a rope which is tied to an iron ring in the bottom of the cart. The rope holds him in such a manner that he has to kneel, in a position which makes it more than uncomfortable as the springless cart bumps over the cobblestones. In his expression there is a look of brutish wonder.

143 EXT PLACE DU PARVIS RUNNING INSERT. LARGER SHOT AFTERNOON.
This is a large shot, accentuating the "importance" of the Court group, central in which is Monsieur le Torteru. He struts. He pretends to disdain the attention of the crowd, but he is exceedingly vain and self-conscious. As the procession thus progresses toward the pillory location, CUT TO.

Changed

144 EXT. PLACE DU PARVIS ELEVATED MED. FULL SHOT AFTERNOON.
This shot is from an elevated position, looking down upon the activity. As the procession to the pillory, the lane formed by the parting of the crowd widens. The soldiers form a small hollow square about the pillory; with the crowd good-naturedly pushing in. There is nothing formal about this activity. The soldiers "josh" the people and many quibs are passed. The supernumeraries of the Court now mount the steps of the pillory in the order of, first the clerk of the Court, second the assistant, third Monsieur de Torteru and fourth his assistant. This assistant carries a long leather sack -- about the size of a gunnysack -- from the mouth of which (tied with a pucker-string) projects the handles of Monsieur le Torteru's instruments of torture. Behind them comes two of the jailers in the cart, with Quasimodo, followed by the third, who carries the hour-glass. He seats himself on a corner of the platform and adjusts the glass for business, Quasimodo is placed upon the wheel of the pillory and quickly tied. Two of the three jailers then descend from the platform. Meanwhile, there has been very "important" action upon the clerk of the Court and his assistant and likewise upon the part of Monsieur le Torteru, who feels the eyes of the people upon him in approval. The clerk's assistant now hands the clerk a scroll . . . . .

145 EXT. PLACE DU PARVIS C.U. ON PILLORY. AFTERNOON
The clerk, feeling his importance, unrolls the scroll and clearing his throat, reads aloud in a voice for all to hear:

SUBTITLE (74) " . . . FOR NOCTURNAL ATTACK AND DISTURBING THE PEACE OF HIS MAJESTY, OUR KING."

He finishes the proclamation of the sentence and hands the scroll to his assistant, who descends. Then the clerk smiles upon Monsieur Torteru with an air of wishing him luck and likewise descends the steps. CUT TO

146 EXT. PLACE DU PARVIS. LARGER SHOT AFTERNOON
The chief clerk of the Court descends the steps from the pillory and takes his position with the other Court officials, inside the hollow square formed by the soldiery. A cry goes up -- a cry of impatience for the whipping to proceed -- a howl that makes Monsieur Torteru all the more deliberate in his movements. CUT TO

147 EXT. PLACE DU PARVIS C.U. OF MONSIEUR TORTERU AFTERNOON
Torteru's assistant is opening the official bag, and exposing to better view the three leather-covered handles of the scourges in the sack. Torteru, with grand importance, is rolling up his sleeves, smiling upon the crowd. He blows a kiss to a pretty girl, who responds in turn. Quasimodo, tied to the wheel, is in this view, is rolling his eyes about, in a manner which indicates that he has no knowledge of the punishment about to be inflicted. His back is to Torteru. The assistant now brings from the sack the three scourges. Torteru takes the heft of one of these, fondling it. Then he selects the second one, shakes it critically, and in the manner of testing it, whirls it thru the air around his head CUT TO.

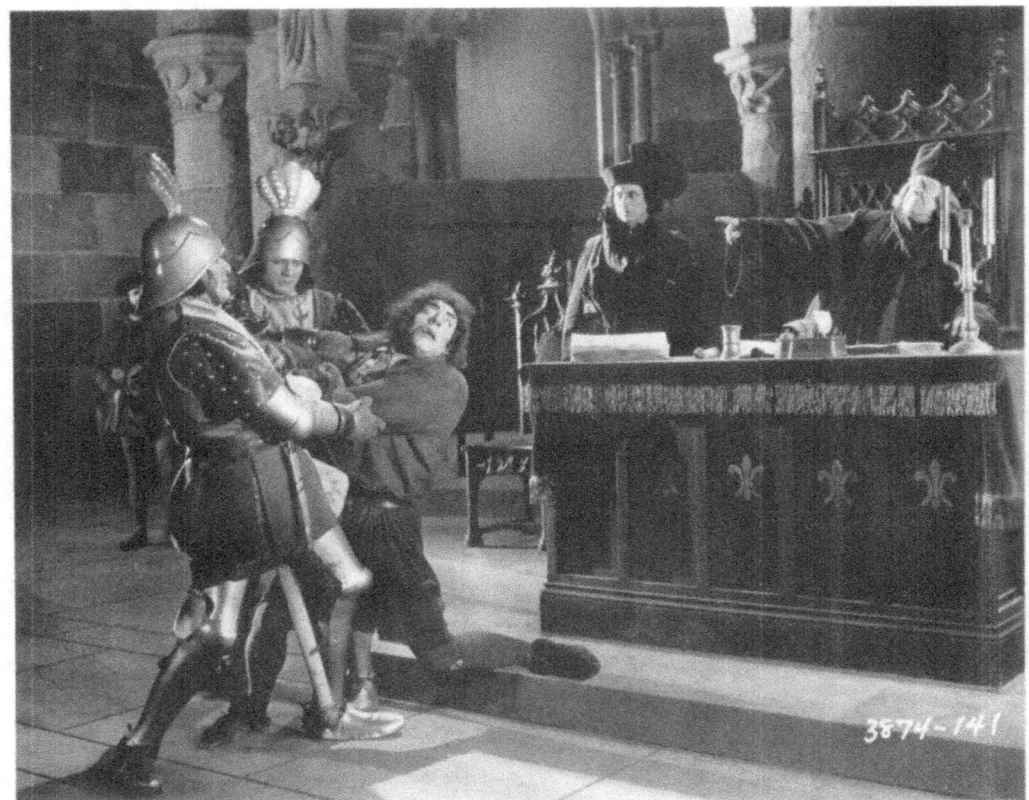

Previous scene - where Quasimodo is sentenced for the kidnapping attempt on Esmeralda.

148   EXT. PLACE DU PARVIS   LARGER SHOT AT PILLORY   AFTERNOON.
All of this serves to increase the suspense. The crowd applauds him, cheers him. To all of which Torteru, showing off, responds with seeming indifference in the importance of inspecting and selecting the proper scourge. During this action, the people nearest the pillory hurl insults and jeers at Quasimodo. The hunchback is impassive, wondering what is going to happen next.   CUT TO

149   EXT. PLACE DU PARVIS   C.U. MONSIEUR TORTERU   AFTERNOON.
He is enjoying himself immensely, as this closeup shows. The second scourge which he has tested in the same manner as the first, he decides wont do. Therefore, he takes the third one. He inspects it critically, examining the fastening of the lead strips fastened to the thongs of the scourge, about six to every thong. The handle of the instrument of torteru is about two feet long, with a leather covered handle. The thongs are about three feet long and there are six of them. It is a wicked looking thing, which Monsieur Torteru, however, regards with affectionate appreciation. This one he approves of and tests in the same manner as before. The assistant now squats on the edge of the platform, with legs dangling over the side, beside the jailer and hour-glass. He comes in for his share of approval likewise. All set, Torteru, with a final look about him, nods his head. It is the signal to proceed. His assistant, who has been watching for this, signals to those below.   CUT TO

150   EXT. PLACE DU PARVIS   MED. SHOT AT PILLORY.   AFTERNOON
The cries and plaudits of the spectators swell. The assistant, on the edge of the platform, has just given a signal with his hand. This is taken up on turn by the two jailers on the ground, underneath, who now, with perfect indifference, leans against the iron handle of the windlass, eating his apple. With a nod, he turns, lays hold of the handle, with two hands to get it started, the while he holds the apple between his teeth. With the ponderous mechanism in motion, one hand is sufficient and he uses the free hand to hold the fruit, which he continues to relish as he works,   CUT TO

151   EXT. PLACE DU PARVIS.   C.U. ON WHEEL   AFTERNOON
The wheel is slowly turning now, bringing Quasimodo around so that he faces Torteru, who as yet does not use his scourge. As Quasimodo comes within convenient reaching distance, Torteru leans over and with a swift jerk, rips Quasimodo's shirt from his back, exposing the deformed back. On Quasimodo's face there is a vacuous look of misconception of what it is all about, but now, with this act, his teeth show in protest. As Torteru rips Quasimodo's shirt off, CUT TO

152   EXT. PLACE DU PARVIS   LARGER SHOT   AFTERNOON.
The larger shot shows the approval of the spectators who yell and jeer as they see the expression on Quasimodo's face. The wheel by this time has turned, so that Quasimodo's back is toward Torteru, who with the deftness of practice, swings his scourge swishing thru the air and brings it down with slashing violence across Quasimodo's back, from which Torteru drags it, thus making the leaded thongs tear into Quasimodo's back. At the instant of this super-brutality, a great cry of approval and admiration for Torteru's skill rises into the air, as we   CUT TO

153   EXT. PLACE DU PARVIS   C.U. OF QUASIMODO   AFTERNOON.
As the blow falls and the scourge is jerked away, with the leaded thongs cutting into his back, Quasimodo's face changes and he gives a straining lurch. For the first time, he realizes what he has been brought here to suffer. He lunges, straining at his bonds, he makes a terrific effort to free himself. His teeth show and beads of perspiration, from rage, and suffering, suddenly stand out upon his forehead. For a flash of this, then   CUT TO

154   EXT. PLACE DU PARVIS   C.U. UNDER PILLORY   AFTERNOON
Just for a flash of this to show the pillory-keeper still
relishing the apple upon which he munches, even while he
works the windlass with his other hand. With the apple
finished, he tosses the core to a gamin and then lays his
whole interest in his work.   CUT TO

155   EXT. PLACE DU PARVIS   LONG SHOT FROM ELEVATION   AFTERNOON
This long shot shows the action at the pillory and the
cries of approval which fill the air as Torteru lays on
the blows with increasing force and skill every time
Quasimodo's back passes him, faster as the pillory-keeper
lays added strength to the windlass. The crowd cheers.
After a few feet of this,   QUICK FADE OUT

SUBTITLE   (75)   IT WAS THE DAY UPON WHICH DOM CLAUDE
HAD INVITED KING LOUIS TO INSPECT THE
TREASURE OF NOTRE DAME.

156   INT. CORRIDOR TO TREASURE ROOM OF NOTRE DAME.   LONG SHOT
AFTERNOON   QUICK FADE IN
The scene fades in quickly on a long shot down a long and
narrow corridor dimly lighted by a slant of light coming
from the upper right. This natural light is confined mostly
to the f.g. and is sufficient to indicate along the left-
hand wall of the corridor a receding vista of small stone
gables let into the wall three feet above the floor level,
each gable surmounted by a small cross, representing the
crypts in which dead church dignitaries are buried. Dimly
seen on the nearest funeral crypt is the engraved inscription
"HIC JACET JOSEPHUS". The inscription is broken as if from
time. The masonry of the entire corridor is flaked with age.
All that can be seen on the second funeral crypt are the words,
"HIC JACET..." And so on down the corridor. The light is so
dim that all this is merely suggested rather than seen. In
the b.g. where they have just paused before a door opening
into the wall on the right are King Louis, Dom Claude and
Phoebus. Phoebus lights this group by a short but very thick
candle which he holds aloft while Dom Claude fits an ancient
key into the lock of the door. This scene has just been fairly registered when into the scene from f.g., left, comes Jehan
(CONTINUED)

156   CONTINUED
who is manifesting uncertain of his direction as he has
been following the group from a distance. His first
glance is in the direction of the camera, fully registering
his expression of fear and excitement. Then he sees the
group disappearing into the door of the treasure chamber.
As he slinks into pursuit,   CUT TO

157   INT. TREASURE CHAMBER OF NOTRE DAME   MED. FULL SHOT AFTERNOON.
This shot is in the direction of the door upscene, center of
wall. This room is a cavernous subcellar of Notre Dame with
a mere suggestion of heavy masonry. The door through which
Louis, the Arch-deacon and Phoebus have just entered is of
massive planks. It is left open. While the group are in
the shadows, strongly illuminated by the candle which Phoebus
continues to hold upraised, there is a source of light above
which sends down a dim truncated cone of illumination softly
suffused over the center of the scene while the rest of the
scene remains in comparative darkness. The lighting effect
generally is misty, with a suggestion of floating dust --
the dust of ages disturbed -- by the opening of the door. In
the center of the room half revealed by this dim illumination
are a number of antique chests, both large and small. These
are loosely grouped and rest on the floor. Dom Claude leads
the way toward these, ushering his Royal guest forward with
respect but dignity. It must not be forgotten that here Dom
Claude is the host and his word is supreme. It is the King
who is now subject. This action brings the trio into the
immediate f.g., closeup. While Dom Claude lifts one lid of
one of the larger chests, Jehan is seen to appear at the open
door, upscene, Jehan seeks cover of the shadows. King
Louis gazes into the open chest with thoughtful absorption.
Phoebus politely stifles a yawn. His thoughts are not of
gold. Dom Claude explains to his Majesty the purpose that
is in his mind and speaks with dignity.

SUBTITLE: (76)   "YOUR MAJESTY IS AWARE THAT MISERY
BREEDS REVOLT."

As Dom Claude completes this title, Louis gives him a side-
ward glance as if to say "There is no danger so long as I
am King." Phoebus also reacts to the title by a lurch of
interest. He'd like to see anyone try revolt. But Dom Claude
with quiet dignity and persuasion continues:

SUBTITLE: (77) "THE PROPERTY OF GOD BELONGS TO HIS CHILDREN. IT WERE BEST THAT YOUR MAJESTY TAKE THIS TREASURE AND ESTABLISH HOSPITALS FOR THE POOR."

While Dom Claude serenely continues to expound his charitable plans and the King lends a willing ear, CUT TO

158 INT. TREASURE CHAMBER OF NOTRE DAME C.U. OF JEHAN AFTERNOON.
This closeup shows Jehan, in the shadows near the door. His face registers amazement and disgust at his brother's offer, then a swift spasm of alarm registers as he sees that he is in danger of discovery. As he starts to escape into the corridor, CUT TO

159 INT. TREASURE ROOM OF NOTRE DAME MED. SHOT AFTERNOON.
This is as before, showing Dom Claude, Louis and Phoebus in fairly close foreground. As Phoebus respectfully aids the placid, dignified Dom Claude to close the treasure chest and Louis strokes his chin pensively, Jehan is seen to disappear into the corridor. Dom Claude and Phoebus straighten up and as the party slowly turns to exit, the scene FADES OUT.

160 CLOSE UP OF HOUR GLASS
IRIS IN ON GLASS as the last grains run out.

161 EXT. PLACE DU PARVIS MED. CLOSE ON PILLORY AFTERNOON
The whipping is over. Torteru stands there, with the scourge dripping blood, looking down at Quasimodo, whose body is almost in collapse, his great shaggy head leaning forward, loosely, tongue out, panting. He suffers. Torteru, with the air of a man well satisfied with his duty accomplished, tosses the scourge to his assistant and starts rolling down his sleeves. Assistant moves over toward the hour-glass.

162 EXT. PLACE DU PARVIS C.U. HOUR GLASS AFTERNOON
There is a fractional pause and then the jailer's hand enters scene and turns the glass upside down so that the sand starts running again, CUT TO

163 EXT. PLACE DU PARVIS MED. CLOSE ON PILLORY AFTERNOON.
We pick up the action as in 161. Torteru completes rolling down his sleeves and adjusting his garments, well satisfied with himself and no longer interested in the prisoner. The crowd is seen beginning to scatter. Torteru nods to the jailer at the side of the hour-glass and the jailer responds by holding up two fingers. As Torteru starts to descend the steps, followed by his assistant, CUT TO.

164 EXT. PLACE DU PARVIS MED. SHOT AT PILLORY.TOWARD RIGHT-HAND CORNER OF NOTRE DAME AFTERNOON
Under the structure, the keeper of the pillory is talking with one or two of the soldiers. The crowd is seen to be scattering. Torteru now joins the clerk and assistant of the Court who are waiting for him, and they melt off into the general movement from the pillory. Groups of admiring youngsters follow Torteru, such as children of today follow in admiration a drum-major. The jailers crowd into the cart, with perhaps two or three of the soldiers. What little formality existed at the beginning disappears. The jailer with the hour-glass stays behind, cracking jokes with some of those about. In this general movement, with the (CONTINUED)

164 CONTINUED
crowd gradually scattering, Esmeralda can be discerned, appearing in the Place Du Parvis near Gudule's cell. CUT TO.

165 EXT PLACE DU PARVIS   MED. SHOT AT GUDULE'S CELL   AFTERNOON.
At the opening of the scene, Sister Gudule is seen partly in profile just within the bars of her arched window, looking in the direction of Notre Dame. Gudule gives a start of crazy rage as Esmeralda comes into the scene from left. ~~Hurriedly she opens from her window quickly and flings open the planked door of her cell and~~ shrieks at Esmeralda. Esmeralda shrinks and starts to hurry. Gudule shakes her fist after her and shrieks:

SUBTITLE (78)   "CURSED GYPSY . . . DAUGHTER OF SATAN . . . CHILD STEALER . . . 'TIS THOU THAT OUGHT TO BE WHIPPED!"

Gudule has let her frenzy get the better of her. She still stands in her doorway and is cursing things in general, rather than Esmeralda in particular, as Esmeralda with mingled sympathy and horror hastens on her way. CUT TO

166 EXT. PLACE DU PARVIS   C.U. AT PILLORY   AFTERNOON
This is Quasimodo's closeup, though a general background of the scenes show the cart, laden down with jailers, soldiers, etc., progressing out of scene in direction of entrance. Torture ~~is still the center of an admiring throng.~~ Now, in immediate foreground, Quasimodo stirs. In agony of suffering, he lifts his head. His eyes roll. His parched tongue protrudes from his mouth. From the background some of the spectators, moving away, hurl dirt at him, even as he bellows:

SUBTITLE: (79)   ~~"A DRINK!"~~

Just for a flash of this, and then CUT TO.

167 EXT. PLACE DU PARVIS   MED. CLOSE AT SMALL FOUNTAIN-AFTERNOON—
There is general activity about as the crowd scatters. Esmeralda is approaching toward foreground and now stops near a public water-tap as she hears the agonized plea of Quasimodo. Her pretty face takes on an expression of compassion. She turns. Here, right at her side, is the fountain, a square stone structure, similar to a tombstone, from which is a spout, giving forth water. At the edge of the stone basin, at the foot of the fountain, is a broken earthen jug, the bottom of which, however, is intact to the extent that it will hold water. Esmeralda hesitates, but as she hears the remarks of the crowd about her, her face becomes decisive, and on impulse, she holds the broken jug under the spout, fills it and starts toward the pillory.   CUT TO

168 INT. A CHAPEL OF NOTRE DAME   MED. SHOT   AFTERNOON.
This is a deep alcove about twenty-five feet high by fifteen broad, and is flooded by the light of hundreds of candles which surround and cause to disappear in a shimmer of light, a dimly seen altar surmounted by a Saint. Across the front of the chapel is a small railing. The rest of the shot indicates that this chapel is but one of a series. As we pick up the action, King Louis, Phoebus and Dom Claude have just come this far from the nave of Notre Dame, and now King Louis, indicating the chapel, dismisses the Archdeacon and says that he will pray. Phoebus, to whom this is evidently a familiar and tiresome part of his official duty, reclines against one of the fluted stone pillars across the aisle from the chapel. Now as Louis sinks to his knees at the railing and lifts his face to the flood of light from the candles, Dom Claude exits from the scene, thoughtfully, in the direction of the front left-hand portal.   CUT TO

169   EXT. PLACE DU PARVIS MED. SHOT AT PILLORY AFTERNOON.
In the medium shot, Quasimodo with his strength fast
failing him is crying, "I thirst!" A gamin gathers up a
double-handful of mud and throws it in his face. Through
all of this, the jailer sitting on the edge of the platform
registers a blissful indifference. It is nothing in his
life. Esmeralda, defiant in her manner, reaches the steps
of the pillory and ascends. Quasimodo's face is slightly
away from this point, so that he cannot see who it is that
approaches. CUT TO.

170   EXT. PLACE DU PARVIS C.U. OF QUASIMODO AFTERNOON
Quasimodo summons his strength and manages to raise his
head again to cry pitifully, "I thirst, I thirst!"
Esmeralda enters the scene. Quasimodo looks up, for an
instant he misinterprets her presence. She too has come
to spit upon him, to torture and revile. He is filled with
terror -- a dumb appeal for mercy, But he expects no
mercy from Esmeralda. His eye lifts to her, expecting
torture. Then his expression changes as he sees that he
has misjudged her. With an inarticulate gasp he leans
forward, and Esmeralda, shrinking with horror at the
horrible sight he presents, holds the bowl to his lips,
her face an expression commingling horror with infinite
compassion and pity. CUT TO.

171   EXT. STEPS OF NOTRE DAME SHOT TOWARD PARVIS. AFTERNOON
This shot is from the left portal of Notre Dame, shooting
out over the Parvis toward the pillory. Dom Claude enters
scene from over foreground. Dom Claude is still pensive
and as he comes to the top of the steps he lifts his face
and looks out over the Parvis. At first this is with
passing interest. Then he sees the crowd scattering. Then
this back view of the priest indicates a sudden interest
as he sees the pillory and recognizes who it is thereon.
While this scene is played with Dom Claude's back to the
camera, the pantomime should suggest as great an intensity
of emotions as if the Arch-deacon's face were visible. Now
as he starts to descend the steps, intent upon hurrying to
Quasimodo, CUT TO

172   EXT. PLACE DU PARVIS C.U. ESMERALDA AFTERNOON.
Esmeralda, in the attitude described, looking down at
Quasimodo with a tear of sympathy.

173   EXT. PLACE DU PARVIS C.U. QUASIMODO AFTERNOON
Esmeralda's hands holding the broken jug to Quasimodo's
lips, while he gulps the water with relief. He looks up
now. On his face there is an expression never before seen.
He is suffocated with love and gratitude. It is in this
moment that Quasimodo's great love for Esmeralda is born
and quickens into fire. A tear starts from his eye and
rolls down his cheek. He is Esmeralda's slave for life.

174   EXT. PLACE DU PARVIS MED. SHOT AT PILLORY. AFTERNOON
Esmeralda, held for an instant in fascinated horror as she
looks down at Quasimodo. She is turning away, just as Dom
Claude enters the scene. At the same moment, the jailer
with the hour glass at his side, turns. He has a momentary
impulse to interfere as he sees Dom Claude's intent to
untie Quasimodo. But their eyes meet, and under the
accusing, dignified demand in Dom Claude's eyes, the jailer
is abashed. Dom Claude has seen Esmeralda's act of kindness
and smiles his peace upon her as she exits. She looks at
him with mystic deference, as she exits. Dom Claude reaches
Quasimodo and sinks to his knees at the victim's side.
Quasimodo's body relaxes in Dom Claude's arms. Dom Claude
starts to loosen Quasimodo's bonds, upon which action the
scene FADES OUT

SUBTITLE: (80) IN THE HOPE OF CEMENTING AN ALLIANCE BETWEEN
HER NIECE, FLEUR DE LYS, AND HER NEPHEW,
PHOEBUS, MME. DE GONDELAURIER GIVES A BALL
IN THE NEW CAPTAIN'S HONOR.

175 INT. GONDELAURIER SALON MED. FULL DAIS NIGHT FADE IN
The scene fades in on medium full shot at Madame de Gondelaurier's dais. The view shows the dais in center and
incorporates a goodly portion of the main salon. Seated
on the chair on the dais is Madame de Gondelaurier, very
smiling and gracious as she chats with such guests as happen
to be standing about her, or, as in the case of the younger
people, seated on the one step of the dais. Other guests
are promenading or chatting in groups. The scene is one
of light animation. At the large door at left of angle
leading into hall, can be seen a number of servants, young
and old of both sexes, peering in as children do nowadays.
So far as possible, the older male guests present should
be such notables as are cast for the more important roles
elsewhere in the story. Thus we have the King's chancellor,
Maitre Charmolu, the King's procurer, and two or three of the
judges who appear at the trial of Esmeralda. ....
is M. de Neufchatel. One of these is Madame de Gondelaurier with whom he
carries on a discreet flirtation . CUT TO

176 INT. GONDELAURIER SALON CLOSER SHOT AT DAIS. NIGHT
This shot shows Fleur de Lys among the younger people to
one side of Madame de Gondelaurier. They are primly chatting
and coquettish. On Madame's other side is Neufchatel. She
playfully shakes under his nose, a lace handkerchief which
is evidently perfumed. He reacts to this, and then suspecting
that some of the younger people are making fun of him, he
scowls in a military way and speaks to Madame de Gondelaurier:

SUBTITLE: (81) "WHERE IS THAT YOUNG JACKANAPES, YOUR
NEPHEW PHOEBUS?"

176 CONTINUED
F. dL: Madame de Gondelaurier responds with a gesture of
mock despair and then speaks with petulant seriousness:

SUBTITLE: (82) "EVER SINCE THE POOR BOY WAS MADE
CAPTAIN OF THE GUARDS HE'S BEEN
SUCH A SLAVE TO DUTY."

Neufchatel is about to say, "Ho-ho, what a joke!" when he
stifles his words and gets over his thought with his eyebrows. In other words, he knows well enough that Phoebus
hasn't been so dutiful as his aunt thinks. As this conversation touches this little climax. CUT TO

SUBTITLE: (83) (THIS IS A PARCHMENT SCROLL AND IS SIMPLY
ANOTHER OF THE APHORISMS WRITTEN BY GRINGOIRE).

"TOT OU TARD CELUI QUI JOUE A L'AMOUR
RECOIT UNE FLECHE AU COEUR."

. . . Les Poemes de Gringoire.

LAP DISSOLVE THIS INTO THE ENGLISH
"SOONER OR LATER HE WHO PLAYS AT LOVE
GETS AN ARROW THROUGH THE HEART."

. . . The Poems of Gringoire

177 EXT. A PARIS STREET (ANY) C.U. FOR TWO NIGHT
This could be shot almost anywhere, no special set being
required. All that is needed is a tree by a bit of wall
and a muddy bit of pavement. The light is off scene, rather
dim, but sufficient to spot up Esmeralda, as if the light
came from an open door or window. Phoebus, in the gorgeous
costume, already dressed for the ball, is lurking behind
the tree, his place of rendezvous with Esmeralda. Esmeralda
comes into scene as if looking for Phoebus and a little
frightened and disappointed at not seeing him. Phoebus
hides for a moment or two, then springs forward to greet

(CONTINUED)

177 (CONTINUED)

Their joy is mutual. But there is no longer any suggestion og yhr madyrtgul malr snouy Phoebus. When Esmeralda, checking her own expression of joy, to a little pout, at the trick that Phoebus has played on her, Phoebus instantly catches her hand as if she were a great lady and bows low to kiss her finger-tips. She accepts his tribute with a feigned air of hauteur and then melts as he caressingly takes her arm under his and indicates that he wants to take her to his Aunt's ball. She starts to protest. Now Phoebus does show himself masterfully insistent. He speaks:

SUBTITLE (84) "THOU MUST COME WITH ME! ART THOU NOT MY BRIDE-TO-BE? IS NOT THIS BALL GIVEN IN MY HONOR?"

BACK. Esmeralda is filled with misgivings but Phoebus is increasingly exuberant and enthusiastic. Esmeralda yields and consents to be led away. As they exit, CUT TO:

178 INT. CLOPIN'S HAUNT   MED FULL SHOT   NIGHT
(Clopin's haunt to be described in later sequence.)
Seated at his table is Clopin. He is in an evil mood. His eyes are on a wicked looking knife which he is whetting upon a stone with all the intensity of a person who loves the thing he fondles tenderly. Upscene there are a few of the familiars of the COUR DEMIRACLES gathered in front of the fireplace, drinking, gnawing at chunks of meat, and singing ribald songs. The door is open. Through it and to a certain extent, through the dirty panes of the windows, is cast a ruddy, flickering glow, from the torches and fires outside. Hold this picture for a few seconds. Clopin with loving eyes inspects the edge of his knife, then rises, sheathing the blade in his broad and tattered sash. He starts toward the door. Just as he does so, Marie enters. She meets Clopin's eyes and starts to sidle away, but stops as Clopin, seeing that Esmeralda hasn't followed her in, bellows:

SUBTITLE (85) "WHERE IS ESMERALDA?"

BACK. Marie backs away from Clopin, abject in gesturing fear as she says she doesn't know. Clopin hurls a curse at her and exits to Cowrt.

179 EXT. PLACE DU PARVIS   MED SHOT OF GONDELAURIES HOME
NIGHT
This medium shot is at the entrance to the porte-cochere of the mansion. There are two massive, iron-studded doors, deeply recessed into the stone structure. These doors are panelled and the lower lefthand panel of the left door is a door itself, to admit entrance to those who arrive on foot, the big doors only being opened for horses or carriages. On the left, recessed in the wall, is a little iron grilled window through which the concierge from within can inspect any person who demands admittance. Entering the scene from right is a vagabond of the Cour de Miracles. He is fat, gross, dirty, tattered, greasy; a human pig, repulsive of face. He is just in the act of crossing the scene as Phoebus enters with Esmeralda. There is a flash of the concierge's face at the little window. Then a few seconds pass, during which Phoebus and Esmeralda are excellently lighted by the flare from the two great flaming torches in the brackets on either side of the porte-cocheres. The vagabond glimpses Esmeralda's face, and then, with greater haste than when he entered, shuffles from the scene. The small door swings open and Phoebus and Esmeralda pass through. The concierge, a man of about fifty, wearing a woolen tassel cap and house slippers of carpet, salaa ms, then stares after Phoebus in whimsical surprise before he starts to close the door. CUT TO:

180 EXT. A PARIS STREET   MED FULL SHOT   NIGHT
This street can be any of the streets previously shown. Coming toward the camera is the fat beggar who saw Phoebus and Esmeralda enter the Gondelauries house. He is puffing, out of wind and running with monstrous effort. There is excitement and determination in his round eyes. A short scene of this, then CUT TO:

125

181 INT. ~~HALL DE GON~~DELAURIER RESIDENCE   NIGHT
This is a grand hallway, ~~at least twenty feet wide~~ and
twenty feet broad. ~~The angle is toward the grand staircase.~~
The upper background is ~~a wall hung with a large~~ tapestry.
The parquet floor is covered partly with ~~a woolen~~ carpet.
At the left is a broad ~~arched doorway connecting~~ the hall
with the grand salon previously described. ~~The~~ hall is less
brilliantly lighted ~~than~~ the Grand Salon, ~~but the~~ latter
practically furnishes the source of ~~light in this location.~~
As the scene opens the only persons visible in the hall are
the group of servants in medieval attire, who sit on the
floor or stand about the side of the large door, looking in
at the festivities beyond. ~~There is nothing formal looking~~
about these servants. ~~They belong to a period when such~~
~~menials were treated largely as children, say like our own~~
~~darkies in the old slave days.~~ In this ~~group are~~ two or
three ~~women~~, two or three men ~~and a number of page~~ boys,
from ~~ten to fifteen years of age~~. They are so engrossed in
what they see, laughing and commenting among themselves,
that they do not notice the arrival of Phoebus and Esmeralda, until these latter, coming from the direction of
the stairs, are almost up to the door. From the moment Phoebus
arrives, it is evident he has been assuring the timid Esmeralda that everything is alright. He does this in a
grandiloquent way. His pantomime registers his claim that
the whole world is at his disposition and he is placing
this at Esmeralda's command. This attitude is further em-
phasised when he presents Esmeralda to the servants. He
does this with a sweeping gesture of exaggerated gallantry
that causes the servants to draw back, abashed and over-
whelmed. There is an old nurse who dares to suggest to
Phoebus that his aunt will take exception. To this Phoebus
merely pooh-poohs and bids the timorous Esmeralda to take
a look at the splendors of the salon beyond. Esmeralda
looks up at him to reassure herself that all this is real,
then shrinking closer to him, is spellbound as she sees,
in greater detail:

182 INT. GONDELAURIER SALON   MED SHOT FROM HALL   NIGHT
This is a cross ~~shot into~~ the salon from the position ~~of~~
the door which opens into the hall. In ~~the right corner~~
upscene is ~~the high platform for the musicians~~, previously
described. ~~The musicians are four in number, a small harp,~~
~~a flute, a drum and a flageolet. The musicians, like all~~
~~the other men in the room, wear their hats.~~ The dance is
just coming to an end. There are at least one dozen couples
who promenade hand in hand with exaggerated grace and dignity. It must be ~~emphasized that~~ there is nothing quick
about this ~~dance. It is a cross between the primitive min-~~
~~uet and a modern~~ ~~musicians~~ ~~solo with. This scene~~ is short
(CONTINUED NEXT PAGE)

182 (CONTINUED)
and is merely to indicate the flash of splendor and
beauty which has made Esmeralda gasp. CUT TO:

183 INT. HALL DE GONDELAURIER RESIDENCE   NIGHT   CU
This shot is from the direction of the salon and shows
Esmeralda transfigured, beautiful, round-eyed, like a child
living in a fairy story. At the conclusion of the dance,
Esmeralda turns to look up at Phoebus. CUT TO:

184 INT. UPPER HALL DE GONDELAURIER RESIDENCE   NIGHT   MED SHOT
~~This close-up~~ ~~~~ ~~~~ ~~~~ ~~~~ Esmeralda. ~~She~~
~~sees in~~ ~~~~ ~~~~ ~~~~ ~~~~ ~~~~ ~~~~
~~shows the approach of Madame de Gondelaurier. Her~~ face
is smiling at her wide-eyed ~~eagerness. For,~~ ~~~~ to
conduct her into the salon, Phoebus takes Esmeralda by the
hand. Esmeralda, quickly understanding his intention, hangs
back, protesting that her appearance is against any such
procedure. Her pretty picture of protest makes Phoebus
think. Quickly, and without analyzing the results which
might ensue, Phoebus smiles and with a nod, calls out of
scene toward the servants. Two of the women enter, courtesy-
ing low and smiling upon Phoebus as he explains that Esmeralda is to be taken upstairs and dressed like a lady. Esmeralda gasps in delight at the thought. The older of the
servant women nods for Esmeralda to follow. The younger of
the two sizes Esmeralda up and finds her good. With a grateful flash toward Phoebus, hardly daring to believe that
such a dream as being dressed like a lady could come true,
Esmeralda exits with the servants. Phoebus looks after her,
smiling with a devil-may-care manner--never weighing the
possible consequences. As he stands thus, CUT TO:

185 INT. DE GONDELAURIER SALON MED SHOT IN D.H. NIGHT
This shot is from a point near the entrance of the hall,
toward the throne chair, where Fleur de lys, dressed in
all the splendor of the times, holds polite conversation
with a smooth faced dandy. Madame de Gondelaurier ~~enters
scene, starting toward the upstage action~~, but ~~stops~~ with
a little cry of delight as she espies Phoebus in the hall.
With a quick glance about to locate Fleur de lys, she
sweeps majestically upscene. CUT TO:

186 INT. DE GONDELAURIER SALON MED SHOT INTO HALL NIGHT
This shot shows Phoebus standing about as before, looking
in the direction taken by Esmeralda. Now he turns toward
the ballroom, and for the first time his face shows a trace
of anxiety. He turns. Madame de Gondelaurier and Fleur de
lys enter from right foreground. Madame is more than glad
to see her handsome nephew and scolds him prettily for being so late. Fleur de lys is demurely coy, looking at Phoebus under lowered eyes and then frowning slightly as she
sees her effort wasted. Madame presses Fleur de lys upon
Phoebus and perforce he must dance with her. Fleur de lys
and Phoebus exeunt, leaving Madame de Gondelaurier looking
after them, beaming. CUT TO:

187 INT. DE GONDELAURIER SALON FULL SHOT NIGHT
The couples are just forming for a minuet as Phoebus and
Fleur de lys take their positions upscene. Now, as the
figure starts, the couples (opposite each other) fall back
in the solemn--almost Phoebus takes Fleur de lys' hands and
~~exaggerated--manner of the dance,~~
comes down scene between the lane formed by the men on the
left and the women on the right. Phoebus and Fleur de lys
are in turn followed by the next couple and so on, with the
dance gradually approximating our modern "Grand March".
Throughout this action, Phoebus is on "needles and pins",
held by his partner, but thinking of Esmeralda. As this
action is in progress, CUT TO:

188   EXT. COUR DE MIRACLES   MED SHOT NEAR THRONE AND GIBBET NIGHT
As the scene opens there is a dance in progress which is a drunken, grotesque parody of the ballroom scene in the Gondelaurier mansion. The dancers, all of whom are old and grotesque, are lighted by the flames of an immense bonfire. Here we use again some of the characters seen in previous shots in the Cour de Miracles. The fat old woman who would have married Gringoire is dancing with a dwarf. There is a bent old witch with a crutch who dances with a cadaverous Don Quixote in queer military attire. It is a dance of grotesques. In the fairly close foreground, near camera, silhouetted against the strong firelight, Clopin strides back and forth with gestures of savage impatience. Where is Esmeralda? On this action, our fat beggar rushes into scene and gasps out his message while he points. He speaks:

SUBTITLE (86)   "ESMERALDA...ESMERALDA...THE CAPTAIN OF THE GUARD...."

BACK. While the messenger continues to pant the rest of his information which we know, there comes into scene from right, Gringoire, who is eager to hear more and has a knowing and happy smile on his face. The fact that Gringoire thus intrudes on the scene is sufficient evidence that he has become a familiar of the Cour de Miracles. Neither Clopin nor the fat beggar, moreover, look at Gringoire as the fat beggar continues to amplify his news and Clopin listens with a terrific and mounting rage. CUT TO:

189   EXT. COUR DE MIRACLES   CU GRINGOIRE   NIGHT
Gringoire is delighted with the information which he is about to give. He is arch. He is going to spring a pleasant surprise. He now announces his news, self-satisfied. He speaks:

SUBTITLE (87)   "FEAR NOT! FEAR NOT! OUR LOVELY ESMERALDA HAS BUT TAKEN HER CAPTOR CAPTIVE. THEY LOVE EACH OTHER."

BACK. As Gringoire recites this information he closes his eyes in ecstatic appreciation of the delicious love affair and opens his eyes to smile up at Clopin. Then there is a rapid transition to shocked surprise and dismay as Clopin's powerful and tense hand comes into scene and plants itself against Gringoire's face and shoves him backward. CUT TO:

128

190   EXT. COUR DE MIRACLES   MED SHOT NEAR THRONE AND GIBBET NIGHT
As we pick up the action, Gringoire is being catapulted backward by the force of Clopin's shove and ends up in a sitting position with a look of pained dismay on his face. Concurrent to this there is a converging movement of Clopin's followers toward him as he lets out a savage shout:

SUBTITLE (88)   "TO THE RESCUE! THE ARISTOCRATS HAVE TAKEN OUR ESMERALDA"

BACK. Clopin explains and exhorts to the stalwart beggars who strain to hear him and agree with him. With a savage snarl and gesture he jerks his knife from his sash and thrusts it upward for all to see and starts forward with a wave of his left hand for those about him to accompany him. On this movement forward, CUT TO:

191   EXT. COUR DE MIRACLES   LONG SHOT THROUGH ARCH   NIGHT
The movement as established in the previous scene is picked up here as Clopin's menacing group follows him down scene. The fat beggar is at Clopin's side, still volubly explaining what he has seen. Clopin does not speak at all. He is taciturn and sinister. As they exeunt the activity of the Cour de Miracles shows a centering of interest about Gringoire.

192   INT. GONDELAURIER HALL   REVERSE ANGLE   MED SHOT   NIGHT
The view is toward a door in the center of wall at the end of the hallway. The door is closed. It opens and through it, in a glory of light from many candles, is seen Esmeralda, coiffed and dressed in a beautiful costume, befitting a princess. She is just starting down scene, a picture of exquisite grace and beauty. The younger maid is at the door, keeping her eyes on Esmeralda in unmistakable admiration. Now, in the hallway, from over foreground, appears Phoebus, accompanied by the older maid, who obviously has gone to summon him. In foreground Phoebus stops with a gasp of delighted admiration as he sees Esmeralda, who now steps through the door into the hall. The elder woman passes behind her through the door. Both she and the younger maid, with a final look of supreme admiration at Esmeralda, retire into the room, as we CUT TO:

193   INT. GONDELAURIER HALL   REVERSE ANGLE   NIGHT
      CU ESMERALDA AND PHOEBUS
      Esmeralda looking toward Phoebus, basking happily in the
      approval which she sees in his eyes as he enters. He looks
      at her, feasts his eyes upon her, to such an extent that
      Esmeralda's heart flutters and she drops her eyes for an
      instant. Phoebus takes a step toward her. He is the per-
      sonification of romance as he leans slightly forward, in-
      spired, pouring out a flood of endearment and praise into
      Esmeralda's ear. She turns. Their eyes meet for seconds.
      Phoebus' arm goes about her waist. Still they look into
      each other's eyes. Now, no words are necessary. He loves
      her. She loves him. She relaxes slightly--happy to feel
      his touch. Then slowly Phoebus draws her to him and with
      eyes still looking into each other's soul, he kisses her.
      Esmeralda's eyes close. Her hand rests on his shoulder.
      For Esmeralda this is not merely a love affair, but a
      glimpse of heaven. Now, in the manner of two happy chil-
      dren, they turn toward camera. CUT TO:

194   EXT. A PARIS STREET   MED LONG SHOT   NIGHT
      This street can be a reverse shot of one of the streets
      previously established. Its lighting is solely by the haze
      of MOONLIGHT and should be in harmony with the sinister
      movement through it, as Clopin, with the fat beggar by his
      side and followed by twenty menacing vagabonds, comes down
      the scene. The movement is silent, sinister and tense.
      CUT TO:

195   INT. GONDELAURIER SALON   MED SHOT   NIGHT
      This view is from the main salon, in the direction of the
      French windows which open upon the Parvis. In the Petit
      Salon are Madame de Gondelaurier and Fleur de lys, with
      several of the guests. Fleur de lys, slightly apart from
      the others, glances into the Salon, as though seeking
      Phoebus. Suddenly her expression changes and she takes a
      quick step toward her mother. CUT TO:

196   INT. GONDELAURIER SALON   NIGHT
      CU MADAME AND FLEUR DE LYS
      Fleur de lys steps into scene from right and lays a hand
      upon her mother's arm. Madame de Gondelaurier turns, and
      glimpsing the expression on Fleur de lys' face, follows the
      direction of the girl's astounded gaze out of scene past
      camera. When she sees what Fleur de lys' eyes have seen,
      her expression likewise changes and she gasps in transfixed
      surprise as she sees.

197   INT. GONDELAURIER SALON   LONG SHOT   NIGHT
      This view is from the arch of the Petit Salon, toward the
      canopied chair at the end of same. Coming down the center
      of the Salon are Phoebus and Esmeralda. Phoebus, on the
      right, is escorting Esmeralda with all the super-courtesy
      of a romance-swept youth and his whole attitude is one of
      high pride as he senses the eyes of the guests in the Salon
      upon them. Esmeralda is prettily amazed and held in awe by
      the splendor of the scene. She is radiant. She is beautiful.
      The action has been picked up with Phoebus and Esmeralda
      well within the room, about half way down scene, and should
      be continuous in uninterrupted movement until they reach
      fairly close foreground just within the arch of the Petit
      Salon. Esmeralda clings somewhat closer to Phoebus. He
      now bows low to his aunt while he holds Esmeralda's hand
      and speaks:

      SUBTITLE (89)
                     "ESMERALDA, PRINCESS DE L'EGYPTE."

      BACK. Esmeralda, after a moment of amazement, takes her
      cue from Phoebus and sweeps into a low courtesy. As she
      straightens up, CUT TO:

198 INT. GONDELAURIER SALON   MED SHOT   NIGHT
This view is from end of the smaller Salon, placing the
French windows on the back and to the right. Through the
arch on the right. Just within the room, vista of arch,
stand Esmeralda and Phoebus. On the left is Madame de
Gondelaurier and nearer to center and slightly behind her is
Fleur de lys. Phoebus has just spoken and is straightening
from his bow. There is an interval of wide-mouthed interest
in "The Princess of Egypt" upon the parts of all. Neufchatel
registers disapproval. Madame de Gondelaurier and Fleur de
lys look on dismayed, but trying as best they may to cover
the thoughts which flash in their minds, i.e., that Phoebus
has found a new and more beautiful sweetheart. In Esmeralda's new attire, it is obvious that she is not recognized
by Fleur de lys as the street dancer in whom Phoebus dis-
played such interest. Two or three of the young gentlemen
among the guests comment in whispers behind their hands.
Phoebus stands very straight, smiling, confident, ready
to challenge any who question Esmeralda's right. Madame de
Gondelaurier appears for a second uncertain. Fleur de lys
looks on in suppressed anger. Before time has elapsed for
definite action by Madame de Gondelaurier, CUT TO:

199 EXT. GONDELAURIER HOME   MED SHOT AT DOOR   NIGHT
The medium shot includes a view of the iron-barred window
of the concierge. At this window is Clopin, suave, graceful, meek. Within can be seen the concierge, doubtful, but
gradually being persuaded as Clopin, suavely, craftily,
pleads. He has come on business--business of vital importance, a communication which must be conveyed personally
to Monsieur de Chateaupers. Will he open the door, please,
and let him through? There must be no delay.

SUBTITLE (90)   "EVEN NOW THY MASTER AWAITETH ME. I WOULD
SEE HIM FOR AN INSTANT ONLY. WITHER,
SWEET COMRADE, OPEN ME THE DOOR."

BACK. Contrasting with Clopin's suave words and gestures,
the others of his group are seen, pressed into a little
knot near the doors, on right. They have their knives drawn
and are in readiness to rush the door, once the concierge
accedes to Clopin's request. The concierge is still in
doubt. Now, as the concierge finally agrees to admit Clopin
and disappears from his fellows, almost instantly the small
door opens and a couple of Clopin's followers fling themselves against. Clopin, with a look to the left and right,
swiftly enters followed by the rest of the band. CUT TO:

200 EXT. PORTE COCHERE GONDELAURIER HOUSE   MED SHOT   NIGHT
This shot is toward the doors which open into the Parvis.
The foremost ruffian is seen flinging the concierge back
into his loge through the small door to the right. The
action is swift and dimly lighted. The band is assembled
within the space and the small door leading to the street
through which the men entered is now being closed. With a
swift movement, Clopin indicates the grand stairway and
motions to his men to follow him. As they start out of
scene, CUT TO:

201 INT. GONDELAURIER SALON   MED CLOSE SHOT   NIGHT
This is viewed from the direction of the main salon. The
guests are all assembled about a group consisting of Phoebus, Esmeralda, Madame de Gondelaurier and Fleur de lys.
Madame de Gondelaurier is not yet convinced of the identity
of this guest that her harum-scarum nephew had introduced.
Fleur de lys is frankly rebellious and disturbed. Esmeralda
is clinging somewhat protestingly to Phoebus. All the guests
are in a quandary, rather inclined to side with the aunt,
but none the less bedazzled by Esmeralda's beauty. Phoebus
is bluffing magnificently. He says:

INSERT TITLE (91)   "SHE DESCENDS FROM A LINE MORE ANCIENT
THAN THAT OF THE KINGS OF FRANCE."

BACK. As he finishes the title there is a swift counter-
interest established among some of the guests which rapidly involves everyone else in the scene. All now turn to
look past the camera in the direction of the arched doorway
leading from the main hall into the Salon. There is a general shrinking. In Esmeralda's face there is a flash of horror
and dismay. Phoebus registers a challenge and a readiness
to fight for Esmeralda who almost collapses into the embrace of his one arm while his right hand goes to a poignard
at his belt. Hold this long enough to register the imminence
of a catastrophe and then CUT TO:

202 INT. GONDELAURIER SALON   MED SHOT   NIGHT
This shot is toward the canopied chair upstage. Camera is on truck ready to follow action. Inimmediate foreground is Clopin flanked by two of his most atrocious followers with the heads and faces of the rest of his gang forming a compact and menacing background. Clopin's expression is fierce and terrible, touched with amusement at his certainty of triumph. They are like a bunch of wild animals who suddenly find themselves in the presence of all they hunger for. On all faces visible in the camera are greed and lust and inflamed imagination. The camera now starts into movement as Clopin and his gang start forward. Clopin's expression is no longer quite so fixed. His eyes never deviate but he is speakingto his followers in a whisper from the corner of his mouth. This movement continues until the camera progresses to a point representing the positions of Phoebus and Esmeralda. In other words, we have been watching this progress through their eyes. CUT TO:

203 INT. GONDELAURIER SALON   MED CLOSE SHOT   NIGHT
This shot is from a position within the Petit Salon, shooting toward the scene with the arch into the main Salon on the left. This places Clopin on the left in immediate foreground profile. Phoebus is slightly further upscene on the right. Center, with his arm about her, is Esmeralda. While the focus of the camera is concentrated on these three main characters, also in two shot to the left and on the right Madame de Gondelaurier and Fleur-de-lys. The incidental business is of Clopin's followers ogling the women and the horror and distress of the women as a reaction to this. This is just atmosphere. The main action is centered wholly on the conflict of Phoebus and Clopin with Esmeralda holding the balance between them. Both Phoebus and Clopin have drawn their weapons. Now, as Phoebus' hand moves, CUT TO:

204 INT. GONDELAURIER SALON   CU PHOEBUS' HAND & POIGNARD   NIGHT
This is just a flash of Phoebus' jeweled hand and richly embossed poignard opposed to the hairy and somewhat deformed hand of Clopin which is now thrust into the scene, holding his crude and murderous knife. The two weapons are a foot or so apart, point on, when into the scene comes the dainty delicate hand of Esmeralda between them. CUT TO:

205 INT. GONDELAURIER SALON   MED CLOSE AS BEFORE   NIGHT
Esmeralda has now begun to plead. Her face is tearful, passionate, filled with desperation. She is looking up, alternately from Phoebus to Clopin. She cries out, "Oh, for the love of God, no violence! No harm has been done." Her pleading is cut short by Clopin who swiftly seizes her wrist with his left hand. Phoebus has a movement to poignard Clopin, but is seized by Neufchatel. CUT TO:

206 INT. GONDELAURIER SALON   CU FOR FOUR   NIGHT
The angle of the camera gives most importance to Clopin and Phoebus who are the straining antagonists, while Clopin is restrained by Esmeralda and Phoebus is restrained by Neufchatel. Esmeralda is tearful and tremulous. Neufchatel is grimly outraged. Phoebus is still straining with a desire to kill Clopin. But Clopin, as if aware that he is safe from attack and sure of his strength, is bitterly and sneeringly self-possessed. Clopin speaks:

INSERT TITLE (92)   "THINK YE TO TAKE OUR ESMERALDA
                    FOR A PLAYTHING? HAVE DONE WITH
                    HER OR I'LL SLIT THY THROAT."

BACK. As Clopin speaks this title and emphasizes it with a flickering gesture of his knife, Esmeralda has a fresh spasm of horror. Phoebus strains forward but is roughly constrained by the glowering Neufchatel. Esmeralda has now definitely withdrawn from Phoebus and stands with her back to Clopin, pressing Clopin back somewhat while her arms are rigidly held back as if to prevent Clopin from coming forward. She cries out to Phoebus, sobbingly:

INSERT TITLE (93)   "MY PLACE IS WITH HIM. I AM NOT
                    FOR SUCH AS THEE."

BACK. In response to this, Phoebus suddenly shakes himself free of Neufchatel, who would restrain him. It is a movement which leaves him alone so far as the aristocrats are concerned and brings him once again face to face with Clopin and Clopin's followers. His hand goes out to Esmeralda's arm as Clopin also seizes her. The attitude of Phoebus is that he is defying Clopin and his gang--that he will fight them all single-handed. He flings this challenge at them as he swings his dagger back, ready to fight. But it is to Esmeralda principally that he shouts the title:

INSERT TITLE (94)   "LOVE SUPPLANTS ALL OTHER CLAIMS.
                    LOVE SWEEPS AWAY ALL BARRIERS."

138

206	(CONTINUED	

BACK. While Phoebus is getting over this title, there is
a tightening of menace in Clopin. He is ready to kill
Phoebus on the spot.

207 CLOSE UP ESMERALDA   NIGHT
Esmeralda desperately casting about her, is aware of this
imminent peril to Phoebus and she cries out to him:

INSERT TITLE (95)   " I DO NOT LOVE THEE."

BACK. As Esmeralda makes this declaration, the falsity of
which is obvious to the camera but not to Phoebus, and she
frees herself from Phoebus's grasp, recoiling closer to
Clopin.

208 CLOSE UP PHOEBUS   NIGHT
Phoebus is like a man who has received a bullet in his
chest. He is amazed. He will not believe it at first.

209 INT. GONDELAURIER SALON   MED SHOT   NIGHT
Esmeralda again shakes her head and again puts out her
hand to fend Phoebus off. This causes a further collapse
on his part. This is a cross shot from the left, placing
Clopin's gang on the left of picture. Phoebus is in a
state of collapse. The occasion is sufficient for three or
four of the young gallants present to seize him from behind, drag him back and disarm him at Neufchatel's command.
By this time Clopin and his gang have reassured themselves
of Esmeralda's capture. While Phoebus' captors still struggle with him, Madame de Gondelaurier takes command of the
situation. She is imperious. She commands Clopin and his
followers to be gone. Clopin is ready enough to obey, now
that he has accomplished the purpose for which he has come.
But he is triumphant, insolent. He sneers loud enough for
all to hear and be struck by what he says as he speaks:

209 (CONTINUED)

INSERT TITLE (96)   "SOON THE DAY WHEN ME AND MINE WILL FEED
FAT AND FLING THE BONES TO SUCH AS YOU."

BACK. As Clopin hurls this defiance there is a movement
among the men aristocrats to resent the insult. But they
are stopped by Neufchatel and a general movement among
the women present. On this, Clopin with his arm not too
savagely about Esmeralda, starts his exit with a word of
command to his men to follow him. They exeunt. Phoebus is
still held by some of his companions, but there is evident
in Phoebus' face the fact that he is held most of all by
Esmeralda's declaration that she did not love him. All
stare after the exeunt of Clopin and his gang in consternation as the scene FADES OUT.

SUBTITLE (97)   JUST THEN PHOEBUS HAD DECIDED THAT
LIFE HELD NO FURTHER INTEREST....

210 INT. PHOEBUS' ROOM   FULL SHOT   MORNING   FADE IN
The scene fades in on a medieval bedroom of rather large
proportions. Left wall, center, a Gothic door which opens
into the upper hall; right, two French windows, the panes
of which are opaque glass in small lozenges, leaded; the
windows are closed. Center of upstage wall, a massive four-
poster bed, with a canopy over it, a regular roof effect.
This bed is high. On the right, built onto the floor, a
series of three steps which give access to the bed. Floor
and steps are partly covered by a rough woolen carpet. On
the other side of the bed is a small night table, on which
is an oil lamp; down scene in fairly close foreground, a
small table of heavy structure, covered with a cloth. Near
the table is a chair and a small bench. Stretched across
the bed is Phoebus. He is dressed in a soft white shirt,
open at the throat, and a heavy dressing robe, trimmed with
fur. Down scene, a man servant is just placing a large and
heavy tray upon the table. This tray is covered with a cloth
and holds crescent-shaped rolls on a platter and a large pot
of chocolate with one medium-sized bowl. The servant debates
for a moment as to whether or not he should disturb Phoebus,
and then turns sharply as he hears a knock at the door. This
also rouses Phoebus, who sits up and looks toward the
door. Phoebus commands the servant to open the door, and
while the servant is crossing, Phoebus shuffles from the
bed, into his slippers, and starts down scene. He has taken
but a step or two toward the center of the room when the
door is thrown more widely open, revealing the poet, Gringoire, who has evidently come this far against the wishes
of the Major Domo. (CONTINUED NEXT PAGE)

210   (CONTINUED)
        Now, as Gringoire sees Phoebus, Gringoire bursts into the
        room eagerly, holding out a folded piece of paper. Phoebus,
        looking at Gringoire, in no very pleasant manner, takes the
        note. As he does so, Gringoire's eyes glimpse the breakfast
        platter and his nose sniffs the food. During this business
        the servants linger at the door as if half expecting to be
        ordered to fling the intruder out. Phoebus opens the note.
        As he does so, CUT TO:

211   INT.PHOEBUS' ROOM AT GONDELAURIER HOME   CLOSER SHOT
        MORNING
        Phoebus is opening the note, not with any great interest.
        He does not even suspect that it might be from Esmeralda.
        Now, as he glimpses the first words, his expression chang-
        es. As a dazzled smile changes his face, CUT IN:

INSERT NOTE written in French Gothic letters on a piece of
        parchment or a piece of hand-made paper torn from a
        book. This note reads:

            IF MONSIEUR PHOEBUS DE CHATEAUPERS
            WOULD HEAL A BROKEN HEART BEFORE A
            LAST FAREWELL, LET HIM COME THIS EVE
            TO NOTRE DAME AT ARBELURE.
                                    ESMERALDA.

        BACK. With the reading of the note, Phoebus' face becomes
        again that of the happy young D'Artagnan. He is going to
        see her again--again--again! His heart fairly sings.
        CUT TO:

212   INT.PHOEBUS' ROOM   MED CLOSE   MORNING
        Gringoire at the moment is lost in blissful contemplation
        of the breakfast, which makes his mouth water. Phoebus
        looks at Gringoire, then in sudden impulse, he grabs Grin-
        goire and kisses him on the cheek with an exuberance of joy
        which makes Gringoire smile. Gringoire understands. As Phoe-
        bus draws back with his hands on Gringoire's shoulders,
        Gringoire speaks:

        (CONTINUED NEXT PAGE)

212   (CONTINUED)
SUBTITLE (98)   "SHE SAVED MY LIFE IN THE COUR DE MIRACLES.
                 E'EN WERE IT NOT SO, HER BEAUTY WOULD HAVE
                 MADE ME HER SLAVE."

        BACK. Gringoire recites this title with such poetic fervor
        that Phoebus laughs and slaps him on the shoulder, and bids
        him to be his guest at breakfast. Gringoire at first is
        delighted, inwardly, for the way in which his face lights
        up shows it; then he catches himself and with rather weak
        excuse that he has already breakfasted, starts to turn away;
        but Phoebus, however, senses the reluctance in Gringoire's
        polite manner, and understanding that the fellow only needs
        a bit of urging, grabs Gringoire by the arm, turns him
        about and speaks:

SUBTITLE (98x)   "THOU HAST BROUGHT ME BACK TO LIFE!
                 LET ME COMMAND THIS HONOR OF THE
                 PRINCE OF POETS."

        BACK. As he speaks this, CUT TO:

213   INT. PHOEBUS' ROOM   MORNING   CU GRINGOIRE
        Phoebus' words contain just the right amount of flattery,
        combined with a genuine sincerity, needed to sway Grin-
        goire. Gringoire starts to make another polite protest,
        then, in the manner of one who has been persuaded against
        his will, Gringoire, glancing at the breakfast again, nods
        his head. CUT TO:

INT. PHOEBUS' ROOM MED CLOSE FOR THE READING
Whereupon Phoebus slaps Gringoire upon the shoulder in a
manner which makes it obvious that they are going to be
good friends. Phoebus motions Gringoire to the chair, his
manner putting Gringoire at ease. Gringoire protests at
the honor thus imposed upon him, but Phoebus insists and
himself sits upon the bench. He passes the rolls to Gringoire. As he does so, Phoebus says, "And so she saved your
life...?" Gringoire has taken a roll and now with this in
his hand, he delivers himself of a poetic, two-armed gesture,
lifting his face with a seraphic smile and half closing his
eyes; then, swiftly, he re-enacts the horror that was his
and he begins his narrative as Phoebus leans forward with
sympathetic interest, momentarily both forgetting their
food. Both have an air of concentrated interest. Hold this
for a second, then Phoebus pours the wine into the large
bowl, motions Gringoire to help himself. Both dip their
rolls into the same bowl, as Gringoire goes on to give
further details. On the action the scene FADES OUT

SUBTITLE   EVER SINCE THAT NIGHT WHEN HE HAD SNATCHED
                        ESMERALDA FROM THE HOUSE OF THE ARISTOCRATS,
                        CLOPIN HAD FELT THAT HIS HOLD ON THE GIRL
                        WAS SLIPPING.

added scene over this, listen of the ...

216   INT. CLOPIN'S HAUNT   FULL SHOT   NOON FADE IN
The scene fades in on a room in Clopin's house, a squalid,
turgid, grimy, dark and foreboding place with a stone floor,
serving as a sort of council-room where Clopin can talk
with his lieutenants and dispense hospitality; down stage,
right, there is a table, at which Clopin sits; center right,
another, but longer table, with benches on either side. Upscene, right wall, a large open fireplace with spit, which
is worked by an old hag. Opposite this, across set, a third
table with benches. The rear of the room fades into a comparative obscurity, yet showing in a suggestive way the
winding stairs which give access to the floor above. The
place is lighted chiefly by the flames in the huge fireplace. In right wall, however, are two grimy windows, and
between those windows, a low-arched doorway, rather wide
in proportion to its height, which gives into a court, the
Court of Miracles, by two or three steps to the higher
level. Gathered about the tables, or squatting cross-legged
in front of the fireplace, are about twenty vagabonds;
women, men, children, dirty, boisterous, sinister; thieves,
beggars, prostitutes, young and old. At the down-stage

table is Clopin, listening with mouth partly open, lip hanging, to the comments of his lieutenants, three in number,
on Esmeralda's treason. Clopin, with the air of one who
recites a crowning infamy, turns and bursts forth
blasphemously:

SUBTITLE   "AS IF ONE CURSED BISHOP WERE NOT ENOUGH,
                   THE GIRL NOW PLANS ON TAKING THE VEIL."

BACK: Clopin narrows his eyes and crisps his hands in a
pantomime of seizing and holding her. In this he is abetted
by his shifty, toadying lieutenants. Clopin now dismisses
his men as if he wanted to be alone with his own bitter
thoughts. The men join those upscene and are lost as individuals as they mingle with the others. Clopin stretches
out, with a long leg in front of him, the other partly
drawn under it, and under slightly lowered eyes, looks at
a definite point past the camera. It should be clear that
he is not looking merely into space, but at a very definite
object. Hold this attitude for a few feet, then he rises,
coming toward the camera as we CUT TO

216   INT. CLOPIN'S HAUNT MED SHOT REVERSE ANGLE DOWN
This view is shooting toward the door in the center of
the wall toward which Clopin moves. Clopin begins to open
the door. The latch slowly lifts. Suddenly the door is
jerked partly open, and there, as though she had just
sprung to this position, is the person whom we shall call
Marie. Marie is not ugly. She retains traces of her former
beauty; but her years with Clopin and her years in this
atmosphere have hardened her, made her cynical and desper-
ate. That she is not the person Clopin expected to see is
apparent from his manner. His lips twist in a snarl and he
draws back as Marie, simultaneous with the opening of the
door, whips from her breast a wicked looking poinard, upon
which Clopin's eyes rest for a moment. Marie hisses
warningly:

Subtitle   (101)   "SHE'LL GO WHITHER SHE WILL AND NONE
                     SHALL STOP HER!"

BACK: Clopin raises his eyes to hers and for a second there
is a clash, then Clopin, unable to stand Marie's gaze,
shifts and snarls. Marie's expression relaxes into a con-
temptuous and mocking sneer. She slams the door in his face.
Clopin's lips tighten in a menacing line as he stands thus
for a second, then he turns, starting to exit scene as we
CUT TO

117 INT. ESMERALDA'S ROOM AT CLOPIN'S MED FULL AFTERNOON
This room, like Clopin's haunt, has a stone floor, of
large flags, worn smooth by use. Upstage, center of wall,
is the door which opens into the main room. In the right-
hand corner, a narrow bed, making it obvious that Esmeralda sleeps alone. Near this bed, against upstage wall, a
large chest, open, with indications that this holds Esmeralda's clothing, etc. Against the left wall, a massive
wardrobe, like the other furnishings, giving the impression
of great age. In the foreground of the scene stands Esmeralda. She wears a plain ――― dress, dancing slippers, no
jewelry. Marie is coming down-stage to Esmeralda, who is
turned toward her approach. Esmeralda is tremulous.
Marie's face, as she approaches Esmeralda, reflects love and
sorrow. Esmeralda is about to leave her forever. Hold this
for just a few seconds, then Marie offers Esmeralda the
dagger. Esmeralda refuses the dagger, embraces Marie and
kisses her as she speaks the title:

SUBTITLE #102)   "I AM GIVING MYSELF TO GOD....
                       HE WILL PROTECT ME."

BACK; Marie bows her head, trying to conceal her grief, and
Esmeralda consoles her. CUT TO

219 INT. CLOPIN'S HAUNT MED FULL SHOT TOWARD DOOR NOON
Clopin is standing in a quandary after his rebuff at Esmeralda's door. Clopin's position is so that he is standing
almost back to camera. He looks over his shoulder toward
Esmeralda's door and then upstage in the direction opposite,
as if at such of his followers who are present. The effect
of his action is to indicate a bitter quandary. He doesn't
know what to do. He would like to restrain Esmeralda by
force. He doesn't dare. He suspects that she is about to
escape from him. She is necessary to his career. He is in
an agony of baffled ferocity. Now, his train of thought is
sharply broken by the arrival through the door of Jehan,
not recognizable immediately because of the cloak with
which Jehan has muffled his face. Jehan from just within
the door sees Clopin and makes a small sign with his hand
which Clopin obviously recognizes. Clopin himself makes a
gesture to indicate the table at which he formerly sat,
and both converge on this as we CUT TO

29 219 INT. CLOPIN'S HAUNT CLOSER SHOT AT TABLE NOON
Clopin's table is with the length of the set. This view
is across the table toward Esmeralda's door. The angle
places Clopin on the right and Jehan on the left so that
as they sit at the table they will face each other, but
in such a position that when Esmeralda's door opens, they
can look in that direction by merely turning their heads.
Jehan has let his cloak drop about his shoulders and makes
no further attempt to hide his features. His pantomime indicates that he has come to report what he has seen in the
treasure crypt of Notre Dame. He is terribly in earnest and
explicit. Clopin has the air of one who is still held by
his thoughts of Esmeralda, still meditative, unaroused by
the word that Jehan brings. This causes Jehan to insist
with a greater vehemence on the necessity for speedy action.
Jehan speaks:

SUBTITLE (103)   "STRIKE QUICKLY, ELSE THE TREASURE WILL
                       BE GONE."

Clopin stirs uneasily, but he savagely asserts the counter-
thought. He speaks:

SUBTITLE (104)   "THE HOUR FOR AN UPRISING IS NOT YET!
                       THERE LACKETH THE SPARK TO
                       MAKE MY PEOPLE FLAME."

As Jehan starts to protest further and Clopin sullenly
shakes his head, the attention of both is diverted by the
opening of Esmeralda's door. Both peer on the direction
as Esmeralda pauses for a moment in the door ―――――――
final word to Marie who is back of her and still clinging
to her ―――. ―――――― ――――― ――――――――― ――――――――
―――――――― the door. Esmeralda takes a step forward and
again pauses, there is a look of mystical sweetness, tinged
with sadness and noble purpose on her face. She is looking
on this scene and on all these people for the last time.
This expression is still on her face as she looks toward
Clopin. Even him she would bless and forgive. But at Clopin's side is the leering and lecherous face of Jehan.
Without taking in the significance of Jehan's look, she
diverts her eyes once more with a touch of sadness toward
the people in the room. CUT TO

220 INT. CLOPIN'S HAUNT CU OF ESMERALDA NOON
This merely meant to point upon the fact that Esmeralda is
ready to consecrate herself to the Church--to renounce the
world, that she loves and pities, and will pray for, these
people she is leaving. CUT TO

221	INT. CLOPIN'S HAUNT MED FULL SHOT REVERSE ANGLE NOON	

~~This shot is from the normal angle, shooting toward the fire-place upscene. This places Clopin's table on the right. Clopin sits on the left and on the right Jehan,~~ ~~facing~~ ~~Esmeralda is on the left in fairly close foreground.~~ Everyone within the range of the camera is looking at Esmeralda with a degree of fascination, having paused in the midst of any other action. All remain practically motionless as Esmeralda starts to cross scene toward the door leading into THE OUTER COURT, except Clopin's three lieutenants who now work in that direction as though to intercept her at the door. These men range themselves side by side across the door, scowling but unseemly. Esmeralda's progress toward the door is smooth and uninterrupted. Jehan and Clopin do not move except to follow her with their eyes. The scene is tense. Now as she nears the door, CUT TO:

222   INT. CLOPIN'S HAUNT GROUP SHOT AT DOOR NOON
~~This view shows the three beggars lined up to intercept Esmeralda's exit. Esmeralda comes into scene and as if she fails to understand why the beggars are there. She smiles at them sweetly and speaking to each by name, conquers them one by one. The first almost timidly wipes hands with her. The second wipes his hand on his own sleeve and barely touches her hand. The third almost kneels, but he and his companions are shoved to one side by the first beggar, who in a gust of boldness jerks open the door to let Esmeralda pass. She exits. Then the beggar gets a fright tremor as he looks out of the scene in the direction of Clopin.~~

223   INT. CLOPIN'S HAUNT CU JEHAN AND CLOPIN NOON
In this closeup Clopin is the spectacle of a ferocious nature momentarily quailed by the passage of the superior spirit. Clopin's whole instinct is to seize upon the girl and bring her back, but a higher power for the present holds him riveted where he sits. It is otherwise with Jehan. Sight of Esmeralda has stirred all the evil in Jehan's heart. At the same time he is fearful of Clopin, but the working of Jehan's mind is clearly indicated in his crafty eyes as he shifts these from the disappearing Esmeralda to Clopin, then back again with a dawning purpose to pursue Esmeralda and make her his own. Upon this scene FADE OUT.

SUBTITLE (105)   HIGH UP UNDER HIS BELOVED BELLS WAS THE ONLY HOME THAT QUASIMODO HAD EVER KNOWN.

224   INT. QUASIMODO'S CELL MED SHOT MED AFTERNOON FADE IN
This is a medium shot of Quasimodo's cell in the left hand tower of Notre Dame, a square room, with massive, deeply indented masonry walls, the ceiling is not seen, but the general enclosure overhead is indicated by the slant of masonry buttresses in the right and left hand corners, at the left, upscene, is a narrow aperture in the masonry, serving as a door, through which may be seen (when open) the slender columns of the high gallery, at the right, and at right angles to the door, is another narrow aperture serving as a window, both door and window indicate in their treatment that they are merely incidental to the structural design of the tower. Under the window is a straw mattress which serves Quasimodo as bed, this is covered by several woolen blankets that were formerly the robes of monks, against the upstage wall is an iron basket used as a brazier and is now half filled with charcoal and ashes. At the side of this is a battered old chest with a padlock and iron-hasp. Near the foot of the mattress is a large crockery water jug and a crockery bowl. Back of this is one of the plain, wrought iron candelabra, with places for many tapers, such as used in the Cathedral. On this now is a single candle-end. Quasimodo is recumbent on the mattress, he lies face down with his arms drawn up about his head and his knees up in such a position as might be taken by a suffering ape. His wounds have been bandaged, he is properly dressed, his general attitude is that of one who is in some sort of mental agony, rather than that of physical suffering. With Quasimodo and his room established the door swings open and Dom Claude comes in as one familiar with the place and with Quasimodo's mood. Dom Claude, leaving the door open, stands for a second with a gentle and benignant smile as he contemplates the hunchback, then goes over and puts a hand on Quasimodo's shoulder, Quasimodo sits up, recognises his caller with a wild gust of gratitude and brings Dom Claude's robe caressingly against his cheek. CUT IN

SUBTITLE (106)   INTO THE DARK ABYSS OF QUASIMODO'S SOUL THERE HAD COME A FURTHER RAY OF LOVE.

224 x   INT. QUASIMODO'S CELL   CLOSER SHOT   LATE AFTERNOON
Quasimodo, seated on his mattress, is looking up at Dom
Claude with a sort of greedy desire, for love and consolation
like a whipped dog, Dom Claude is caressing Quasimodo's head
and looking down at him with a gentle and good-natured smile,
a smile not devoid of humor, as he speaks the words:

SUBTITLE (107)
"POOR DEAR CREATURE, IN THY GROPING
THOU MAYST YET FIND GOD."

Quasimodo has the air of one who, although he has not heard,
wishes to assure Dom Claude that he, the Hunchback, will do
everything that Dom Claude wants him to do, upon this scene
FADE OUT

subtitle (108)   A N G E L U S

225   INT. TOWER ROOM OF NOTRE DAME   MED SHOT   EARLY TWILIGHT
FADE IN
The scene fades in on the tower room, into which hang several
large hemp bell ropes, shoot this through a vignette mask to
concentrate on Quasimodo. The tempo of his movements is slow
as he throws his weight into the pulling of one of the bell
ropes, just a few feet of this and then CUT TO

226   INT. BELFRY ON NOTRE DAME   MED SHOT   EARLY TWILIGHT
The view shows one of the medium sized bells, swinging in the
same tempo in which Quasimodo pulled the rope in previous
scene, shoot this through a soft edged iris aperture, in soft
lighting, harmonious with the Cathedral spirit, for only a
short scene then CUT TO

227   EXT. FULL SHOT OF LOWER PORTION FACADE OF NOTRE DAME
EARLY TWILIGHT
This view incorporates the three portals of Notre Dame, with
the angle so that the left hand door is nearest the camera,
across the entire front of the Cathedral is a narrow terrace,
reached by eleven stone steps from the street level. The
Street, (a portion of the Place du Parvis) is paved with the
so-called "Kidney" cobbles, but with flat flags inserted to
make foot paths leading to each door, these foot paths are
at least five feet wide, clustered on these steps, nearest
to the left hand portal is a group of at least eight beggars
who have previously been seen in the Cour de Miracles, one
of these is a hag who shakes with a palsy at the approach of
a worshipper, but is still as soon as the worshipper passes,
there is a cripple with a crutch, another woman with her face
usually covered with a shawl, as the worshipper passes, she
draws back the shawl, revealing in a flash a face without a
nose, our legless man who captured Gringoire is busily beg-
ging at the top of the steps. To the right of the door, facing
camera, is the blind man. Our one-armed beggar is also seated on the steps, with a little bucket hung on the hook of his
wooden arm, he thrusts this insolently at all who pass, two
of the beggars are ghastly children, almost naked, others of
similar type may be furnished for atmosphere, all of this is
in the nature of preliminary atmosphere before Esmeralda
enters the scene. Esmeralda enters the scene from upstage
right and progresses toward foreground, her whole attitude
from the first indicates eagerness, timidity, and awe, she
is about to take a tremendous step, she is going to surrender
herself to the Church and put the world behind her. She
pauses for a moment of final hesitation and then hurries up
the steps. It is not until now that the beggars discover
her, their recognition of her causes an instant reaction
among them, they are stricken with astonishment and a gradual
awe by her presence, she does not notice them immediately, her
whole attention on the open door of the Cathedral, as she
reaches the top of the steps, she pauses.   CUT TO

228   EXT. PORCH OF NOTRE DAME   MED SHOT   EARLY TWILIGHT
This view is from a point just under the arch of the portal,
shooting toward Esmeralda, the b. g. of the scene is the view
across the Parvis, toward the medieval houses on that side of
the square, in fairly close f. g. is Esmeralda, in the same
position as in the long shot, she stands there, oblivious to
anything for several seconds, while she gazes thru the portal
of Notre Dame, in back of her, the beggars still stare at her
transfixed, an impression of humanity in the depths, all save
one remain in their positions while the legless man, suddenly
realizing that Esmeralda is about to be lost to them, stealth
ily shoves his barrow toward her and fiercely, but slowly
plucks at her dress with a claw-like hand, Esmeralda is

228   CONTINUED
brought out of her contemplation by his touch, as she
turns, CUT TO

229   EXT. PORCH OF NOTRE DAME   CU OF ESMERALDA AND BEGGAR
EARLY TWILIGHT
Esmeralda turns, looks down and realizes with horror what
is trying to hold her, she cringes away from the beggar who
is triumphant leers up at her with a mingling of menace and
appeal, for several seconds they should be held thus, during
this interval her shrinking continues as the beggar slowly
smiles, NOW CUT TO

230   EXT. PORCH OF NOTRE DAME   CU ESMERALDA   EARLY TWILIGHT
Esmeralda shrinking away from the beggar, toward whom she
looks with full realization of all that he means, hold her
attitude for a few seconds and then cut in,

SUBTITLE (109)
IT WAS LIKE THE CLUTCH OF CLOPIN.....
SHE FELT LIKE A SOUL 'T LXT HEAVEN AND
HELL. ON ONE SIDE THE COUR DE MIRACLE....
ON THE OTHER THE SAFE SHELTER OF NOTRE DAME.

This title gives an indication of the decision of Esmeralda's
mind, now she cringes still further away from the beggar,
the view being large enough to suggest by the movement of
her dress that the beggar's hand still clutches her - CUT TO

231   EXT. PORCH OF NOTRE DAME   MED. SHOT   EARLY TWILIGHT
This view, shot partly from within the arch of the left door,
is large enough to show all of the beggars, who are looking
toward Esmeralda and the legless man, who are in fairly close
f. g. Esmeralda breaks away from the beggar's clutch and with
her hands on her breast, comes toward camera, with dilated

231 CONTINUED
eyes and the purpose to consecrate herself registers on her face, the beggar remains for a moment, with his hand outstretched toward her, then, with sudden resolution on his own part, he turns and ~~hurries away to his burrow.~~ CUT TO

232 INT. ~~BELFRY~~ [illegible] ~~EARLY TWILIGHT~~
For a flash of the bell slowly coming to a stop, hold for only a few seconds and then

233 INT. NOTRE DAME LONG SHOT ? ON APSE LATER TWILIGHT
The camera is placed at a position on the right hand side of the apse, shooting toward the front of the Cathedral, this gives us a long shot of practically the entire aisle of the Cathedral, on the left, looking along the aisle, are the deeply fluted columns that support the roof of the nave. On the right hand side in the immediate f. g. are three large arched openings giving onto as many chapels, from these three opens emerge a soft flood of lights as if from many candles, beyond these chapels is the huge and cavernous opening of the right transept and beyond this a continuation of the aisle with shadowy columns to left and right, at the extreme end of the aisle is the dimly discerned door, the whole shot should give an impression of Cathedral size and beauty, it should be rich in suggested detail, every pillar has its saint or group of saints, there should be a suggestion of banners and flags suspended from aloft, thru apertures between the columns to the left and accentuating the architectural richness of the Cathedral, there is a very subdued glimmer of light as of shrines and chapels elsewhere. The set may be further touched up where advantageous by clusters of twinkling candles on primitive iron candelabra. Esmeralda is coming down scene to a point near chapel, her eyes are directed into the chapel and are somewhat lifted in contemplation of the saint which is out of sight, as she holds this we see Phoebus enter from left, he comes forward rapidly and is obviously looking for Esmeralda, he is dandified, dressed up for a love tryst, play this for several seconds as Phoebus approaches. CUT TO

234 INT. NOTRE DAME LONG SHOT LATER TWILIGHT
This is practically the same shot as before, except that the camera is moved forward to a point opposite the last chapel on the right. Phoebus is hurrying toward the camera and now slows down and then stops in fairly close f. g. as his first expression of joyful eagerness slowly becomes one of almost awed inspiration as he catches Esmeralda's mood, hold this for a few seconds and then, as Phoebus starts toward Esmeralda's direction, with subdued fervor, CUT TO

235 INT. NOTRE DAME LONG SHOT LATER TWILIGHT
This is practically the same as before, except that the angle puts Esmeralda in close f. g. on the left, lighted by the flow from the chapel. Phoebus, coming down scene, enters view, she is unaware of his presence and does not turn until Phoebus reaches a point two or three feet from her, where he stops, puts out his hand and speaks, "Esmeralda?" – with loving appeal, she turns, for a matter of seconds they simply look at each other, with Phoebus' expression showing that he senses some tragedy. CUT TO

236 INT. NOTRE DAME CU OF ESMERALDA LATER TWILIGHT.
This is a super closeup of Esmeralda, the light from the chapel illuminates her face, lighting it to an angelic beauty, she is sympathetic but exalted as she speaks:

SUBTITLE (110) "PHOEBUS...... I [illegible] have you [illegible]
to see, [illegible] to send you... to save my own soul
from being [illegible] by darkness... THE
CHURCH WILL RECEIVE ME."

CUT DIRECT FROM TITLE TO

[handwritten: changed #] [handwritten: Jurer ensues down stairs for candles]

237 INT. NOTRE DAME LARGER SHOT FOR ? O LATER TWILIGHT
Phoebus gasps a protest, but before he can find words to voice the protest, they are interrupted by the entrance of Quasimodo, Quasimodo is at first absorbed in his occupations

237 CONTINUED
about the church, he has an armful of long, slim, tapering
wax candles, he is about to go into the chapel with these
when with a slow realizing expression of wonder he sees
Esmeralda, her reaction on him causes him to forget all else,
his mouth drops open, he crouches slightly, for an instant it
looks almost as if he would drop to his knees, at her feet,
the reaction of all this on Phoebus is one of protest, anger
and even of challenge. This is the Hunchback he saw trying
to drag Esmeralda away and whom he himself has had whipped.
Esmeralda herself has given Quasimodo a look of tender pity,
then she has given a glance of appeal to Phoebus, but Phoebus
slipping his arm under hers draws her somewhat ~~haughtily and~~
~~Phoebus and they extend~~. Quasimodo stands there still forgetful of his duty, looking after Esmeralda and disregarding
the candles that are slipping from his arm, leaving him thus,
we CUT TO

Sc 2 238 INT. NOTRE DAME A GALLERY TREFOIL MED SHOT DUSK
This trefoil is a clever shaped Gothic aperture, in the
upper part of the nave. It opens onto a narrow passageway
in back of it. There is no source of light in the passageway
Jehan enters scene from right end in passing, stops sharply
as he looks through the trefoil, down into the nave. His
evil face changes as evidently glimpses Phoebus and
Esmeralda. CUT TO

239 INT. NOTRE DAME LONG SHOT INTO NAVE DUSK
This long shot is from an elevated position, presumably
from the trefoil. It shows the chapels, through arched
columns, the details of which are almost lost at this
distance, as is also the figure of Quasimodo, and shows the
movements of Phoebus and Esmeralda toward the little door
in the transept, and opening into the garden. For a flash
of this then, CUT TO

240 INT. NOTRE DAME A GALLERY TREFOIL CLOSER SHOT TWILIGHT
As Jehan sees Esmeralda and Phoebus, his face registers
satisfaction and cunning purposes. His thought is murder.
His intensity is so great that he almost swoons, almost
prays to the powers of darkness for victory. He does not
turn, but slowly withdraws into the darkness with this
expression still on his face and melts into the gloom of
the gallery. CUT TO

241 EXT. GARDEN OF NOTRE DAME MED LONG SHOT TWILIGHT
(The intervening action ~~has changed twilight to full night~~)
The scene presents the small garden of Notre Dame, situated
in this shot between the apse of the Cathedral and overhung
by flying buttresses. It is limited on the outer side by
a wall of Gothic masonry about ten feet high and cut in the
center by a door leading to the street. From this door there
winds a narrow path which joins a wider path along which
move Phoebus and Esmeralda. As much of the garden as we can
see represents it as a place of mystery and great beauty,
filled not only with flowering bushes but also monumental
relics of discarded primitive masonry. Down scene fairly
close f. g. is a marble bench. ~~The bench is partly screened~~
by bushes. As Phoebus and Esmeralda approach this bench,
it is seen that Esmeralda is still in her religious mood,
but this is softened as she listens to the compassionate
love making of Phoebus. It is in response to his pleading
and somewhat against her own will that she allows him to
place her on the bench and seat himself at her side. CUT TO

242 EXT. GARDEN OF NOTRE DAME CLOSER SHOT AT BENCH TWILIGHT
Esmeralda for the moment swayed by Phoebus' eloquence. She
now turns, raising her eyes to his as he presses her hand
to his breast. She is deeply moved. She says:

SUBTITLE
"DEAR HEART, O MY PHOEBUS, CANST THOU
NOT SEE THAT I AM DOING THIS BUT FOR
THEE....THY GREAT NAME, POSITION,
CAREER,..THY VERY LIFE?"

back; Her protest merely increases Phoebus' fervor. He
still holds her two hands to his breast with one hand,
while his other hand is extended to go about her waist.
He shifts his ~~position enough so that one of his knees~~
CONTINUED

242 CONTINUED
is bent, almost as if he were kneeling to her. For a moment he brings her hands to his lips, then lifts his face more imperative and impassioned than ever. He says:

SUBTITLE (112) "THOU SPEAKEST OF TRIFLES WHEN HEAVEN ITSELF IS AT STAKE."

As Phoebus still speaks the title, we see the shadowy form of Jehan furtively approaching from background, almost a part of the shadows themselves. His movement is toward the gargoyle. So stealthily is his approach that neither Esmeralda nor Phoebus are aware of his presence. Jehan reaches the gargoyle, and in its protection, only partially concealed, leans toward the lovers, the better to hear and see. He is the personification of evil. He is like a hawk, stooping over two unconscious doves. Unaware of his presence, Phoebus and Esmeralda continue their colloquy with increasing tenderness and passion. As Esmeralda shows signs of yielding, Phoebus with a slow intensity of rapturous passion, slips his arms about her shoulders and draws her over until she is reclining in his arms with her hands embracing his shoulders. Without precipitation, with a distinct impression of holiness, Phoebus lowers his face to the rapturous swooning face of Esmeralda and kisses her. Concurrent with his action, there has been a gradual, surging forward of the otherwise impassioned Jehan. Now in contrast to the slow reverence of the movements of the lovers, Jehan, with a savage ferocity, raises his hand to strike. A trick of the light causes a momentary gleam from the blade as it plunges downward into Phoebus' back. CUT TO:

243 EXT. GARDEN OF NOTRE DAME AT SAME BENCH CLOSER SHOT TWILIGHT
The action is continued, at the moment of the stabbing. This Cut may serve to eliminate the actual murder, which would cause censor-board complications. Esmeralda looks up into the face of Jehan, leaping over her, with Phoebus already in agony from the blow he has just received. She screams. While the action is swift, the expression of the three characters must be distinctly registered, the horrified recognition on the face of Esmeralda; the gloating ferocity in the face of Jehan. Now, before any other action, Jehan draws back and casts the knife to the ground before slinking away into the darkness. Instantly (NEXT PAGE)

243
Following this action on the part of Jehan, Esmeralda is filled with a frenzy of concern for Phoebus. The light in Phoebus' eye is fading as he sinks into unconsciousness.

244
This larger shot shows Esmeralda as she frantically eases the unconscious Phoebus to the ground and continues to hold his head. Already in response to Esmeralda's screams, there is a movement of shadowy figures, who come running toward the scene of the crime. One of these is an old sexton, the others are a couple of beadles of the church and a burger who has been at prayers, as they reach Esmeralda and rather in consternation while Esmeralda attempts to explain.

245
This wall is a plain masonry wall with Gothic trimming. Set in the wall is the narrow door, solidly constructed of planks. At the opening of the scene, Monsieur de Neufchatel and two archers come running into the scene, and after a momentary dull bang, hammer upon the door.

246
There is general excitement as those who have entered the scene crowd about Esmeralda, who is supporting Phoebus' head in her arms. Note, that the old sexton is out of the scene, but now re-enters, followed by Neufchatel and the two archers who pounded upon the garden door. At the same moment of their entrance another beadle appears with a lantern, which floods the immediate foreground with light. The swinging light catches the knife upon the ground, and one of the archers, seeing it, picks it up with an exclamation. During this, the old sexton has been volubly explaining that he saw Esmeralda bring the young captain into the

CONTINUED NEXT PAGE

246 (CONTINUED)
Garden. From all these expressions, it now becomes obvious that they think Esmeralda committed the crime, especially Monsieur Neufchatel, who picked up the knife. He issues a command, whereupon his companions seize upon Esmeralda, with military brutality, and drag her away from Phoebus, whose body is taken hold of by the beadles. Upon this action, the scene FADES OUT

subtitle (113)

FADE IN ON:
AVIS NEA PHYS...MAIPPCHE SE LITER.
La PROVERBE DE GRINGOIRE.

247 EXT. COUR DE MIRACLES. MED LONG SHOT NIGHT. FADE IN
The scene fades in on a medium shot near the gibbet. The place is less crowded than in previous shots. The scene is lighted by the fires which burn in the court. The central activity shows a crowd of the familiars gathered about the space, in the center of which is Gringoire, "learning a trade." Gringoire is attempting to balance a long stick on his nose and at the same time, juggle three balls. Gringoire's first attempt fails as the stick topples and falls to the ground, and shouts of laughter arise from the crowd. In this shot establish the entrance of the cul-de-jatte, the "legless" man, clattering across the stones toward Clopin, who is one of the spectators watching Gringoire. CUT TO:

48 EXT. COUR DE MIRACLES   MED CLOSE GRINGOIRE   NIGHT
This view shows the laughter of the beggars as Gringoire's first attempt fails. From their manner it is evident that they have accepted him as one of their tribe, so to speak. More evident is the fact that Gringoire is trying to please, for he accepts their cries of derisive laughter in good nature. Gringoire is established in this shot, standing with legs outstretched, looking upon Gringoire with an expression which shows that even he can be amused to the point of laughter. Likewise, Marie is seen. Her attitude toward Gringoire is encouraging. Gringoire picks up the stick, and with a "do or die" expression on his face, raises it again to his chin. He is succeeding admirably now and cries of approval and encouragement fill the air as Gringoire struggles to maintain the balance. The cul-de-jatte now clatters into the scene, kicking aside his barrow and standing to his feet, running to Clopin and clutching Clopin's sleeve. Clopin turns. CUT TO:

49 EXT. COUR DE MIRACLES   MED CLOSE OF CLOPIN   NIGHT
Clopin turns to the beggar who is clutching his sleeve. Clopin senses in the man's manner that he is going to impart information of importance and his amused expression changes into one of attention. The vagabond's attitude toward Clopin has something of fear for he doesn't know exactly how Clopin is going to take his information. He whispers:

(SPOKEN 11a) "ESMERALDA HAS FLED TO SANCTUARY.
              IN CHURCH."

Clopin's reaction is instantaneous. He draws back, in surprise and growing anger. The beggar, seeing that he is not to be kicked - at least not yet, continues, punctuating his mimicry of what happened with words. He gives a vivid, exaggerated pantomime of Esmeralda's attitude as she stood within the door of Notre Dame; of her shrinking in horror as he clutched at her dress, and of the evident determination of her manner as she broke away from him and entered the Cathedral. Clopin's face shows his increasing wrath.

50 EXT. COUR DE MIRACLES   MED CU OF GRINGOIRE   NIGHT
Gringoire is succeeding quite admirably with his balancing, but now, having sensed the cul-de-jatte's recital of what happened at Notre Dame and knowing of Esmeralda's purpose, forgets to concentrate and accordingly the stick starts wobbling. Too late Gringoire tries to catch it. He wavers from side to side trying to regain the lost balance. In the action his gyrations carry him closer and closer to Clopin.

51 EXT. COUR DE MIRACLES   MED CLOSE CLOPIN   NIGHT
With the action picked up from preceding scene, Gringoire gyrates closer and closer to Clopin who is reflecting over what the cul-de-jatte has just finished telling him. Clopin's face is menacing anger. As a culmination to Clopin's wrath, Gringoire backs into Clopin. Gringoire turns, apologetic. Clopin scowls and with an imprecation, places his hand flat on Gringoire's face and sends him reeling. Gringoire falls over himself and brings up in a sitting position, looking at Clopin in a sort of dazed manner as Clopin brushes his way through the crowd toward his haunt. The scene FADES OUT.

QUICK FADE IN ON:
An atmospheric art drawing, representing a long shot of Paris with Notre Dame the center of the composition. With this established and keeping the shot as a background, SUPRIMP IN THE TITLE:

(SUPRIMP 11b)   "THE CITY OF A MILLION INDUSTRIES, GRAB
                AND GO, GRAB AND LIVE - THAT YOUNG
                WOULD SURVIVE MUST GRAB AND LEAVE
                NO TRACE."

IT DISSOLVES FOR THE TIME BEING.

152 EXT. NOTRE DAME MED SHOT AT LEFT DOOR EARLY MORNING
The scene fades in on a shot large enough to show the left
portal in its full height. The camera should be at an elevation. The scene (taking a liberty to get a desired effect) is deserted except for Clopin who is ascending the
eleven steps. With each step, his movement becomes slower,
for in spite of his attitude towards things religious, there
is something which holds him back. At the top step he stops
He is held rooted to the spot by a superstitious fear which
he cannot analyze nor understand. It is as though an invisible barrier had stopped his progress, a barrier against
which he fights. CUT TO:

SUBTITLE   NO FURTHER WORD HAD COME TO CLOPIN CONCERN-
                ING THE WHEREABOUTS OF ESMERALDA. HE HAD
                THE COURAGE OF THE DEVIL, BUT HE SHUDDERED
                AT CROSSING THE THRESHOLD OF NOTRE DAME.

253 EXT. PORCH OF NOTRE DAME   MED CU OF CLOPIN   MORNING
This is the reverse angle of previous shot. Clopin's face
shows that he is the prey of fear, a twitching palsy. But
he is determined. He curses himself inwardly for his fear,
and moves forward slightly, his movement giving the impression of fighting against an invisible barrier. Then
with a curse, he partly dominates his dread and pushes
forward. As he moves, recede the camera before him, following his progress. The effect desired here is for the
camera to move at a faster speed than he does, so that
the full value of his movement as he fights his way into
Notre Dame against an invisible host, may be realized. The
movement is continued until Clopin is within Notre Dame.
The details of his facial expression will be lost, but,
silhouetted against the light of the portal through which
he has entered, the expression of his body will show the
fight he is still making against the unseen force which
holds him. Camera movement stops. Clopin progresses now
to close foreground. His fists tighten now and his eyes
light up as he sees Dom Claude, the person he has come to
see. He again summons courage, and as he starts toward
camera, CUT to

254 INT. NOTRE DAME MED SHOT AT CHAPEL   MORNING
The view is shooting directly into the chapel, the figure
of the Saint therein being lost in the shimmer of light
from the candles which burn at its feet. In the foreground
on his knees, like a child at prayer, is Quasimodo. Dom
Claude, by his side on the left, is looking down at him
with a tender smile, prompting his devotions. An interpretation of the scene is that Dom Claude, preaching forgive-
ness, has brought Quasimodo to pray before the image for
the souls of those who scourged him. CUT TO:

255 INT. NOTRE DAME LARGE SHOT AT CHAPEL   MORNING
Hold the above scene for a matter of several seconds, with
Dom Claude and Quasimodo silhouetted against the shimmer-
ing light from the chapel. Clopin, on his guard, somewhat
crouched, enters from the left, unseen, unheard. The scene
stops him. He is held again by the fear he doesn't realize
...the fear of God which is in the mind of every man.
CUT TO:

256 INT. NOTRE DAME CU OF CLOPIN   MORNING
Shoot this closeup full on Clopin's face. His lips twitch.
His eyes shift and glow. His hands work in unconscious
hatred. Yet he is held by the fear as he glares in the
direction of Dom Claude. CUT TO:

257 INT. NOTRE DAME MED SHOT AT CHAPEL   MORNING
Dom Claude and Quasimodo still in the same position.
Clopin hesitant, Dom Claude feels Clopin's gaze upon him.
He turns. For two or three seconds the men look at each
other. Then, in contrast to the effort with which Clopin
forced himself to this spot, Dom Claude crosses slowly to
him, with graceful dignity. Quasimodo, being dead, is unaware of Dom Claude's movement. He is lost in a spiritual
moment as he looks up toward the image in the chapel. As
Dom Claude now reaches a point near to Clopin, CUT TO:

258 INT. NOTRE DAME   MED CU FOR TWO   MORNING
Clopin, with a spasmodic shudder, stands his ground as Dom Claude enters. Clopin's attitude is servile, cringeing, yet hyena-like, ready to spring. For a second the men look into each other's souls. Yet Dom Claude, in spite of the hatred he sees in Clopin's eyes, speaks softly. "Can I help you, Mon enfant?" Clopin's face changes into a smile. He shifts his eyes, his head, his body, as he nods, "Oui..." Dom Claude looks at him, serene, contemplative. Now Clopin, with an effort, works himself to the point of looking at Dom Claude again. He gathers courage. There is a flash of his old menace as the thing which brought him there moves him to speak. He says:

SUBTITLE (117)   "I COME TO GET ESMERALDA."

BACK. At the mention of Esmeralda's name, Dom Claude gives a visible start. He recognizes the name, the girl who was arrested in the Cathedral garden. Clopin's face now, which is a dawning accusation, a manner of hurling into Dom Claude's face a sneer and a taunt. Clopin believes that Dom Claude has the girl in his keeping. All this in Clopin's look. Dom Claude sees what Clopin means. His horror at the thought paralyses his tongue. Clopin suddenly finds his nerve, seeing that he is not struck dead, and reaches out his hand as though to grasp Dom Claude's wrist. Dom Claude withdraws a step, quickly speaking:

SUBTITLE (118)   "SHE HAS BEEN CARRIED TO PRISON BY HIS MAJESTY'S SERVANTS."

BACK. This stuns Clopin for a moment. To his mind it is only an excuse upon the part of the Priest to cover his act--all part of a plot. Then suddenly, hand on hips, Clopin spreads his legs slightly and bursts into raucous, mocking laughter, which rings through the spaces of the Cathedral. CUT TO:

259 INT. NOTRE DAME   QUASIMODO AT CHAPEL   MORNING
It is not the intent here that the action should give the impression that Quasimodo hears Clopin's laugh. He does not. Kneeling before the chapel, Quasimodo finishes his prayer and crosses himself. Then, he gets to his feet, turning as though to look up to Dom Claude, and then quickly taking in the scene with a glance, as he sees that Dom Claude is not at his side. Clopin in the attitude described, is still laughing, harsh and raucous, a mirthless menace, en-
(CONTINUED NEXT PAGE)

259 (CONTINUED)
joying in his exaggerated way what he considers a great joke and an obvious lie. CUT TO:

260 INT. NOTRE DAME   CU OF QUASIMODO   MORNING
Quasimodo cannot hear what is taking place, but he can see. Silhouetted against the shimmer of light from the chapel, Quasimodo's form gradually assumes the posture of menace as he sees the obvious contempt in which Dom Claude is being treated. His teeth show. He moves out of scene, quickly, quietly.

261 INT. NOTRE DAME   MED SHOT FOR GROUP   MORNING
Clopin is still laughing. Neither he nor Dom Claude is aware of Quasimodo's approach. Quasimodo enters. He looks up at Dom Claude, and then over at Clopin, who, unaware of his presence, now ceases his laughter and suddenly assumes a manner full of savage menace, taking a quick step toward Dom Claude. As Quasimodo, with a leap, jumps between him and Dom Claude, Clopin steps on guard. On Quasimodo's face there is a look well calculated to inspire fear. For a matter of seconds, Clopin looks down at Quasimodo. CUT TO:

262 INT. NOTRE DAME   CU OF QUASIMODO   MORNING
He is in front of Dom Claude, who is calmly looking toward Clopin. Without shifting the line of his gaze, Dom Claude's hand comes to Quasimodo's shoulder, restraining him, as a master would restrain a faithful dog. Quasimodo crouches, a more menacing figure than Clopin ever presented. The Hunchback's eye burns with anger against any who might dare to threaten Dom Claude. He is like a great beast, ready to spring upon his enemy and tear him limb from limb. CUT TO:

263   INT. NOTRE DAME   MED SHOT FOR GROUP   MORNING   264   (CONTINUED)
Dom Claude is silent as he looks at Clopin. Yet on his
face is a righteous indignation, a high dignity, a command
for Clopin to go. Clopin gives ground, the hyena still.
In surroundings which are unnatural to him, he is beaten.
From Quasimodo, he looks sidewise, furtively, up at Dom
Claude and speaks:

SUBTITLE (119)   "I'M GOING...BUT I'LL GET HER, IF I HAVE
                 TO TEAR DOWN NOTRE DAME ROCK BY ROCK."

BACK. With this, Clopin, unconsciously admitting the
superiority of the man before him, backs out of the scene.
Quasimodo, the faithful dog, looks up at Dom Claude for a
word--a word which would send him after Clopin, a word
which would mean Clopin's death. But Dom Claude, looking
after Clopin, only shakes his head, slowly, forgivingly,
and restrains Quasimodo's head. Upon this action the scene
FADES OUT.

SUBTITLE (120)   BLIND JUSTICE

264   INT. COURT ROOM   MED FULL SHOT   MID AFTERNOON   FADE IN
The scene fades in a medium full shot, from a corner angle
of a courtroom in the Palais de Justice. The courtroom is
a large hall, presumably at least sixty feet long by thirty
broad, although the angle reveals only about half of the
right and rear walls. In the righthand wall are three
lofty, narrow, pointed windows, through which slants sunlight, dimmed by stained glass set in leaded lozenges. In
the rear wall are two doors, also narrow, lofty and pointed,
the general type of architecture being much older than that
of Notre Dame. The walls are wainscoted to a height of
twelve feet, that is to a line on a level with the lower
sills of the windows. Above the wainscoting, the plaster is
painted with a geometrical design of fleur de lys. Under the
windows is a dais, running the full length of the room,
reached by a flight of two steps which run the length of the
dais. On the dais is a long and narrow table desk of Gothic
design, behind which are seated the judges. The judges are
thirteen in number, all of them dressed in black and wearing
black caps. They are elderly men, with solemn, eerie,
haunting faces. All of them sit almost motionless and ex-
pressionless, except for the President of the Court, himself
one of the judges, seated in the center and slightly in advance of his colleagues. Seated on the steps of the dais
(CONTINUED NEXT PAGE)

are various pages and servants of the Court. At right angles
to the dais are various tables at which lawyers are seated,
working at piles of manuscripts. Between these tables and
in front of the President of the Court, however, there is
a wide free space, to be occupied later by the prisoner and
her guards. In the general background and filling the
scene with subdued movement, are numerous officials of the
Court, including Charmolu, the King's Proctor, and Maitre
Torteru, the official torturer already seen. Charmolu and
Torteru are each the centers of various followers and assistants. Beyond them, there is a cluster of halberds and
pikestaffs in the hands of soldiery. Above the heads of
the judges, between two of the windows, is a very large
crucifix, but dimly seen in the shadows. In a prominent
position back of Charmolu, as a privileged onlooker, is
Jehan, furtive and alertly interested. This whole scene is
one of soft light, centering about the President of the
Court and the open space in front of him. The general
lighting of the room is so dim that there is already a
candle or two flickering on the tables of the lawyers,
wherever advantageous to the picture. As we pick up the
action, the trial is in momentary suspension, while the
President of the Court affixes his signature to a parchment which, with an air of satisfaction, he passes to one
of his colleagues. As the colleague nods and takes the
document and prepares to read it, the President of the
Court, with a change of his amiable smile for his colleagues to one of official severity, makes a slight motion
to attract the attention of Maitre Charmolu, and tells
Charmolu that the court is ready to proceed. Charmolu
turns with a sharp and officious word of command, whereupon
there is a movement among the halberds and pikestaffs.
From this mass of armed men, Esmeralda, barefootedly dressed
in white, is dragged somewhat roughly into the open space
immediately in front of the President. She immediately
becomes the center of a group. The bailiffs, who brought
her to this position, release her arms and fall back somewhat. Charmolu, standing on the steps of the dais, in a
position of easy familiarity with the President of the
Court, scowls at the prisoner coldly. He and the President
of the Court interchange various derogatory whispers as
they look at Esmeralda. Other lawyers, soldiers, Torteru
and his men crowd about her. The attitude of all there is
that either of mere vulgar curiosity, contempt, cheap lust
or open hatred. The attitude of Esmeralda in the presence
of all this is merely that of dignified and self-forgetful
grief. It is to be deducted from the action and bearing of
all concerned that the trial has already proceeded far.
She is a tender Joan d'Arc. CUT TO:

265   INT. COURT ROOM   CU ESMERALDA   MED AFTERNOON
      Esmeralda is thinking of Phoebus. She doesn't know whether
      he is alive or dead. She lifts her eyes to the dim cruci-
      fix above the judges, in a sort of silent prayer. She has
      wept. She has not been able to sleep. She has been brutally
      threatened. She knows that she is in danger of death. Her
      face is very white. There are circles under her eyes. Her
      hair is loose. Her dress is of the simplest, white and
      plain. CUT TO:

266   INT. COURT ROOM   MED CLOSE SHOT   MID AFTERNOON
      This shot is centered almost entirely upon Esmeralda, the
      President of the Court, and Maitre Charmolu, what we would
      call the Prosecuting Attorney, with Jehan in the back-
      ground. They are utterly unmoved by Esmeralda's obvious
      innocence, her youth and beauty. Both of them regard her
      with superior and self righteous contempt. At a nod from
      Charmolu, the President of the Court leans forward with
      harsh emphasis, and demands:

SUBTITLE (121)   "GIRL, DO YOU PERSIST IN DENYING THAT
                 YOU STABBED PHOEBUS DE CHATEAUPERS?"

      BACK. Esmeralda has the air of one who merely repeats
      something that she has said many times before, yet with no
      lessening of passionate conviction. There is desperation
      in her manner as she says:

SUBTITLE (122)   "HOW COULD I HAVE STABBED HIM!
                 I LOVED HIM!"

      BACK. As Esmeralda completes her title. Jehan in the back-
      ground leans forward with a sneer occasioned by Esmeralda's
      reference to her love for Phoebus, and now Esmeralda sees
      him for the first time. There is a rapid transition in her
      expression to one of acute horror and fury. As she flings
      her hand toward Jehan in denunciation and Jehan recoils
      slightly, Esmeralda cries:

SUBTITLE (123)   "'TWAS HE STABBED HIM!"

      BACK. As Esmeralda continues her denunciation, one of the
      soldiers restrains her with a rough hand on her shoulder.
      Charmolu and the Judges turn sharply to look at Jehan.
      Jehan has immediately recovered his poise. CUT TO:

267   INT. COURT ROOM   C.U. JEHAN, JUDGE AND CHARMOLU   MID AFTERNOON
      Jehan smiles deprecatingly at Charmolu and the Judge
      smoothly remarks:

SUBTITLE (124)   "THE GIRL IS BEWITCHED."

      At this declaration of Jehan, Maitre Charmolu smiles slightly
      and only partly turning his head toward the President of the
      Court speaks:

SUBTITLE (125)   "PUT HER TO THE QUESTION."

      As he finishes speaking this title, Maitre Charmolu turns
      with his quizzical smile and the President of the Court
      roars the suggestion in the form of an order: "Put her
      to the question!"   CUT TO

268   INT. COURT ROOM   MED SHOT   MID AFTERNOON.
      The President of the Court is still leaning forward, having
      just spoken the words, "Put her to the question!" Jehan
      flashes a Satanic smile. Because the instant reaction upon
      the part of the lawyers and officials of the Court, it is
      as if they were a lot of schoolboys and had just heard the
      bell for recess. Hitherto, they have been rather dull and
      apathetic. Now, a little tremor of excitement reaches every-
      one in view of the camera. A number of the frozen judges
      back of the President of the Court smile grimly and nod to
      each other. Some of the lawyers look up from their scribbling.
      A couple of the pages on the steps of the dais whisper to
      each other, "Come on, Bill, let's go down and see the fun."
      But the center of activity is about Esmeralda herself, she
      hasn't understood the significance of what has been said. Nor
      does she even when the bailiffs again seize her by the arms
      and start to drag her away, almost gleefully, in the direction
      of the door in the left-hand or back wall. But the greatest
      alacrity is shown by Torteru and his followers who bustle off
      to proceed Esmeralda to the torture chamber to have all in
      readiness. There is a general alignment of soldiers with the
      pikes and halberds to the left and right, thus forming a lane
      toward the left hand door in the back wall. Down this lane
      and toward the door, Esmeralda is conducted by her bailiffs,
      while Charmolu, the Persecutor, stifles a yawn, says a parting
      (CONTINUED)

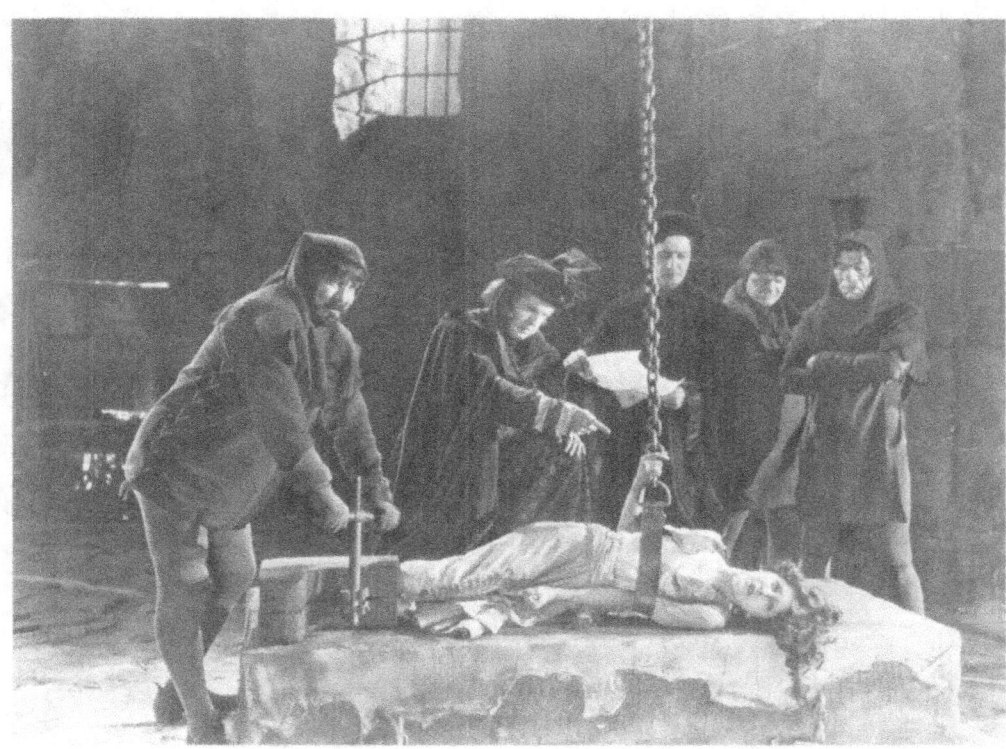

268 Continued
word of friendly "au revoir" to the President of the Court, and Jehan, and starts in pursuit with a following of lawyers and other officials.   CUT TO

Asst. carrying ——

269 INT. TORTURE CHAMBER MED. C.U. AT DOOR MID AFTERNOON
The medium closeup is at the bottom of the circular staircase, down which the crowd has descended. Maitre Torteru and his followers are entering the scene and passing from view over f.g. They are in high good humor, Esmeralda now appears and as the scene before her eyes bursts upon her gaze, she stops stock still in horror. The bailiffs behind her exchange glances of amusement. Make it perfectly clear that what Esmeralda has seen is horrible. She shudders.   CUT TO

270 INT. TORTURE CHAMBER. FULL SHOT MID AFTERNOON. RED TINT.
The torture-room is a vast chamber of exceedingly heavy stone masonry and paved with irregular flags. There is nothing Gothic about this. The masonry is Roman. The stones are huge. The wall is broken by a round foundation pillar of at least ten feet in diameter. There is a heavy curve of masonry blotting off part of the upper f.g. The whole idea is to show that this is in the sub-cellar of the Palais de Justice. The light flickers as from torches and candles. In the background is a huge elevated hearth, somewhat like that of a forge and in this, there is a glowing fire of charcoal. Silhouetted against this red glow are various iron implements, suggested rather than seen in detail. This hearth occupies about a third of the rear wall, somewhat to one side. The remainder of the rear wall is broken by a cranelike effair from which is suspended a rope ending in a hook. To the left of this again, there is a gibbet-like construction, but little higher than a man. Suspended to this from his bound wrists there is a motionless figure of an unconscious man. All of this is seen rather by suggestion than in detail. In the middle distance against the wall, there is a leather covered divan of massive construction, about one foot high, seven feet long and five feet wide. This is the torture-bed. From the stout framework are suspended various straps and chains. From overhead, pendant from the unseen roof, are other chains and ropes, terminating in hooks and buckles.
(CONTINUED)

270 CONTINUED
Sufficiently far front in the f.g. to be clearly revealed by the camera are such implements of torture as long handled pincers, hammers, ladles for melting lead or boiling fat, iron racks and screw arrangements for squeezing heads and various other parts of the human anatomy. At the foot of this collection of implements of torture is the "Boot," which is to be used in Esmeralda's case. This is a loosely constructed portable vise like a box of heavy planks, two feet high and eighteen inches wide, open at the top, one side of which is actuated inward by a letter "S" crank with a longish handle. As we pick up the action, Torteru, bent over, is just pulling the boot over in front of him to see that it is in proper condition, while a couple of his assistants look off in the direction of the door.
CUT TO.

271 INT. TORTURE CHAMBER IND. FULL REVERSE SHOT. MID AFTERNOON.
This scene, shot in the direction of the door from the circular staircase, places the torture bed on the right. Esmeralda, transfixed in horror, is standing at the foot of the stairs in the opening, looking toward the scene we have painted. In fairly close f.g. back to the camera, is Torteru and his assistant. At the present, they are bent over, concentrated on the inspection and arrangement of "the boot" so that their bodies do not obstruct the view of Esmeralda. When they straighten, however, and they crowd about her, they will serve the purpose of cutting from view the actual application of the "boot" so that this will not be cut by censors. The bailiffs behind Esmeralda now push her toward the camera. Esmeralda, held back by fear and horror, with growing realization of what "the question" means, is in a daze. She gasps, her hand goes to her breast. But those with her are relentless. Behind her is Maitre Charmolu, with a beak-nosed assistant who carries a scroll. This scroll when unrolled, is seen to have a signature and seal affixed thereto, with a ribbon pendant from the seal. It is presumably a list of the questions which are to be put to Esmeralda. Torteru, back to camera, is looking at Esmeralda (up) whose eyes are fixed in horror of fascination upon the "boot." Torteru now straightens, stepping back to the left slightly and with all the exaggeration of a gallant, taking Esmeralda by the arm and leading her, unresisting, as though hypnotized, to the foot of the torture bed. He places her there, giving the word to his assistant, who drags the boot close enough, so that Esmeralda's foot can be placed within its two jaws. Meanwhile, in the b.g. have accumulated all the curiosity seekers who followed from the court room and they are looking upon the scene with varying degrees of greedy interest. Maitre Charmolu nods to his assistant, who unrolls the scroll.   CUT TO

272   INT. TORTURE CHAMBER   C.U. ESMERALDA   MID AFTERNOON.
      This closeup is just large enough to show, by suggestion
      the action as Torteru, in the scene kneeling over, lifts
      Esmeralda's left foot with smiling charm and then lowers it,
      evidently into the "boot." Esmeralda is looking down, held
      in horror by the action.   Now CUT TO.

273   INT. TORTURE CHAMBER   MED. SHOT AT FOOT OF BED   MID AFTERNOON.
      Torteru's body, back to camera, covers the fact that Esmeralda's
      foot is in the boot. Torteru, looking up at Esmeralda,
      smiles while on Esmeralda's face there is the growing horror
      of realization as she watches him turn the crank of the
      instrument until her foot is clasped between its jaws.
      Maitre Charmolu and his assistant now enter scene. As yet
      the boot is merely being adjusted and no application of
      its hellish pressure has been applied. Esmeralda, with
      quivering lips, with hand over her breast as though to still
      her heart, now looks up as Maitre Charmolu nods to his clerk
      to ask the questions. The beak-nosed clerk, with a sing-song
      voice, puts the first question: "Do you, Esmeralda, deny
      that you are a witch?" Esmeralda nods her head with
      vehemence. She does. Maitre Charmolu speaks. Torteru
      gives the handle of the "boot" a turn. Esmeralda's face
      changes. She gives a stifled scream and her hand covers
      her mouth. She looks up. The appeal in her eyes meets cyni-
      cal and relentless gaze. Torteru, even though back to camera
      might well be a shoe salesman, solicituously inquiring,
      "A little too tight, madam?" Maitre Charmolu nods again.
      Again the clerk intones his second question:

SUBTITLE: (126)   "DO YOU, ESMERALDA, DENY THAT YOU
                    STABBED HIS MAJESTY'S SERVANT,
                    PHOEBUS DE CHATEAUPERS?"

      Esmeralda appeals:

SUBTITLE: (127)   "I DO DENY IT . . . I LOVED HIM, I
                    LOVED HIM!"

      This is a vehement outburst, forgetful at the moment of the
      torture being applied. Maitre Charmolu indifferently nods
      to Torteru. Torteru, with an exquisite smile, gives the
      handle of the "boot" another turn.   CUT TO

278   INT. PHOEBUS' ROOM AT GONDELAURIER HOME   MORNING   FADE IN
      MED. CLOSE SHOT PHOEBUS IN BED.
      The scene fades in on a medium closeshot of Phoebus in bed.
      He is propped up against a mass of soft linen covered
      pillows, the bandage which goes about his chest visible
      through the open front of the fine cambric shirt which he
      wears. The expression of Phoebus' face is in harmony with
      the thought expressed in the title. Phoebus is wondering
      if the charge can be true. The very thought of it causes
      a reaction in his mind, expressed upon his face, combined
      with a flash of pain. He relaxes against the pillows and
      his eyes close. His face continues to show however, his
      conflicting emotions.   CUT TO

279   INT. PHOEBUS' ROOM AT GONDELAURIER HOME   MORNING   FADE IN
      MED. CLOSE AT BED.   MORNING.
      This view is large enough to show Madame de Gondelaurier
      standing near Phoebus' bed on the right. Near her is the
      leech, a man about forty. He is smooth-shaven, saturnine,
      thin, stoop-shouldered, like a student, and wears a long
      black fur-trimmed cloak, with fur-trimmed cap with a
      folded edges. The leech's manner serves to indicate beyond
      doubt that Phoebus is in no danger and Madame de Gondelaurier's
      reaction, as he expresses this in his voice and manner,
      shows great relief. They turn now, starting down scene as
      he   CUT TO

280   INT. PHOEBUS' ROOM AT GONDELAURIER HOME   MED. FULL SHOT
      MORNING.
      This view is large enough to show one of the windows on
      the right. Through it streams the morning sun, at such
      an angle as to indicate the approximate hour of eleven.
      As Madame de Gondelaurier and the leech come down toward
      f.g. the leech continues to show her in whispered words
      that Phoebus' condition is condition is nothing to cause
      great alarm. Just as they reach fairly close f.g. the
      door on the left opens, and Fleur de lys, looking very
      pretty in a morning dress, her plaited hair down her back,
      enters followed by Jehan. Jehan's outward manner is ad-
      justed to a quiet solicitude and hypocritical sympathy.
      He glances toward the bed, but only for an instant, then
      (CONTINUED)

274   INT. TORTURE CHAMBER   C.U. ESMERALDA   MID AFTERNOON.
      In order that the scene may not be cut by the censors, do not
      have this a too harrowing scene. Esmeralda screams . . .
      but is losing consciousness. She looks up toward Maitre
      Charmolu, crying:

SUBTITLE: (128)   "I CONFESS . . . I CONFESS TO ANYTHING
                    YOU WISH!"

      With this, Esmeralda's eyes close. She is swooning and
      with the swooning, her tortured mind reverts to the one
      happy thought in all her life . . . Phoebus. A little
      smile appears on her face, and even as she sways and before
      her body topples over,   LAP DISSOLVE CUT AND INTO.

275   EXT. AN IDYLLIC EXT   FULL SHOT   NIGHT   LAP DISSOLVE IN.
      The scene lap dissolves in on an idyllic exterior. The
      b.g. is a painting that only love might conceive. It is
      a garden, a garden of love and happiness. Tall poplars
      are silhouetted in a silver light. There is a vista of
      palms and marble balustrades, of a lake and a fountain.
      It is a place of romance, of happiness, of love. And in
      the f.g. coming toward each other from left and right are
      Phoebus and Esmeralda. Their approach to each other's
      arms is slow, but magnetic. They meet, his arms go about
      her. Her hands rest upon his shoulder. His lips bend to
      her. Their lips meet. They have found each other. Upon
      this scene,

276   INT. A SUBTERRANEAN CELL   LS. LS SHOT   MID AFTERNOON.
      The scene dissolves in on a subterranean cell, round, like
      a deep moderate sized cistern, the circular wall of which
      is in rough masonry, in contradiction to the smooth masonry
      of the other cells we have seen. At the opening of the shot,
      the place is illuminated from the top, revealing a ladder
      which leads to a trap-door in the ceiling. On the floor
      (CONTINUED)

280   CONTINUED
      turns to Madame de Gondelaurier and the leech. That they
      are acquainted is obvious, for both Madame and the leech
      bow to Jehan with a certain amount of respect. Is he not
      the arch-deacon's brother? Fleur de lys, with a smile at
      Jehan, turns to her mother and the leech, explaining in
      a quiet voice:

SUBTITLE: (130)   "MONSIEUR, THE BROTHER OF THE ARCH-DEACON,
                    INQUIRES THE HEALTH OF OUR COUSIN."

      Madame de Gondelaurier smiles her most charming smile,
      treating Jehan with obvious respect and a manner of
      social equality. Fleur de lys, with a questioning glance
      at Jehan, turns upscene toward the bed. Jehan bows to the
      leech, and Madame de Gondelaurier, who cross scene to
      exit as Jehan follows Fleur de lys upscene to a point on
      the left of Phoebus' bed.   CUT TO

281   INT. PHOEBUS' ROOM AT GONDELAURIER HOME   MED. CLOSE AT
      BED   MORNING.
      Phoebus' eyes are closed, but the expression on his face
      shows the thoughts which torture his mind. Fleur de lys
      is just reaching the bedside, looking back toward Jehan,
      who now enters. From Fleur de lys' manner it is evident
      that she thinks Phoebus is asleep. But Phoebus now
      opens his eyes, turning his head slightly to look up at
      Fleur de lys and Jehan. Outwardly, Jehan's manner could
      indicate regretful solicitude, but from the flash in
      his eyes, we who understand Jehan, can sense the satisfaction
      he feels in seeing his victim thus. He leans over toward
      Phoebus, knowing full well that his deliberately chosen
      words will stab Phoebus to the heart. He speaks:

SUBTITLE: (131)   "THE WENCH WHO STABBED YOU HAS CONFESSED
                    THE CRIME. SHE HAS BEEN ORDERED HANGED
                    WITHOUT DELAY."

281 CONTINUED

BACK: To us, there is, must be, a devilish satisfaction in Jehan's manner as he speaks thus. Fleur de lys, looking at Phoebus, betrays a certain pleasure in the news. She does not see Jehan's face as he speaks this. Phoebus looks at Jehan's face for an instant . . . then sits straight up. Fleur de lys frowns. CUT TO

282 INT. PHOEBUS' ROOM AT GONDELAURIER HOME C.U. PHOEBUS MORNING.
Phoebus sits straight up. There is a flash of pain upon his face which is subconscious, for now Phoebus is not thinking of his pain, but of Esmeralda. We can presume that he has a touch of fever perhaps. A fever which distorts with vivid reality, the picture which Jehan's words bring to his mind. His eyes dilate slightly in an almost wild look as he pictures . . . . .
LAP DISSOLVE CUT AND INTO.

283 EXT. PLACE DE GREVE LONG SHOT A. GIBBET SUNSET
In this scene, play for what is an almost unnatural lighting value. A shaft of cross-lighting, as though from the setting sun, illuminating the gibbet to make it stand out against a background that is a suggestion of hazy human beings, gone wild at the spectacle of an execution. Mons. Torteru stands ready upon the raised platform of the gibbet. On the crossarm is his assistant, ready to adjust the swinging rope about Esmeralda's neck. Ascending the steps of the gibbet is Esmeralda, dressed in a white robe which shimmers in halo lighting. Her hair is down. Her hands are tied behind her. Her feet are bare, the crowd, suggested rather than in detail, is gleeful. Handkerchiefs wave in the air. Monsieur Torteru stands smiling. Esmeralda, with beautiful resignation, face slightly raised, as though to Heaven, takes her position under the swinging rope. It is placed about her slender white neck. The cries of the crowd increase. Monsieur Torteru turns to perform his task, and THE SCENE LAP DISSOLVES INTO:

284 INT. PHOEBUS' ROOM AT GONDELAURIER HOME CU PHOEBUS MORNING
Phoebus' eyes are wildly dilated as his tortured mind presents this vivid distorted picture. There is a shudder which racks his body. He screams, "No, no, no," making as if to leap from the bed. He collapses against the pillows in a faint. Fleur de lys bends down into scene to adjust the pillows. In spite of her tendency to flirt, she feels genuine sorrow for Phoebus and a certain mental satisfaction that the situation will result to her own advantage as far as Phoebus is concerned. CUT TO

285 INT. PHOEBUS' ROOM AT GONDELAURIER HOME MED SHOT MORNING
Fleur de lys with tender womanly solicitude, bending over Phoebus, and adjusting his pillows. Jehan's face is diabolical in its sneering satisfaction as he sees the effects of his words. Hold this for a few seconds and then FADE OUT

SUBTITLE (132)   AN HOUR BEFORE DAWN ON THE DAY SET FOR
                  HER EXECUTION, ESMERALDA RECEIVED A VISIT.

286   INT. A SUBTERRANEAN CELL   MED SHOT   DAWN   FADE IN
       The opening of the trap at the top of the cell is an
       equivalent of a fade in. A pale shaft of light shows
       Esmeralda crouched on the cell floor, half reclining, half
       in an attitude of prayer. This is no sooner established
       than there is seen slowly descending the ladder from above,
       a cowled figure bringing a lantern. The lantern is the
       source of light. The cowl and the movement suggests the
       coming of Dom Claude. Esmeralda sits up and sees the ad-
       vent of the visitor, who descends leisurely with its back
       to Esmeralda and the camera, until fully established on
       the floor of the cell and the lantern is placed in position
       on a hook. Then the figure slowly turns. Esmeralda dis-
       covers the identity of the visitor before this is revealed
       to the camera. Her expression registers a transition to
       frozen horror. There is now revealed, instead of the
       expected face of Dom Claude, the satanic face of Jehan.
       Hold this for a few seconds. In spite of his evil, Jehan
       has come primarily to plead. As Esmeralda shrinks further
       and Jehan inclines forward, he speaks:

SUBTITLE   "EVEN NOW I CAN SAVE THEE. 'TIS THY
                  ONLY CHANCE. COME WITH ME."

287   INT. A SUBTERRANEAN CELL   CLOSE SHOT   DAWN
       As Jehan completes the title and waits expectantly,
       Esmeralda loses something of her horror, but with a mount-
       ing revulsion, she speaks:

SUBTITLE (134)   "WHY DO YOU COME TO MOCK ME?   I HAD
                  RATHER DIE."

       Jehan hears her reply. His mind is working evilly. He
       states what he thinks is an argument – he speaks:

SUBTITLE (135)   "'TWAS THE DYING WISH OF THY PHOEBUS. LAST
                  NIGHT HE PASSED AWAY."

                                                    (CONTINUED)

287   CONTINUED
       Now as Jehan completes the title, it can be seen that
       Esmeralda is drawing herself up from her crouching position
       and that Jehan is sinking a little lower before her fixed
       look of passionate sadness and accusation. CUT TO

288   INT. A SUBTERRANEAN CELL   MED SHOT   DAWN
       Now as Esmeralda draws herself wholly to her feet and shrink
       as far back as possible against the wall, thinking more of
       this announcement of the death of Phoebus than of any pos-
       sible danger she may be in at the hands of Jehan. Jehan
       slowly sinks completely to his knees with his tense arms
       out and his hands touching her robe. Esmeralda herself is
       tense as if in contact with a creature of horror. Now as
       Jehan sinks his head lower in an attitude of complete
       abasement as Esmeralda looks down at him with groping
       amazement, Jehan speaks:

SUBTITLE (136)   "O ESMERALDA, HAST THOU NO PITY?
                  MAN NEVER LOVED WOMAN AS I LOVE THEE."

       For a flash as Jehan speaks this, then CUT TO

289   INT. A SUBTERRANEAN CELL   CU ESMERALDA   DAWN
       Esmeralda, still looking down, speaks with a mingling of
       horror and grief:

SUBTITLE (137)   "RATHER HAD I BEEN WITH PHOEBUS...BETTER
                  A MOMENT WITH HIM DEAD THAN LIFE WITH
                  THEE."

       For a flash as Esmeralda completes the title and then
       CUT TO:

290 INT. A SUBTERRANEAN CELL — MED. CLOSE — DAWN
As we pick up this shot, Esmeralda is looking down at Jehan and breathing heavily as a reflex to her last title and her loathing. Now Jehan shows a transition from abject pleading to an outburst of frenzied passion. He lifts his face to Esmeralda and clutches her arms with frenzied desire. This merely brings her loathing to a climax. She shudders up and back from his touch. She fairly hisses the words as she speaks:

SUBTITLE (138) "ASSASSIN!"

We hold this scene several seconds before there is any movement. During this time Esmeralda should register an indomitable will, a spiritual force that cannot be gainsaid. Jehan weakens under this gaze. His arms relax. He averts his face. He gets to his feet. (All this very slowly) ~~with an almost stealthy movement, like that of an old man, he reaches for the lantern.~~ Then Jehan turns vengefully and speaks:

SUBTITLE (139) "VERY WELL, THEN, MINX!"

Esmeralda receives the taunt with steady horror but does not move. With the closing of the trap overhead, the scene FADES OUT.

~~RUN TWO OR THREE FEET OF BLACK SCREEN BEFORE FADING IN ON THE FOLLOWING SCENE. THERE IS NO SUBTITLE BETWEEN THESE TWO SEQUENCES.~~

291 INT. BELFRY OF NOTRE DAME — CU GREAT BELL DAWN — FADE IN
The scene fades in on a vignette aperture showing GREAT BELL of Notre Dame. This bell is a ponderous work, six feet high, ornamented with scrolls and Latin inscriptions. This view is toward the East. The movement of the bell is East and West. Its movement is ponderous for its weight is terrific. The bells swing twice, forward, then to the rear. A shower of dust and small debris falls into scene, with, if possible, which will give an impression of the booming sound which vibrates everything in the immediate vicinity. CUT TO

292 INT. BELLRINGER'S ROOM — NOTRE DAME — MED CU — DAWN
This view is toward the East, showing in the rear, to right and left, two of the typical narrow Gothic slits. Thru these slits break shafts of slightly slanting light from the sun which is just rising. In immediate f. g. JUDITH CLOSELY, is Quasimodo. His body is a frenzy of physical exertion as he holds the bell-hawser in his gnarled hands. His position would suggest that he has just completed his last downward pull upon the hawser and he now lets it slip through his hands, upward, as the bell above swings, now looking upward, with his face expressing an ecstatic surging of joy in the physical frenzy of his action; Quasimodo keeps his eyes on the hawser until it is just starting its downward movement. Then he jumps into the air, springing like a cat, clutching the rope again with his hands, lending his entire weight into the downward movement.

SUBTITLE (140) "LITTLE DID DASHNESS KNOW THAT DEATH KNELL WAS RINGING."

His frenzy is not of joy in knowledge of what the tolling means, but a simple forgetfulness of everything in the sheer joy he gets out of hearing the only voice he can hear, the bells of Notre Dame. With the downward sweep of Quasimodo's body, CUT TO

293 INT. ??? OF NOTRE DAME   CU GREAT BELL   DAWN
The bell swings again, with the great clapper hitting the bell with an increased impact as Quasimodo, below, lends his weight to the downward pull   CUT IN

SUBTITLE (141)   WHEN QUASIMODO RANG THE GREAT BELL OF NOTRE DAME LIKE THAT ALL PARIS KNEW THAT A PRISONER WAS BOUND FOR THE PLACE OF EXECUTION.

Continue the movement of the bell until it swings in the opposite direction. The sun has risen a little higher by this time and the belfry has lighted up to the extent that the sifting of fine dust and debris from the vibration can be plainly seen.   CUT TO

294 INT. BELL RINGER'S ROOM OF NOTRE DAME   MED CU QUASIMODO   DAWN
Continue Quasimodo's frenzied action of leaping into the air and clutching the bell hawser as it starts its descent again   CUT TO

295 EXT. A PARIS STREET   MED SHOT   DAWN
This the Paris street at the right looking away from Notre Dame. It must appear different, however, to any view previously seen. Coming toward the camera are a number of horsemen in purple livery, with white crosses on their breasts. They carry drawn swords. These horsemen are flanked by a numerous body of footmen, sergeants of the watch, uniformed like the baliffs we have already seen and armed with nothing but long staves or sticks. As a detail to the progress of the procession, an early prowling rag-picker gets in the way of the procession and is bumped aside by one of these footmen, who not only butts him with his stave, but gives him a kick in the rump as the fellow falls to one side. Back of the horsemen comes a rather low-pitched four-wheeled cart, drawn by a single, very fine, glossy horse. The cart is flanked on each side by officials of the court which tried Esmeralda. These officials are

CONTINUED

295 CONTINUED
MOUNTED BUT are not at home on horseback. This is a special occasion. We see Maitre Cjarmolu and the President of the Court, Tanderau, and various lawyers and clerks. These are attended by their lackeys and assistants on foot, but staying close to the stirrups. Back of the cart is another body of the horsemen in purple livery, with white crosses. The procession is wound up by a company of cross-bowmen marching eight abreast; enough to close the street. Back of the procession and working their way into it at every opportunity, are numerous urchins. Most of the windows of the houses in range of the camera are open and decorated with protruding heads. All of these are people who have just been waked up by an unusual sound. In the cart, but barely seen in this shot, is Esmeralda, dressed in white   CUT TO

296 EXT. A PARIS STREET   MED SHOT CLOSE IN CART   DAWN
The camera is on the cart, keeping Esmeralda in fairly close f. g. Her hands are tied behind her back. Her hair is down. She lifts her eyes to look out of scene, her expression signifies, "Father, forgive them, for they know not what they do."   CUT TO

297 EXT. A PARIS STREET   MED. CLOSE AT WINDOW OF HOUSE   DAWN
This is an upper window, on the second floor. The view shows a CLOSEUP of two heads, those of a staring burgher, looking down at Esmeralda, with his wife. Both are frowsy and adorned with nightcaps. The man has the better position and he laughs coarsely and cries out:

SUBTITLE (142)   "YOU'RE GOING TO DANCE ON AIR!"

At his shoulder is the bleary face of his wife, who grins at her husband's humor. Just a flash of this.   CUT TO

298 EXT. A PARIS STREET   MED SHOT   DAWN
This shot is from an elevated position, the view as seen from the upper window. Progressing into scene from the right, comes the cart with Esmeralda. Esmeralda has her head bowed and slightly to one side. Continue the progress of the procession out of scene until the cart exits off left of view and then CUT TO:

299 EXT. ???   LONG SHOT   PROCESSION   DAWN
In immediate f. g. there is a crowd of people between camera and the background showing the place of the Angelus execution. With this activity established, CUT TO

300 EXT. PLACE DU PARVIS   THIS SCENE IS SHOT FROM THE PLACE OUTSIDE THE ARCHED WINDOW OF GUDULE'S CELL
At the window is Sister Gudule straining to see what is taking place. As she recognizes Esmeralda a look of ferocity comes into her face. As she starts to turn, CUT TO

301 LONG SHOT   PLACE DU PARVIS   MORNING
As procession is brought to temporary halt by the crowd.

302 MED. SHOT OF CART
As Gudule rushes in, screaming, jumps up on hub of cart, reaches for Esmeralda, and speaks title:

302 CONTINUED
SUBTITLE (143)   "LET ME SLAY THE GYPSY FIEND! HER LIFE FOR THE LIFE OF MY CHILD THAT THE GYPSIES STOLE!"

She clutches Esmeralda's dress at the neck, frantically pulling at it, in an attempt to take her by the throat. In this same movement, her fingers close on the chain around Esmeralda's neck supporting the amulet.   CUT TO

303 LONGER SHOT   EXT. PLACE DU PARVIS   OF CART
Longer shot as horseman rides in and pulls Gudule down off the cartwheel. As she is pulled away, she still clutches at the dress, and amulet in her hand. The amulet breaks off and remains in her hand, as she falls to the pavement, still screaming. Esmeralda's reaction to this is one of mingled pity and horror.   CUT TO

304 EXT. P. P.
LONG SHOT AS PROCESSION GETS STARTED AGAIN

305 CLOSEUP GUDULE
As she continues cursing Esmeralda. She glances at the amulet in her hand and recognizes it. There is an instant of horror. She is dazed and speechless. Then a frantic grief as she turns as if to run to Esmeralda, this time to save her. She realizes that Esmeralda is her own daughter. As she starts out of C. U.   CUT TO

306 LONGER SHOT OF GUDULE
As she staggers after cart, calling:

CAPTION (144)   "MY DAUGHTER! MY BABY! SAVE HER.
                   OH! GOD!"

307 EXT. PLACE DU PARVIS   LONGER SHOT KICK OF CROWD   DAWN
As Sister Gudule turns as if to rush once more to Esmeralda, the two soldiers grin at her unfeelingly and restrain her. She beats against them with her bare hands for a moment, receives a shove that sends her reeling forward, and falls. She lifts her hands with amulet in them as if in prayer and then, unmistakably, she dies - CUT TO

308 EXT. GALLERY NOTRE DAME   MED SHOT   DAWN
Quasimodo comes around corner of tower and sees workmen who are already at their task of mending the roof. These workmen, in response to the cry of one of their fellows, clamber across the roof and balcony toward the outer parapet, which commands a view of the Parvis. Their action is full of excitement occasioned by something that they can see in the Parvis. Of this moment, Quasimodo mistily springs to portals in the excitement. As he reaches the parapet of the balcony, CUT TO

309

309 EXT. GALLERY OF NOTRE DAME   MED SHOT   DAWN
This view is a medium shot, shooting from a point in space, in front of the gallery, toward the same. The action is at a point on the gallery near the left hand tower. The other seven workmen are at the gallery, in varying degrees of interest and excitement, peering over the parapet down into the Parvis almost directly beneath them. [scribbled out]
takes a place on the left of the rope. The workmen are on the right. As Quasimodo looks down, CUT TO

310 EXT. GALLERY OF NOTRE DAME   CU   QUASIMODO   DAWN
Quasimodo starts down toward the space in front of the church He is half fascinated by what he sees, without actual realisation at this moment, that the white figure beneath him is that of Esmeralda. The memory of her flashes thru his mind, brought there by a recognition of which he is not certain. He poises his head, staring down, trying to co-ordinate what he sees with something which memory persistently flashes in his mind.   CUT TO

311 EXT. FACADE OF NOTRE DAME   MED SHOT   DAWN
This shot is along the facade of Notre Dame, with the left portal in left f.g. Establish in this view, upscene side of entrance to the left portal, is the rope which dangles into the scene from above. At the foot of this rope which
                                              CONTINUE

311 CONTINUED
terminates in a loose coil on the platform is a group of three workmen, who have been busied in adjusting a piece of rope about one of the rolls of lead. There is a big hook attached to the end of the rope which swings from above. The roll of lead has been tied in such a way that a sort of rope basket or sling, is formed, into which this great hook can fit. Their activity, however, has long since ceased and they are looking with avid interest on the activity of the procession which has progressed to a point almost in front of the left portal of Notre Dame. At the same time, several of the bailiffs break from the procession, and with their staves threatening, run across the platform and drive the workmen into the background. In the f.g. the guard in purple livery with white crosses on their breasts, have backed their horses around into a sort of loosely defined hollow square. The cart with Esmeralda is brought up almost to the steps of the Cathedral, with the back of the cart toward the camera. Now, two of Torteru's assistants leap nimbly into the cart at a word from him. As they start to untie Esmeralda, CUT IN:

312 MED. C.U. TURULE'S BODY IL C.U. DU PARVI.
A monk and two bourgeois men. The monk is just getting up from his knees and waving the men back, and the monk speaks title:

SUBTITLE (145)   "THE EARTHLY PENANCE IS ENDED. PRAY TO HER SOUL!"

313 EXT. FACADE OF NOTRE DAME. MED SHOT L.S. FACE DU DOM.
Esmeralda's position is on the left, between the two men who took her from the cart. The beak-nosed clerk of the court comes up on the right, sniffles importantly, wipes his nose on the back of his hand and begins to read with a sing-song inflection from a partly rolled scroll on which hangs a ribbon and seal. As he reads, CUT IN:

SUBTITLE (146)   ".....AND FIRST APPEAR ON THE STEPS OF THE CATHEDRAL CHURCH OF NOTRE DAME... THERE TO DO PENANCE......"

This completes the clerk's formality. He turns, rolling his scroll as he exits. The bailiffs exeunt to the left with Esmeralda between them. CUT TO

314 GALLERY OF NOTRE DAME C. U. OF QUASIMODO M.S.
Quasimodo is looking down toward the space which we presume is almost directly beneath him. His head is poised in such a manner as to indicate that he is straining the bad vision of his one eye, and from the expression on his face, the fleeting recognition which insistently forces itself into his mind, is just starting to take definite form. It is dawning on Quasimodo that the figure far below him is that of Esmeralda, the girl who gave him succor when he suffered. As Quasimodo leans down, move the camera forward until his face almost fills the entire screen. Then blur the face of Quasimodo, starting a LAP DIS OLVE into the following scene

315 EXT. FACADE OF NOTRE DAME VIEW STRAIGHT DOWN DASH LAP DI OLVE IN FRM. THE BLURRED FACE OF QUASIMODO
Even as the scene lap dissolves in, the camera moves closer and still closer, to the screen, until Quasimodo's eye PRACTICALLY FILLS THE SCREEN. But as this takes place, the scene is also LAP DISSOLVING INTO THE VIEW, which is a kaleidoscopic image of a brain which suddenly responds to knowledge with a burst of revelation. The shot is straight down, showing in the center, the form of Esmeralda. She is a very small figure, but is lighted with a glory of light which makes her sparkle like a diamond in the setting of a whirlpool of distorted chimera, which swim in confusing circles around the central nucleus, as though seen through the eye of a person over whose vision is partly blinded through a film of tears. Her below, Esmeralda is seen in a kneeling position on the steps, face uplifted now as she raises her eyes in a final submission to a power above. LAP DISSOLVE OUT AND INTO

316 EXT. GALLERY OF NOTRE DAME C.U. QUASIMODO SHOOTING
The scene DISSOLVES IN in the same manner in which it lap dissolved out, i.e. on a closeup of Quasimodo's eye upon which the camera recedes to a closeup of his face, fairly blurred, but which takes definite outline to show his expression as he now knows that the figure far below is that of Esmeralda. Supreme rage against those who have touched her, surges in his blood, supreme rage against himself, for has he not with his own hands, tolled the knell for her death? His mouth opens, his teeth clew. There is a hissing intake of his breath.

317 EXT. GALLERY OF NOTRE DAME MED SHOT AT PROJECTION OF WINDLASS MON IRIS.
The windlass projection, with the rope dangling thru the pulley, is in immediate f. g. On the right are the workmen peering down into the Parvis. Quasimodo is looking down. As he tears himself from what he has just seen, he suddenly leans to the parapet and hurls himself into space. Catching the rope with both hands and sliding out of sight below, while the workmen give a cry of horror and look down to see

318 EXT. FACADE OF NOTRE DAME SHOOTING STRAIGHT DOWN LONG SHOT
Supposedly, the eye of the view is right along a line with the rope. Far below can be discerned the figure of Esmeralda kneeling. She is on the right. The figure of Quasimodo can be seen, sliding down the rope, growing smaller and smaller in the narrowing perspective. Shoot this scene thru a soft edge circle iris. Just before Quasimodo reaches the ground, CUT TO

→ Shot of descending camera - Taken from it.

319 EXT. FACADE OF NOTRE DAME MED SHOT LOOKING
The view shows, in the center of b. g. the dangling rope, it is swaying, waving, unsupported at the bottom by anything which would keep it steady, the view shows in fairly close f. g. the kneeling figure of Esmeralda. Her face is upturned. She is lost for the moment in a spiritual submission. Behind her, at a distance of several feet, stand the bailiffs who brought her to this position. The action
CONTINUED

319 CONTINUED
WHICH follows must come with the swiftness and unexpectedness (to those in the scene) of lightning. Quasimodo appears in scene from above. Even as he reaches a point a few feet above the porch, he lets go and springs, landing like a monkey on all fours, but straightening even while in the movement to spring forward, racing down the steps with the speed of a leopard. He seizes Esmeralda, and before the bailiffs or anyone else can overcome their surprise, is bounding across the platform with Esmeralda in his arms. There is an immediate rush after him as we CUT TO

320 EXT. NOTRE DAME MED SHOT AISLE OF PORTAL LOOKING
The doors are open. In the Cathedral, seeing down the aisle toward camera which shoots into the Cathedral from the porch, is seen the stately figure of Dom Claude. Quasimodo dashes into the scene from camera side, taking a position within the portal, turning and screaming in his unnatural voice, the one word:

SPOKEN (147)   "SANCTUARY! SANCTUARY!"

From the position of Esmeralda in Quasimodo's arms, it is perfectly obvious that she has swooned. Quasimodo hardly pauses after screaming the words, but turns and rushes up the aisle, as Dom Claude, with an all-observing glance, takes in the situation and hurries his steps to the f. g. where, at the threshold now appear several of the bailiffs, and soldiers, swords drawn, who have rushed after Quasimodo. Dom Claude raises his hand. The men before him (backs to camera) stop on the threshold of the portal. Seeing that their attitude calls for sternness, Dom Claude speaks:

SPOKEN (148)   "HALT! QUIET, VIOLATE THE SACRED LAW OF SANCTUARY"

BACK: The mengtop, their attitude, even with their backs to the camera and drawn swords, should make it obvious that they are beaten. They cannot follow, that Esmeralda is safe. Upon this scene, QUICKLY FADE OUT [crossed out]

SUBTITLE (149)   TO QUASIMODO, THE ONLY THING THAT MATTERED
                  WAS THAT THIS GIRL HAD ONCE BEEN KIND TO HIM.

321   INT. QUASIMODO'S CELL   MED. CLOSE SHOT   QUICK FADE IN
       MORNING
       The scene fades in on a medium shot in Quasimodo's cell--
       the quick fade out and the quick fade in here will serve in
       the place of a title, which is not necessary. The view is
       toward Quasimodo who is crouched, kneeling on the floor
       near Esmeralda who lies on the mattress with her head
       toward the camera. Her beautiful head is about all we can
       see of her. Quasimodo has just placed her there. He is still
       panting, partly from his physical exertion and partly from
       emotion. He looks at Esmeralda with an expression which is
       haunted, reverent, smitten with wonder -- a suggestion
       that her beauty is a thing which he cannot comprehend. He
       leans forward slightly, poising his head to one side with
       a movement that is at once hopeless, for in his kind, un-
       consciously asserting itself, is the thought that she is
       beyond him. Hold this for several feet and then CUT TO:

322   INT. QUASIMODO'S CELL   CU OF ESMERALDA   MORNING
       Esmeralda's eyes are closed, her breathing is slightly
       faster than normal. Her eyes open slowly; there is no con-
       sciousness of her surroundings, no thoughts, except that
       she has been to face with death. She sees Quasimodo,
       and for the briefest second there is a reaction--the slight
       suggestion of a revulsion, a fear. Quasimodo bows his head,
       humbly. She lifts her hand.

323   INT. QUASIMODO'S CELL   MED. CLOSE SHOT   MORNING
       This view is toward Quasimodo, as in the original shot.
       He has glimpsed the momentary expression on Esmeralda's
       face; he knows the feeling that has flashed through her
       mind; he has lowered his head. Esmeralda's hand is rising.
       Now, for a second, it rests upon his shaggy head, and in-
       dication of the appreciation she feels for his act. Quasi-
       modo does not look up. Esmeralda's hand slips from his
       head and drops, listlessly, to the mattress. For a matter
       of several seconds we hold Quasimodo thus-- CUT TO:

327   INT. QUASIMODO'S CELL   MED. GROUP SHOT   MORNING
       This is as before, shooting toward the door. The angle of
       this shot is such that it will permit us to see into
       the room thru the door when it is opened. Right into
       the room presently, just within the door is Jehan. Esmer-
       alda's position is shifted so that she is at Dom Claude's feet, with her
       head resting upon her knees or his knees. Now she looks up
       for a word from Dom Claude. Quasimodo watches them both,
       loving them both, knowing not which of them he loves the more.
       Dom Claude smiles down upon Esmeralda, encouragingly, consol-
       ingly, as he speaks:

SUBTITLE (150)   "MY DAUGHTER, THE LAWS OF THE SANCTUARY
                  PROTECT YOU, PENDING AN APPEAL. HAVE
                  FAITH...TRUST IN THE FATHER OF US ALL."

       BACK: As he speaks this, the first rays of the early morn-
       ing sun appear and send a narrow shaft of parallel light
       thru the open door. Jehan, seeing that his shadow will
       tell of his presence, shrinks out of sight. The light il-
       luminates Dom Claude's spiritual face and gives him a halo
       lighting to Esmeralda's profile as she looks up at him.
       Quasimodo keeps his eye upon his beloved master and the
       beautiful creature his love for whom he cannot fully grasp.
       Upon this, the scene FADES OUT.

. . . .

SUBTITLE (151)   ESMERALDA BELIEVED THAT PHOEBUS WAS
                  DEAD. LIKE MANY ANOTHER MOURNER
                  BEFORE AND SINCE, SHE WAS FINDING
                  CONSOLATION IN THE BOSOM OF NOTRE DAME.

324   INT. QUASIMODO'S CELL   LARGER SHOT   MORNING
       This is a normal angle for this set, shooting toward the
       narrow slip of a door upscene. The window on the right allows
       the early morning light to fill the room with a soft light,
       but nothing in the nature of direct rays, as the window
       faces west. This view places Quasimodo in a position with
       back almost to camera. He is still in the position as be-
       fore, head upon his breast. The door to the gallery
       opens and Dom Claude appears. Quasimodo notes his entrance
       only when Esmeralda stirs. Dom Claude looks down upon the
       scene, then lifts his hand in blessing, as if both of these
       unfortunates were his children. Dom Claude comes to the
       wooden chest, which is near the mattress. As he sits down,
       CUT TO:

325   INT. QUASIMODO'S CELL   CLOSER GROUP SHOT   MORNING
       Shoot this from the angle of the original shot, placing
       Esmeralda's head in foreground. On the right is Dom Claude,
       sitting down on the chest. Quasimodo is on Esmeralda's
       right, thus placing him at the back of Dom Claude and with
       his back almost to the door through which Dom Claude en-
       tered. The view, thru the opened door, permits a glimpse
       of the roof and gallery. Anyone appearing at the door could
       do so unseen by the members of the group. Dom Claude is look-
       ing down at Esmeralda, with spiritual encouragement and
       consolation. Esmeralda rises to a sitting posture. This
       movement brings her head about on the level of Dom Claude's
       knee, in a manner of self-abandonment and renunciation--
       of memory of all she has been through. She rests her right
       arm on his knees and her face on her arm. She is ready to
       give herself to the Church. In the background of this ac-
       tion, at the door, appears Jehan, furtive, sly, fascinated.
       Dom Claude's hand rests upon Esmeralda's head, consolingly.
       Quasimodo looks from one to the other reverently, trying
       to follow what is being said and done. Dom Claude, under-
       standing Esmeralda's emotion, gently smoothes her hair
       with caressing hand--a Christ and a penitent.   CUT TO:

326   EXT. QUASIMODO'S CELL   CU AT DOOR   MORNING
       Jehan is peering past the camera, taking in the scene. So
       Esmeralda is here! Within the confines of Notre Dame! He
       sees how she clings to Dom Claude, trusting, contented.
       If he, Jehan, were Dom Claude! -- then she would cling to
       him, she would do as he might dictate. The prospect quickens
       his heart and his breath.   CUT TO:

328   PAINTING OF NOTRE DAME   LONG SHOT   NIGHT   FADE IN
       The scene fades in on a long shot of a painting of Notre Dame,
       by moonlight. The moon is near the full, still in the
       East and at a height which would suggest the time for evening,
       about eight o'clock. The outlines of Notre Dame are sil-
       houetted against a movement of clouds in the background. The
       picture should present the Cathedral in a highly beautiful
       and spiritually artistic sense. After several feet of this;

329   EXT. GALLERY OF NOTRE DAME   MED. CLOSE   NIGHT
       This view is from a point of space in front of the gallery
       and shows Esmeralda, leaning on the parapet. The moonlight
       in back of her lights her hair, which is flowing loosely,
       moved by a gentle wind, in a halo of glory. In accord with
       the title, Esmeralda's face has an expression of peace. In
       the spiritual envelopment of Notre Dame, she is finding
       consolation--"Surcease and Nepenthe;" its spirit has reached
       her and has quieted her. She is in a reverie of peaceful
       aspiration.   CUT TO:

330   INT. QUASIMODO'S CELL   MED. SHOT NEAR DOOR.   NIGHT
       This medium shot shows the door, open, and on the left the
       wooden chest previously mentioned. The cell is lighted by
       one small candle end which burns on the candelabrum near
       the door. The flame flickers fitfully, blown by the same
       gentle breeze which moved Esmeralda's hair. Quasimodo
       appears within the doorway now, stopping for an instant to
       look cautiously in what we know to be the direction of Esmer-
       alda. Then, lightly and swiftly, he steps into the room,
       throwing upon the floor near the chest a coarse, unbleached
       canvas sack, which shows signs of age. He fumbles at his
       belt, for the key to the padlock, and finding it, sinks
       upon his knees before the chest and unlocks the padlock,
       lifting the massive lid. The contents of the chest cannot
       be seen from this angle. Quasimodo, back to camera, leans
       over the chest. For a matter of seconds, we can imagine
       that his eye feasts upon what the chest contains; then
       comes a slow, mystical motion, as though a miser were
       sifting between his fingers, pieces of gold.   CUT IN:

SUBTITLE (152)   "QUASIMODO'S TREASURE CHEST...TO HIM
                  THEY WERE AS THE FRAGMENTS OF PRAYERS."

331 INT. QUASIMODO'S CELL   CU AT CHEST   NIGHT
The ~~view of this~~ ~~from the back of the room~~ ~~shows~~ ~~against~~ ~~the darkness~~ wall. In the immediate background, closeup on right, is the chest. This angle discloses the inside of the chest, showing it to be filled with candle ends, large and small. These are Quasimodo's treasures. On the left kneels Quasimodo. The light from the candelabrum throws a wavering, fitful light upon the view from above. In Quasimodo's face is a satisfaction, a happy contemplation, anticipation of the joy of sacrifice. Now, as he reaches down, takes the sack he has brought with him and in great double-handfulls, starts removing the treasure into the sacks. As he progresses in this action, CUT TO:

332 EXT. GALLERY OF NOTRE DAME.   MED. CLOSE   NIGHT
This medium closeup is of Esmeralda. Her expression is even more at peace now than it was in the opening shot. There is something in the spiritual atmosphere of the Cathedral which envelopes her, that lifts her above wordly things. For a few feet of this, and then CUT TO:

333 INT. QUASIMODO'S CELL.   MED. SHOT   NIGHT
This shot is from the normal angle, and shows Quasimodo, back to camera, still kneeling upon the floor at the chest. The sack is a little more than half-full now, and it is evident that Quasimodo has completed his task of joy. Gently, he lowers the heavy lid of the chest, locks it and deposits the key in his belt. The grotesque figure under the light of the solitary candle above him, he stands to his feet, and with but little effort, slings the heavy bag of candle-ends over his shoulder. He goes to the door, pausing for an instant to glance toward Esmeralda. Then cautiously he slips thru the doorway and disappears, in the shadows.   CUT TO:

334 EXT. GALLERY OF NOTRE DAME.   MED. CLOSE   NIGHT
Esmeralda gives no indication of having heard Quasimodo. Her thoughts are far away - with Phoebus, she is roaming, the idyllic paths of love. The picture which brought oblivion to her torture at the Palais de Justice comes before her mind's eyes. She sees him coming toward her—they meet---his arms clasp her to him and their lips meet. Esmeralda's eyes close in peaceful ecstacy. From now on, this
(CONTINUED NEXT PAGE)

334 (CONTINUED)
will be her heaven, her love, her peace. The smile of a mind at peace is upon her face as we CUT TO:

335 INT. PHOEBUS' ROOM   MED. SHOT   NIGHT
The medium shot discloses Phoebus, seated in a large Dagobert chair, richly cushioned. Phoebus is attired, in his tights and a soft cambric shirt, open at the neck and the fur-trimmed robe previously described. The chair is by the large table, on which is a cluster of candelabrum. Under it is a tome of fair proportions, from which Phoebus has been reading. It is open at about one-third. Now, however, Phoebus broods. He thinks Esmeralda dead. He is with her in his thoughts. His head is resting upon his upturned hand, the elbow of which arm is on the arm of the chair. His face is drawn. He is convalescent, but he suffers anguish of mind. ~~Even the matrons of Madame de Gondelaurier does not~~ ~~touch him~~ ~~much~~. She stands, looking down at him with genuine compassion, but not without a pang of resentment, for she knows that it is not of Fleur de lys he is thinking. She takes a step closer to him, resting her hand upon his shoulder. Phoebus stirs, disconsolate. Madame de Gondelaurier gently speaks:

INSERT TITLE (153) "MY DEAR NEPHEW, YOU ARE TOO YOUNG TO MOPE AND PINE. I'M AFRAID THAT MY LITTLE WATER BE LYS WOULD CONSOLE YOU, IF YOU WOULD BUT LET HER."

BACK: Madame de Gondelaurier terminates her speech with an arch manner, which changes into vexation however as she observes that he does not answer, nor give indication even that he has heard her.   CUT TO:

336 INT. PHOEBUS' ROOM   CU PHOEBUS   NIGHT
Phoebus in the attitude described. The closerview, however, shows his expression and dreamy, far-away manner to a better advantage. Somewhere out in the plane of souls, the two spirits which call so strongly to each other, have met. There is just a slight flaming of Phoebus' eyes to indicate this as the scene LAP DISSOLVES OUT AND INTO:

172

340 EXT. NOTRE DAME RADIATING LIGHT
This shot is similar to the opening shot of this sequence, except that it does not give such a large view. Esmeralda can be seen at the parapet, silhouetted against the moonlight, with her hair a glorious halo. Hold this for a few feet and then CUT TO:

SUBTITLE (154)   QUASIMODO ENTERS AT A MERCHANT WHO DEALS IN
                 SECRET TREASURES.

341 INT. THE THIEVES EXCHANGE.   LONG SHOT   NIGHT
This is a long and narrow and rather lofty room which might have been built in between two houses already standing. It is dimly but fantastically lighted, but the source of light is not shown. The idea is to bring out the grotesque and somewhat sinister quality of the place, the den of a receiver of stolen goods. The walls are almost completely hidden by robes and tapestries and materials of all sorts, suggestive of the modern pawn-shop, conducted on a large scale, with everything cast about pell-mell. The proprietor of this place, Josephus, is tall and squeamy, dressed in a rather tight-fitting, fur-trimmed robe that clothes him from chin to foot. On his head is a skull cap. Both cap and robe are black. Josephus has the face of a ghastly rat. He is at once furtive and masterful. He and Quasimodo in a way are equal. Neither is afraid of the other. Both are more or less fierce in their intercourse.

342 INT. THE THIEVES EXCHANGE. CLOSE-UP SHOT NIGHT
On the counter, near the place of the bargaining, is a pair of richly embroidered oriental slippers. Hanging on a hook within reaching distance of Quasimodo, is a robe of yellow velvet, very rich, but plain. Quasimodo's bag of candle ends is upon the counter and Josephus is in the act of belittling their value, as Quasimodo points to the yellow robe which hangs near Josephus. Josephus turns and glances at the robe and goes into a paroxysm of anger at the very thought of such an exchange. He jerks down a robe of much cheaper quality and throws it at Quasimodo, who with hardly a look at it, masses it into a heap, and throws it with a snarl of defiance to the floor back of Josephus. Simultaneous with the action, Quasimodo snatches the yellow robe from the hook

(CONTINUED NEXT PAGE)

342 (CONTINUED)
and there follows a vivid pantomime display of fierce intercourse. Josephus swears that he is being ruined. Quasimodo clutches his bag of candles to him, threatening to go. He knows how to bargain. Josephus restrains him and offers another garment, to which Quasimodo insists that the slippers, which his eye has just caught, also be included in the exchange. Josephus rants and pulls his hair. It is impossible.
CUT TO: FADE OUT.

SUBTITLE (155)   TO ESMERALDA THE NIGHT HAD BROUGHT
                  A DREAMLESS SLEEP.

343 INT. QUASIMODO'S CELL   MEDIUM SHOT EARLY MORNING   FADE IN
The view is large enough to incorporate the mattress upon which Esmeralda lies sleeping, and the candelabrum which stands near the great chest. Hanging upon this candelabrum is the velvet robe for which we saw Quasimodo bargaining the night before. Under the robe, in plain view, are the slippers. The room is filled with the soft early light of the morning. Esmeralda is covered with one of the discarded monk robes previously described. She stirs now, turning so that it is in the line of her vision.   CUT TO:

344 INT. QUASIMODO'S CELL   CU OF ESMERALDA   EARLY MORNING
Esmeralda opens her eyes. At first there is only the ordinary reaction of awakening to find that it is morning. Then the scarlet robe and slippers, in her line of vision, intrude into her waking thoughts and with a little exclamation, she sits upright, with her eyes registering a look of pitiful tenderness as she sees:

345 INT. QUASIMODO'S CELL   CU OF CANDELABRUM   EARLY MORNING
The sides of the aperture should be vignetted so as to show only the robe hanging upon the candelabrum and the little slippers beneath it. Just for a flash of this, then CUT TO:

SUBTITLE (156)   IT IS A DEVOTIONAL OFFERING.
                  ESMERALDA KNEW THINGS IT WAS.

346 INT. QUASIMODO'S CELL   CU OF ESMERALDA   EARLY MORNING
The expression of pitiful tenderness on Esmeralda's face takes more definite form, gives way to joy of sympathetic understanding and appreciation, followed then by a return of delight which first showed upon her face. Esmeralda's expression, however, should be tempered in their emotion, as the reflection of all that she has gone thru would unconsciously control her thoughts.   CUT TO:

347 INT. QUASIMODO'S CELL   MED. SHOT   EARLY MORNING
Esmeralda, with the enthusiasm of her childish nature expressing itself, in her manner, throws aside the robe which covers her and stands to her feet. Esmeralda is attired in the medieval substitute for the modern nightgown, which we can presume has been sent by one of her sisters, at Dome Claude's instruction. The robe which Esmeralda wore the day before is thrown across the corner of the chest. Running to the candelabrum and taking the robe therefrom, she holds it against her, glancing down at it as best she may, to glimpse the effect. For a few seconds Esmeralda stands thus. Then, with her face expressing the simple joy that the gifts afford her, she picks up the slippers and looks at them with delighted eyes. Upon this action, CUT TO:

348   EXT. GALLERY OF NOTRE DAME MED SHOT AT DOOR EARLY MORNING
This is a medium shot at the door which opens into Quasimodo's cell. It is closed. Huddled in a mass on the pavement in front of the door is Quasimodo. He is asleep. The morning sun is not yet up, so the light on him is very soft. His head is resting upon his arm, which is crooked under him. He is the picture of a faithful dog on guard at the door of the person he loves. For a short scene of this, then CUT TO:

349   INT. QUASIMODO'S CELL MED. SHOT NEAR DOOR EARLY MORNING
The intervening scene has given opportunity for Esmeralda to don the robe and slippers. The garment should be of a nature that will accentuate her figure in clinging lines. With her mass of dark hair falling about her shoulders, she presents a picture well calculated to inspire Quasimodo's love. She turns to the door now, laying her hand upon the latch. Her face has an expression of sympathetic understanding and appreciation for the Hunchback whom she knows lies outside her door. Softly, she opens the door. As she does so, CUT TO:

350   EXT. GALLERY OF NOTRE DAME MED. CLOSE AT DOOR TO CELL EARLY MORNING
Quasimodo is still huddled across the threshold of the cell. The door opens and Esmeralda appears looking down at him almost maternally. For a matter of seconds she contemplates him, a faithful and appealing animal. Now, on impulse, she drops to one knee and without revulsion but with sympathy, gently lays her hand upon Quasimodo's mass of tangled hair and smoothes it back. So a mistress would caress a favorite dog. At her touch, Quasimodo stirs, opening his eye to look up at her. His head is toward the East. Esmeralda kneeling at his side, has her face also more toward the East than West. Now, the first rays of the morning sun break thru over the apse of the Cathedral and Esmeralda's face is illuminated in a glory of light. Quasimodo thus beholds her, at first incredulously, almost as if he had been awakened from one dream to behold another. He slowly puts up one of his big hands and tenderly touches his head where Esmeralda caresses him. All the time, he continues looking at her, with a devoted veneration. The scene FADES OUT.

353   INT. BELFRY OF NOTRE DAME DOWNWARD SHOT EARLY MORNING
This shot is shooting straight down into the great depth of the tower, showing the narrowing perspective as the sides pull closer and closer together. The shaft is lighted by the soft haze which filters in from the front of the tower and the side, all the way down. The rear wall, however, admits the sunlight only a portion of the way down. The camera is placed in relation to the great bell so that the side to which Quasimodo clings is slightly off center. Thus, the swinging of the bell will bring him to what is almost a closeup position. Far below can be seen Esmeralda, looking up at him. Upon this scene, FADE OUT.

SUBTITLE (157)   IT WAS QUASIMODO'S DAY OF GLORY. THERE WAS ONLY ONE MEANS BY WHICH HE COULD EXPRESS THE JOYFUL TUMULT IN HIS HEART.

351   INT. BELFRY OF NOTRE DAME. LEFTHAND TOWER EARLY MORNING FADE IN
There are only two bells in this shot, both of them very large, one much larger than the other, the larger bell having a mouth five or six feet in diameter. Both bells,-- only one of which is seen in distinct focus, the larger one,--are supported by heavy beams. These beams are disposed in such fashion that the bells have free play, and yet at the same time the Hunchback, by standing on the framework which surrounds the bell, can conveniently caress the bell and set it in motion, at the risk of breaking his neck. With this established as the scene fades in, Quasimodo appears, his expression and every movement bespeaking joy. He comes to fairly close f.g. and in risk of falling, leans over and caresses the bell, then with huge muscular effort, starts the bell into motion. At first the movement is slow and ponderous. Then the movement is more rapid and of greater swing. As the bell gains momentum in response to Quasimodo's urging, Quasimodo flings himself at the bell in an orgy of joyful expression and clings there, to the ears of the bell, keeping up the movement as a child would work a swing. When the movement has become tumultuous and Quasimodo has reached a delirium of joyful expression, CUT TO:

352   INT. BELFRY OR A ROOM ON TOWER CU ESMERALDA EARLY MORNING
Esmeralda stands here, with her hands clasped, in front of her, face uplifted in exstatic admiration. She is watching Quasimodo. CUT TO:

SUBTITLE (158)   MORE THAN EVER HAD THE COUR DE MIRACLES BECOME A PLACE OF DARKNESS, A CENTER OF SLUMBERING REVOLT. THE CONTINUED ABSENCE OF ESMERALDA HAD BROUGHT ABOUT SULLEN LETHARGY....THE LULL BEFORE A STORM.

354   FADE IN EXT. COUR DE MIRACLES MED LONG SHOT NIGHT
The scene fades in, showing us the Cour de Miracles with a strong impression of almost complete lifelessness. There should be no wind. So far as possible, even the fires and torches should burn small and straight. About these fires and torches are dimly seen groups, almost devoid of movement, and in complete dejection. Men are seated on the ground with their heads on their knees. Women move slowly about their tasks with dragging steps. At one of the improvised tables near the haunt, is seated Clopin in rather indifferent contention with a number of his men. With this apathetic atmosphere established, LAP DISSOLVE INTO:

355   EXT. COUR DE MIRACLES MED CLOSE AT TABLE NIGHT
The scene LAP DISSOLVES in from previous scene, showing Clopin and his six men. They are all sullen. Clopin is disdainful and sour. His men are snarling and barely at pains to conceal their spirit of mutiny. From a leather sack on the table in front of him, Clopin takes coin which he slides across the table to one man after another. He is obviously doling them out their share of a robbery, the whole movement is intended to indicate that not even this wealth is sufficient to divert their minds from the disaster which has befallen the Cour de Miracles and for which Clopin is blamed: the disappearance of Esmeralda.

356 EXT. COUR DE MIRACLES   MED LONG SHOT   NIGHT
A longer shot, as in original scene of this sequence. The action is a continuation of the preceding scene, with Clopin definitely concluding his action of splitting the loot. Concurrent with this, Jehan enters scene from foreground, and goes rapidly in the direction of Clopin. He becomes a center of drifting interest, as various other characters are roused from their apathy, recognizing him as a possible news-bringer, and joining in his wake as he progresses toward Clopin. One of the figures that has been seated near a fire rouses himself with indifference, then with alacrity, and shows his face to the camera. This figure runs to him from another group. They have both been anxiously waiting news of Esmeralda. Perhaps this is the news they wait for. They also follow Jehan, who is now close to Clopin. Clopin's sour ill-humor is instantly translated into vivid expectance at sight of him. CUT TO:

357 EXT. COUR DE MIRACLES   MED GROUP SHOT AT CLOPIN'S TABLE   NIGHT
The angle is such that Clopin is on the left, in fairly close foreground. In the front row of those in the background are Marie and Gringoire. They, like the others, have turned their interest to the new arrival, Jehan, who now enters from the right. As Jehan comes into the scene, his interest is not immediately fixed on Clopin or those about him. His interest is on the vagabonds to left and right of him, who are menacing Clopin speaks a word of command and this quiets the vagabonds and brings the attention of Jehan to the beggar-king. They are face to face. The attitude of both of these arch villains for the moment is challenging and cautious. Clopin says:

SUBTITLE (159)   "WHAT BRINGS YOU HERE WITHOUT ESMERALDA?"

BACK. As Clopin speaks, all eyes are on his face. Now as the question is put to Jehan, the interest shifts to him. CUT TO:

358 EXT. COUR DE MIRACLES   CU OF JEHAN NIGHT
In this shot it is indicated that Jehan has thrust forward his face. He hesitates for a moment as his jaw sets and his eyes blaze. Then he delivers his message in a fierce whisper. CUT IN:

SUBTITLE (160)   "THE HOUR HAS STRUCK. THEY ARE ABOUT TO SURRENDER THE MAID TO THE OFFICERS OF THE KING."

BACK. Jehan finishes the title, registering by his face that the word has gone home, the spark that will fire Paris this night. As Jehan turns his eyes to take in the full value of what he has just said, CUT TO:

359 EXT. COUR DE MIRACLES   MED GROUP SHOT   NIGHT
Clopin instantly perceives that here is his chance to re-assert his sovereignty and satisfy his own purpose utterly. He lets out a terrific shout as he throws up his arms and exhorts his followers, screaming:

SUBTITLE (161)   "HEAR ME, YE TWO-LEGGED CATTLE, AND LEARN HOW TO BECOME MEN. WERE YE NOT ALSO BORN OF WOMEN AFTER THE MANNER OF KINGS?"

BACK. Clopin is the expression, in arms and legs and head, of a terrific energy. His appeal, flung at the people, has wrought them into a sudden frenzy, in violent contrast to their recent lethargy. Everywhere about him in foreground and in the shadowy background, fists are stuck up, some of them armed with knives, bottles and clubs.

SUBTITLE (162)   "WILL YE FOLLOW ME TO NOTRE DAME?"

360 EXT. COUR DE MIRACLES   LONG SHOT TOWARD CLOPIN   NIGHT
This scene is at right angles to previous shot. Clopin has sprung upon the table and is now a towering figure as he screams to those about him. In the immediate foreground the surging melee of vagabonds is oblivious to Jehan, who is craftily backing toward the foreground. He is like a fox, who, having accomplished his purpose, is slinking away. In the foreground he turns. His face is seen to be inflamed with a hellish satisfaction. The whirlwind is started and will soon sweep Notre Dame. Jehan quickens his steps toward camera. CUT TO:

361 EXT. COUR DE MIRACLES   CU OF GRINGOIRE   NIGHT
Gringoire and Marie are looking toward Clopin, out of scene. All about them is the shrieking mob, gone wild at Clopin's words. Fists fill the air. Knives wave. Marie and Gringoire turn to each other. They realize all that the scene portends. They fear for Esmeralda. A silent question passes between them. Marie nods. Instantly Gringoire turns and with his elbows forcing a way for him through the pressing mob, he fights his way out. CUT TO:

362 EXT. COUR DE MIRACLES   MED GROUP SHOT   NIGHT
This view is toward Clopin, who is still on the table. The men referred to as his lieutenants, now scatter. They have been given instructions to arouse every nest of thieves in Paris and order them to arms. The cries grow. Clopin screams at the crowd, "To Arms!" The cry is taken up by a hundred voices. The people turn to each other. The waving of hands and knives becomes more general as the cry rises into the air.

INSERT TITLE (163) "TO ARMS! TO ARMS! RESCUE ESMERALDA! BACK NOTRE DAME!"

BACK. With this, there is a general scattering, a running movement as the crowd turns and with one mind, directs itself toward the arsenal. CUT TO:

363 EXT. COUR DE MIRACLES   LONG SHOT   NIGHT
The long shot shows the sudden mob movement of the people toward the black depths upscene. The movement is in a general direction toward the upper righthand corner. The doors of the arsenal, so called, cannot be distinguished in this shot. As this movement starts, Clopin again screams. Ten or fifteen of his men gather about him. He gives them fierce instructions and they scatter, running toward foreground. All of his movements indicate the most violent excitement, verging on frenzy. With this action established, CUT TO:

364 INT. THE ARSENAL   FULL SHOT   NIGHT
This view is from the interior of the arsenal, shooting toward the double doors upscene. At the opening of the shot, the scene is almost completely dark. Only a few rays of light enter the crevices of the doors. Then the doors are suddenly flung open to the left and right and the crowd from the Court rushes in pellmell, many of them carrying the fire brands, which furnish illumination. The crowd is in a state of unruly madness, bent on nothing except to seize such arms as are available and to get away. The arms are seen, stacked in various piles against the walls of the warehouse. There are antique pike-staffs, spears, swords, and a conglomeration of such improvised weapons as blacksmiths' tools and farming implements, hammers, tongs, iron rods, scythes, sickles lashed to poles, boat hooks, clubs, and even a medieval lance or two of the kind once carried by the Knights. There is a squabbling rush for all of these. A detail of the action, all of which is very swift and tumultuous, is when one ruffian near the camera disputes with a billet of wood and makes off with another for the possession of a sword. The second ruffian clouts the first with a billet of wood and makes off with the sword for his own use. The types in this mob are of the most diverse, women as well as men, children and the very old, cripples and the able-bodied. CUT TO:

SUBTITLE (164) CLOPIN'S CALL TO ARMS REACHED ALL THE HIDDEN CORNERS OF PARIS...A KINGDOM WAS THE STAKE.

181

365 INT. A SEWER   MED SHOT   NIGHT
The sewer is about six feet high and about six feet wide, with an arch of slimy and dripping masonry. This is but dimly seen at the opening of the shot, while a flickering light is visible in the background, a wavering torch which is rapidly being brought forward toward the camera. The torch is carried by a courier from the Cour de Miracles, one of those dispatched by Clopin. He is breathless and muddy with much running. He is already followed by a horde of sewer dwellers, haggard creatures of the utmost squalor and ferocity, the human sewer rats of old Paris.

SUBTITLE (165)   THROUGH ALL THE MAN-MADE RAT-HOLES
                     THAT UNDERLAY THE ANCIENT CITY.

BACK. In the immediate foreground where there is an open space such as would be furnished by the intersection of another sewer and a manhole opening from above, is a man and a woman who have obviously been sleeping on the ground in the midst of their family of four half-naked and starving children. Both man and woman, like the other "sewer rats", are also half-naked and dressed in rags. They hear the summons with an outburst of demoniacal eagerness and mirth. The messenger turns to exit right, followed by the swarm of human rats. As they exeunt, CUT TO:

366 EXT. COUR DE MIRACLES   LONG SHOT   NIGHT
This is the normal long shot except that the camera is elevated to a height which will allow movement underneath it and show the expressions of the mob as they come toward foreground. Presumably the movement has been in progress for several minutes. Clopin is not in sight. The crowd now armed, is slowly gathering, in spite of its terrific intensity, to be on to the goal. They are armed with the implements described in the arsenal, and are fierce but exultant. Only a spot in the moving mass is clearly illumined as from a lighted window back of the arch. All the rest is more or less dimly seen, but this spot of light brings out the detail of weird faces and unusual weapons. The whole purpose of this particular scene is to plant dread and menace. With this movement established, CUT TO:

367 LONG SHOT INT. PHOEBUS' ROOM   NIGHT
Phoebus hears knock at door and starts toward door. Just after he has taken a step or two, the door impetuously is opened, as Gringoire brushes past servant and springs toward Phoebus with the excited announcement. As he reaches Phoebus, CUT TO:

368 INT. PHOEBUS' ROOM   CU FOR TWO   NIGHT
Gringoire excitedly telling Phoebus the news, then speaks:

SUBTITLE (165)   "CLOPIN AND HIS RABBLE ARE ON THEIR
                     WAY TO ATTACK NOTRE DAME!"

BACK. Phoebus is stunned for a moment, turns back to Gringoire and says: "Sack Notre Dame! Why?" Gringoire replies with title:

SUBTITLE (166)   "THEY'VE SWORN TO BRING BACK ESMERALDA!
                     SHE'S IN THE TOWER."

BACK. Now as Gringoire continues his excited recountal, Phoebus is swept into full joy of conviction. He flings out his arms and seizes Gringoire in a swift and ecstatic embrace. This lasts for a second or two, then he is getting the purport of the message that Esmeralda is in danger. This is the time for action. He points toward the door, telling Gringoire to rush below and give an order to prepare horses. With his other hand, he explains that he will get into few clothes and be with him instantly. On this action, as Gringoire rushes from the scene, CUT TO:

369 INT. A MEDIEVAL TAVERN   MED SHOT   NIGHT
There is a large room of vaulted masonry, with a stone floor. There are no windows. There is a small planked door upstage. The room is lighted by numerous decrepit candlesticks in the iron bands that surround the stone pillars supporting the roof. There may be a further strong source of light from off scene, to the left, suggesting a huge open fireplace. Scattered throughout the room are numerous heavy tables surrounded by benches. The benches and the room generally are crowded by a maudlin, boisterous mob of men and women, all of them more or less drunk. The women are mostly fat and young, fair enough representatives of their calling. The men are all sorts, some of them in armor as if they were deserters from the King's army. There is no reserve in the behavior of these, nor of the other male roisterers present. It is a scene of maudlin debauch. After this atmosphere is established in a few feet, the door upstage is flung open and one of Clopin's emissaries appears. This emissary is bedraggled and breathless as if he also had been running. He carries a long-handled hatchet which he waves about his head and shouts the news:

SUBTITLE (167)   "TO ARMS! WE'RE GOING TO LOOT NOTRE DAME!"

BACK. His first cry causes a general cessation of movement in the crowd, focuses all interest on himself. Then as he comes swaggering upscene toward camera, he continues to proclaim the news to left and right as there is a general rising to meet his summons. One of the soldier deserters waves a flagon, exhorting everybody to join. One of the drinkers near the messenger offers him a tankard from which the messenger drinks as the excitement grows. Everybody is now afoot and there is preparation for a general exit as we CUT TO:

368** [crossed out]

370 EXT. ANY STREET CORNER NEAR ARCH   MED SHOT   NIGHT
This shot is from within the porte-cochere and under the high arch, shooting toward the doors. There is a strong flare of light from the right. A horse comes plunging into the scene from foreground mounted by the partly dressed Phoebus, with a drawn sword. Phoebus checks his horse in the full light from the door, to give an order over his shoulder to the second horseman, Gringoire, who now appears. Phoebus points with his sword out into the direction of the Bastille and shouts his final instructions to Gringoire, saying:

(CONTINUED NEXT PAGE)

SUBTITLE (168)   "........! ROUSE THE GARRISON!"

BACK. Phoebus whirls his horse as Gringoire nods comprehension and bows over his horse's back, as both animals start out into the night at a gallop. CUT TO:

371 EXT. A PARIS STREET   LONG SHOT   NIGHT
This shot is at foreground intersection of this street with another one. The streets are dark, but the intersection is illuminated by a Madonna in a niche of one of the corner houses. The general aspect of this set is like the Carrefour de Notre Dame, previously used, but should be sufficiently changed to indicate another location. As we pick up the action, Clopin and his immediate lieutenants with torches are coming into the zone of light. They are marching steadily, but at no great speed, indicating they are followed by a large company. This company is seen in the background, bobbing along in marching time, but with a prevailing sense of disorder. The mob that follows Clopin bristles with the improvised arms we have already seen. Clopin himself is armed with the knife in his belt and an archaic sword at least seven feet long, which he brandishes now and then to exhort silence and closer ranks. His immediate lieutenants are dreadful scoundrels, burly and full of menace. One of them carries a pitchfork, another carries a huge axe. A third carries a sledge-hammer. A fourth carries a crowbar. Several of the rabble carry scythes. There is no doubt now but that Clopin is King again. The camera, mounted on truck, is ready to pick up the action as Clopin and his immediate followers approach foreground. Just as Clopin and the head of the procession comes into full light of the Madonna, there enters by cross street from the right, a rush of the sewer-rats whom we have seen previously roused. Their rush is stopped in the full light of the Madonna by their sight of Clopin. Clopin, with a gesture of his sword, gives them ferocious welcome, and waves them to fall in behind. The attitude of the sewer people has been touched with timidity and cringeing from their first sight of Clopin, but now, at this welcome from their acknowledged King, they scamper joyfully to join the procession. The camera meanwhile has taken up the action and the slow moving horde moves forward. Clopin and those about him lean slightly forward, menacing intent upon the march. In the background the mob masses in the light of the Madonna, a terrible picture of fierce faces and weapons. CUT TO:

372 EXT. NOTRE DAME   CU AT SIDE OF PORTE LOUP   NIGHT
This places the left portal of the Cathedral on the right. The angle should be such that this is indicated. The side of the tower is thus placed on the left of aperture. Joined to the tower and jogging then at right angles some distance from the tower, is a wall of smooth masonry about seven feet high, with a triangular Gothic coping. Over this wall at a height of perhaps ten feet can be seen a small arched door, let into the wall of the tower proper. Outside of this door is a restricted stone platform, reached by a flight of stone steps built against the wall of the tower. A few vines may be utilized to dress the wall and some shrubbery extending over the wall to indicate generally that this is a continuation of the garden back of the Cathedral. We pick up the scene empty, in [illegible]. Then, after a second or two, Jehan enters from the corner of the wall and there lurks as if expecting the instant arrival of Clopin and his people. After his first glance off scene in the direction from which he has just come, which assures him that he has arrived ahead of time, he draws a breath of relief and still holding his position with his body toward the camera, turns his head and looks up with satisfaction at the small door in the side of the tower. It is by this door that he knows he can enter the Cathedral as soon as the excitement begins. CUT TO:

373 A PARIS STREET   LONG SHOT   NIGHT
This can be the reverse shot of some street used before. It should be disguised, however, to give the impression of an entirely new location. Phoebus is coming toward camera on his big horse, at a hard gallop. As he approaches foreground there comes into the scene from a narrow alley-way four or five vagabonds, all of them armed with clubs and knives. They are led by one especially stalwart ruffian who carries a long staff. As the vagabonds see Phoebus, the leader (who was dispatched by Clopin) thrusts his followers back of him, grabs his staff in both hands to strike Phoebus as he passes. Phoebus sees the danger and without slackening speed, dodges the blow and lunges at the vagabond with his sword. The vagabond falls over backward as Phoebus dashes on out of scene. CUT TO:

374 EXT. PLACE DU PARVIS   LONG SHOT   NIGHT
This shot is across the Parvis from Notre Dame. Clopin's forces debouche into the Parvis from a narrow street on the right. As the mass emerges from the street, it scatters somewhat and begins a much quicker movement. Hold this long enough to show that Clopin's army has grown immensely. Other bands are arriving by lefthand street and other entrances. There is a sense of hundreds and hundreds of armed ruffians, male and female, pouring into the Parvis. Some of these carry torches and some bundles of fagots. There are two or three whirlpools of activity, where bonfires will soon be lit. Apart from these so-called whirlpools, the general drift of the mob is straight up toward Notre Dame, principally toward the middle portal. All members of the mob are now running, gesticulating, and shouting to each other. CUT TO:

375 EXT. NOTRE DAME   CU AT SIDE OF NOTRE DAME   NIGHT
This is a closeup of Jehan. His face registers his satanic satisfaction and almost delirious excitement at the arrival of the mob. This is the time he has waited for. Now, as he turns, CUT TO:

376 EXT. NOTRE DAME   CU AT SIDE   LARGER SHOT   NIGHT
This shot is large enough to show the doorway out into the left wall. Jehan springs and catches the coping of the wall with his hands and with the agility of a cat, reaches the top of the wall, springs over to the stone steps leading to the small door. His action at the small door registers the fact that he has a key to it. With this he opens the door and enters, closing it after him. CUT TO:

377 INT. QUASIMODO'S CELL   MED SHOT   NIGHT
This is the normal angle, placing the slit of a window on the right. The cell is lighted by a couple of candles. This window overlooks the Parvis. Esmeralda stirs from her sleep and sits up. Her eyes are wide with sudden alarm as she hears the noise in the Parvis. After a second of hesitation she springs up and looks out of the window. CUT TO:

378 EXT. PLACE DU PARVIS   LONG SHOT   NIGHT
This shot is from an elevated position, shooting down toward the Parvis, as though from Esmeralda's cell. There is no longer quite the same loose disordered movement of the mob as was seen in preceding shot. There are now two definite groups around bonfires which have been started and there is a slower drift of people toward the front of the Cathedral, marshalled in that direction by the small figure with the long sword--Clopin. A flash of this and then CUT TO:

379 INT. QUASIMODO'S CELL   CU OF ESMERALDA   NIGHT
This closeup is at the window, showing Esmeralda. She begins fully to realise that this is an attack on Notre Dame, by Clopin and his followers. She has a moment of horrified doubt as to what to do, and then, as she decides to appeal to Quasimodo and begins to turn to exit, CUT TO:

380 EXT. GALLERY OF NOTRE DAME   MED SHOT   NIGHT
This is a medium close shot at the door into Quasimodo's cell. Quasimodo is huddled on the threshold of the door, without mattress or covering. He sleeps with his legs drawn up and his head down between his arms. There is no movement about him--he is in profound slumber. Just for a flash of this--then the door opens and Esmeralda appears. Without hesitation, or other sentiment than that of the perfect faith that a mistress would have in her watch-dog, she stoops down and gently shakes Quasimodo's shoulders. At the first contact of her hand, Quasimodo thrills and starts up to a sitting posture. He easily catches Esmeralda's alarm and is as quickly on his feet, crouching slightly before her and ready to do her bidding. She explains with a gesture what she has seen--one hand pointing toward the Parvis and the other on her heart. As Quasimodo starts to move toward the front parapet of the gallery with a sort of stealthy ferocity, we CUT TO:

381 EXT. GALLERY OF NOTRE DAME   MED SHOT   NIGHT
This shot is from the rear parapet of the gallery, toward the direction of the Parvis. Quasimodo and Esmeralda are entering the view from the right, Quasimodo now in advance. As he rests his hands upon the stone parapet of the gallery and peers over with what is rumble, his whole body indicates his consternation at such a movement, at such an hour. He is ready for any kind of violent reaction to this and Esmeralda expresses a mounting horror as her first fears are confirmed. Quasimodo with a movement that is swift and lithe, now half turns to seize a loose bit of masonry at his feet. He has already picked this up, with the idea of hurling it at the mob below, before Esmeralda divines his purpose, and stops him. They are still in a position of controversy, as we CUT TO:

382 EXT. BASTILLE   MED SHOT   NIGHT
This is a shot of the Bastille gate as previously identified. After the first flash of an empty scene, Phoebus gallops into the scene from foreground. He pulls in his horse immediately in front of the closed gates of the Bastille. At the same instant, two heavily armed and armoured guardsmen spring from the places of concealment on either side of the gate. The two guardsmen start to menace him, but recognize him and hastily run to throw open the gates. As the gates open and Phoebus canters his horse forward, CUT TO:

383 EXT. NOTRE DAME   MED CU AT CENTER PORTAL   NIGHT
This is designed as a medium closeup, but the immense proportions of Notre Dame should be borne in mind. The view is large enough to show the entire center doors to the Cathedral. Around this central door there is a compact center of interest. There are at least a dozen of Clopin's workers now struggling to tear this door to pieces. Three or four of them are beating it with sledge-hammers; others are pulling at its iron work with pincers and prying at it with crowbars. They are lit by a dozen torch-bearers who roughly indicate a semi-circular open space in the midst of which is Clopin urging the workers on. The crowd is vociferous. This forms the center of the picture. Somewhat to the left, there is another minor center of interest where four or five stalwart ruffians are blasphemously and gleefully stoning the front of the Cathedral. The bonfires are now throwing over the entire scene a livid shaking light. Just enough of this to indicate that the attack is but fairly started, and then CUT TO:

384   INT. HARRISON   MED SHOT   NIGHT
This is a large room of smooth, clean masonry, with an
arched roof and a very large fireplace upstage; there is
a fairly large door to the left. The place is very severe
and neat, suggesting the purely military. Arms of the period are racked along the wall. Over the fireplace there
is a panoply of a shield and lances, draped with flags.
We pick up the action as one of the soldiery, in part uniform, is about to pull the bolt of the door. Beside the
fireplace are a group of his companions who have been playing checkers and who now watch him. There is perplexity on
the faces of all of them. They have heard a rush of hoofs
at the door. All this for a mere flash, andthen the man
pulls the door open. Just inside is seen Gringoire on his
horse. Gringoire flings himself down and in with the cry:

SUBTITLE (169)   "AUX ARMES! AUX ARMES!"

BACK. As Gringoire completes his cry and begins to shout
an explanation, there is an instant reaction of joy and
military alacrity. With this action in progress, CUT TO:

385   EXT. GALLERY OF NOTRE DAME   MED SHOT   NIGHT
This is a cross shot from the direction of the righthand
tower, shooting across the gallery to the left. The view
incorporates the rolls of lead, the rocks used to weigh
down the windlass and the great timbers. As we pick up
this action, Quasimodo has already overcome the qualms of
Esmeralda to the extent that he is actively engaged in the
defense of the Cathedral. He has the large piece of loose
masonry that we saw in the previous shot, uplifted ready
to hurl it to the Parvis below. His whole action indicates
a devoted ferocity. In the defense of Esmeralda and the
Cathedral he will gladly die. There is thus a certain ela-
tion about him as he hurls the mass of stone out into the
night. Concurrent with this action, Esmeralda is seen shud-
dering back and away from him, with her clenched hands to
her temples. As Quasimodo hurls the rock, he leans over the
parapet to see the result of his first shot. This scene and
all subsequent scenes about the Cathedral are vividly lit
as though from the bonfires in the Parvis. CUT TO.

386   EXT. NOTRE DAME   MED LONG SHOT   NIGHT
This shot is toward the center portal, but is large enough to show the effect upon the majority of Clopin's followers of the falling stone. Back of the torch bearers and the general center of interest about the activity around the central doorway, is the group which has been stoning Notre Dame. This is a compact group all of whom are shouting and cheering as the stone-throwers break the windows. This is of the shortest duration before there is a momentary confusion such as would come from a cry of "Look out!" and then the huge rock that Quasimodo threw crashes into the midst of the group, knocking down and crushing a dozen of them and causing a movement in the crowd like that of an exploding bomb. The effect of the falling rock is to stun everyone in the immediate vicinity for several seconds and then, as those who staggered back recover themselves, there is an inward rush of hundreds of people from all sides to see what has happened. Those who know what has happened are now shrieking imprecations and shaking their fists upward toward the gallery.

387   EXT. BASTILLE   NIGHT   LONG SHOT
The gates are open and the two guardsmen previously established, stand back from the gates to make room. They barely are out of the way, when Phoebus, followed by thirty mounted guardsmen, come out at a swift canter. Phoebus turns in his saddle and waves his sword. His followers cheer and wave their lances in response. They are off at a gallop toward Notre Dame. CUT TO:

388   EXT. CORNER PARIS STREET   NIGHT   LONG SHOT
There is a slant of light from a source off scene, suggesting a lighted window which illumines the corner of the street. At the moment of opening this shot, a white dog dashes out of scene as if frightened. Immediately afterward appears the head of a cavalcade of mounted soldiers. At the head of the cavalcade is Neufchatel. At the side of Neufchatel, and a little to the rear, is Gringoire crouched low and clinging to his horse in the manner of an inexperienced rider. The other horsemen follow closely. Just enough of this to register the speed and dash. CUT TO:

389   EXT. GALLERY OF NOTRE DAME   MED CROSS SHOT   NIGHT
This is a cross shot, the same as before. As we pick up
Quasimodo, he has already armed himself again. This time,
as he rushes toward the parapet, he has a big rock in each
of his hands. At the parapet, he hurls first his right-
hand missile andthen the left-hand one, showing that he
can use either hand eq ually well. He is now in a joyful
frenzy, like that which thrilled him when he rode the great
bell. As he delivers his left-hand throw and without looking to see the effect of it, he turns for further missiles.
During Quasimodo's business, Esmeralda is actively helping
him. CUT TO:

390   EXT. PLACE DU PARVIS   NIGHT   LONG SHOT TOWARD DOORS
The missiles hurled by Quasimodo fall into the crowd.
There are numerous victims, but these get no pity and are
left to shift for themselves. Some members of the crowd
shake their fists and curse, looking upward toward parapet,
but the general mob movement and frenzied attack on the
central door continues. CUT TO:

391   INT. DOM CLAUDE'S CELL   MED SHOT   NIGHT
Dom Claude seated on chair by light of candles, reading.
Beatific expression on his face. CUT TO:

392   EXT. A PARIS STREET   MED LONG SHOT   NIGHT
This street can be one of the streets of the Carrefour de
Notre Dame, shot from a reverse angle and disguised. The
street is in gloomy shadow, except for a slant of light
that comes from a single open window on the second floor
of one of the houses in fairly close foreground. Approaching at a mad gallop down the street come thirty guards with
Phoebus at their head. They pass through the shaft of light
toward camera. This is a short flash, but gives a sense of
Phoebus urging his troup to greater speed. CUT TO:

393   INT. CORRIDOR OF NOTRE DAME   LONG SHOT   NIGHT
This is a long shot down a narrow masonry corridor, with
a pointed Gothic arched roof. This is a lateral gallery
in the upper part of the interior of Notre Dame. On the
left are a series of four dimly seen doors. At the extreme
end of the corridor, farthest away from the camera, the
corridor ends in a winding stone staircase, leading to a
lower level. We have just registered the locale when up
this stairway and into the corridor comes Jehan, still on
a crouching run. He thus rapidly and cautiously approaches
camera. Here at the door nearest foreground he pauses and
listens, then comes to an evil decision. He knocks on the
door...then steps to one side. A second or so later the
door is opened, letting out a flood of light. In this flood
of light appears Dom Claude. He has a benevolent look of
surprise. A moment later he is seized by Jehan from the
shadowy background. There is just a flash of this and then
Dom Claude goes over backward, disappearing into the room
with Jehan trying to throttle him. For a second or two the
scene is left empty, except for a shadow on the wall of the
corridor opposite the door, denoting a violent struggle
within the cell. Then we see Jehan backing from the door
with a look of horror but also of satanic triumph on his
face. In his hands is a key-ring at least ten inches in
diameter from which hang a number of heavy keys--the keys
of the treasure chamber which we have previously seen.
Jehan still standing in the flood of light contempletes
these keys. CUT TO:

394   EXT. GALLERY OF NOTRE DAME   MED SHOT   NIGHT
This is a medium shot on the gallery, shooting from a position on the right, toward the left tower. In immediate
foreground Quasimodo is struggling with one of the enormous
beams previously planted as a part of the workmen's equipment. This beam is a tree trunk, roughly hewn and not absolutely straight. It is about twenty feet long and ten by
twelve inches. Quasimodo's back is to camera. The far end
of the beam already overhangs the parapet and Quasimodo is
now lifting the other end with a mighty effort, preparatory
to hurling the beam into space. The pantomime of his whole
body indicates a fierce and tireless energy. For just a
flash of this, then CUT TO:

395   SET IN JEHAN   INT CORNER NOTRE DAME
      Still standing at side of lighted door. He has found the
      key to the treasure room. He contemplates this with gloat-
      ing avarice, but gets a second thought--a thought of Es-
      meralda, that causes him to look upward in the general di-
      rection of the tower where Esmeralda is. His expression
      changes to one of cunning and lustful desire. As he starts
      to exit in response to this thought. CUT TO:

396   EXT. NOTRE DAME - MED LONG SHOT TOWARD CATHEDRAL   NIGHT
      The beam thrown by Quasimodo has fallen on the panic-
      stricken mob. There is a tumultuous movement of horror-
      stricken men and women from where the beam has crushed
      its victims, some of whom are trying to drag themselves
      away. Against the panic movement, to get away, Clopin
      fights his way in and commands those about him to seize
      up the beam and use it as a battering-ram.

397   EXT. NOTRE DAME   MED CU CLOPIN   NIGHT
      Clopin with bitter frenzy exhorts his people and cries:

SUBTITLE (170)   "THE HUNCHBACK HAS SENT US A BATTERING-RAM!"

      BACK. As he finishes title and some of his fearful follow-
      ers stoop to obey.

398   EXT. NOTRE DAME   LONG SHOT   NIGHT
      Clopin commands as his people lift beam and start to rush
      it toward central door. CUT TO:

192

399 EXT. GALLERY OF NOTRE DAME   CU OF QUASIMODO   NIGHT
This shot of Quasimodo is from a point in space in front of the gallery. He sees the battering ram brought into use. His face registers a fresh rage and resolution. As he leaves his place at the gallery and turns, ready for action, CUT TO:

400 EXT. GALLERY OF NOTRE DAME   MED SHOT   NIGHT
This is a cross shot toward the left tower and is large enough to incorporate the rolls of lead, scaffolding, beams, etc., which have been previously established. As Quasimodo turns from the parapet, every movement of his body is instinctive with ferocious energy. He drags scaffoldings, tubs presumably filled with pitch, coils of rope, to a point upstage left, against the parapet near the inside wall of the left tower. As he starts to stack this material with the purpose of starting a fire, CUT TO:

407 [handwritten, replacing 401]

EXT. PLACE DU PARVIS   LONG SHOT   NIGHT
The shot is away from Notre Dame and in the direction of the righthand street. Phoebus and his guardsmen come into scene and immediately deploy and begin to fight separately with the mob. The guardsmen are armed with lances. As they come into the Place, some of Clopin's people are storming the Cathedral, others are stoning the adjacent houses, some are engaged in clearing away the dead and wounded, others are in wild movement about the great bonfires. Immediately upon reaching the Place, Phoebus turns and signals to some of his followers to come with him and they charge straight on through the mob, to the Cathedral past camera. The fifteen or so remaining cavaliers deploy and become scattered and each of these become an individual center of action. This whole scene can be slipped into the most effective shots. CUT TO:

402 EXT. GALLERY NOTRE DAME MED. CLOSE NIGHT
On the gallery can be seen the flames of a fire which Quasimodo is firing with tireless energy. In the immediate foreground is Esmeralda almost dropping from exhaustion from her efforts at helping Quasimodo. CUT TO:

403 EXT. PLACE DU PARVIS NIGHT LONG SHOT AWAY FROM NOTRE DAME
This shot will be as long as possible and in the direction of the lefthand street. The fight is raging and only a couple of Phoebus' knights are left in scene when from the lefthand street come Gringoire and Neufchatel, followed by their horsemen, riding furiously to the attack. Almost at the same instant, archers and other foot soldiery arrive, cover the side lines from left and right and it is seen that the tide of battle turns in favor of the King's men. (NOTE: This action may also be split into favorable shots.) CUT TO:

404 MED. LONG SHOT EXT. NOTRE DAME NIGHT
Shooting toward Notre Dame. This shot picks up Phoebus and a number of his knights, battling desperately against overwhelming odds. All action of the mob is directing against the riders. We see in this action Clopin with a scythe. CUT TO:

401 EXT. PLACE DU PARVIS MED SHOT NIGHT
While Phoebus and a few of his men continue to struggle valiantly in the background, the camera picks up Clopin close to camera as he hamstrings a horse with a sweep of his scythe. The horse goes to his haunches and the knight is dragged to destruction. As Clopin registers his fiendish glee, and turns for a fresh victim, CUT TO:

402 EXT. GALLERY OF NOTRE DAME MED CLOSE NIGHT
This shot is as close to the fire as it is possible to get. Half concealed in the fierce glow of the flames and yet clearly recognizable is one of the rolls of lead. On the lefthand and from under the parapet. We pick up Quasimodo and Esmeralda shoving another roll of lead into the fire by side of a long pole. They both shrink somewhat from the heat, which is so intense that the end of their pole, toward the fire, itself catches fire, while still some distance from the flames. This much established, we see the roll of lead already in the flames suddenly collapse and begin to flow into the stone gutter. As Quasimodo frees this, he grins reproachfully and indicates to Esmeralda what is happening. She shudders somewhat and backs away toward cell. CUT TO:

403 MED SHOT OF GARGOYLE NIGHT
This gargoyle on the exterior of gallery matches up with the action on gallery and shows the start of flowing lead. CUT TO:

404 EXT. NOTRE DAME LONG SHOT NIGHT
The shot is toward the Cathedral on the lefthand side. The action shows the cascade of melted lead as it strikes the surprised and horrified mob. Many of them are caught in the shower, and crumple, or flee, or shrink. CUT TO:

409　　EXT. NOTRE DAME   MED CU ON GROUP   NIGHT
　　　This is the same action as in preceding shot showing the
　　　effect of the burning lead on foreground group--some try-
　　　ing to snatch away the pain, others screaming and cursing,
　　　some fleeing with their arms over their heads. CUT TO:

　　　GALLERY NOTRE DAME   MED SHOT   NIGHT
　　　The camera shoots full on Quasimodo who leans over parapet
　　　watching the effect of his molten lead. Esmeralda is in the
　　　door of Quasimodo's cell, looking toward Quasimodo with a
　　　feeling of horror almost amounting to suffocation. While
　　　they are thus engrossed, Jehan comes stealthily from around
　　　the back of the tower. As he starts cautiously toward Es-
　　　meralda, CUT TO:

411　　GALLERY NOTRE DAME   MED SHOT   NIGHT
　　　Change angle, holding fire in foreground, Quasimodo in
　　　background, as Quasimodo turns from looking over the para-
　　　pet and runs toward the fire, dumping on another roll of
　　　lead. CUT TO:

412　　GALLERY   NOTRE DAME   SHOT ON QUASIMODO'S CELL DOOR   NIGHT
　　　As Jehan grabs Esmeralda, she screams, as he forces her into
　　　the cell and closes the door. CUT TO:

413　　GALLERY   NOTRE DAME   MED CLOSE QUASIMODO
　　　Fire, in background, as he swings once more to parapet to
　　　gloat over the effect of his efforts. CUT TO:

414. [...] NIGHT
This is a down shot from Quasimodo's position, showing the battle under way in the Parvis. The troops, including the foot soldiers, are getting the best of it. There are several milling beginnings of panic. CUT TO:

415. INT. QUASIMODO'S CELL NIGHT
Esmeralda is shrinking away from Jehan who is at once plausible and menacing. She is terror stricken. He is smiling. He speaks title:

SUBTITLE (171):   "FOR ALL MY DEFORMITY OF BODY MINE, YOU AND ARE FAIRWAYS, MY DEAR."

ACTN: As he comes closer to Esmeralda and she shrinks and shudders, CUT TO:

416. GALLERY NOTRE DAME NIGHT C.U. QUASIMODO
Quasimodo still peering over parapet expressing his exaltation. ~~Now as he shifts his gaze to his left, he sees~~ -
CUT TO:

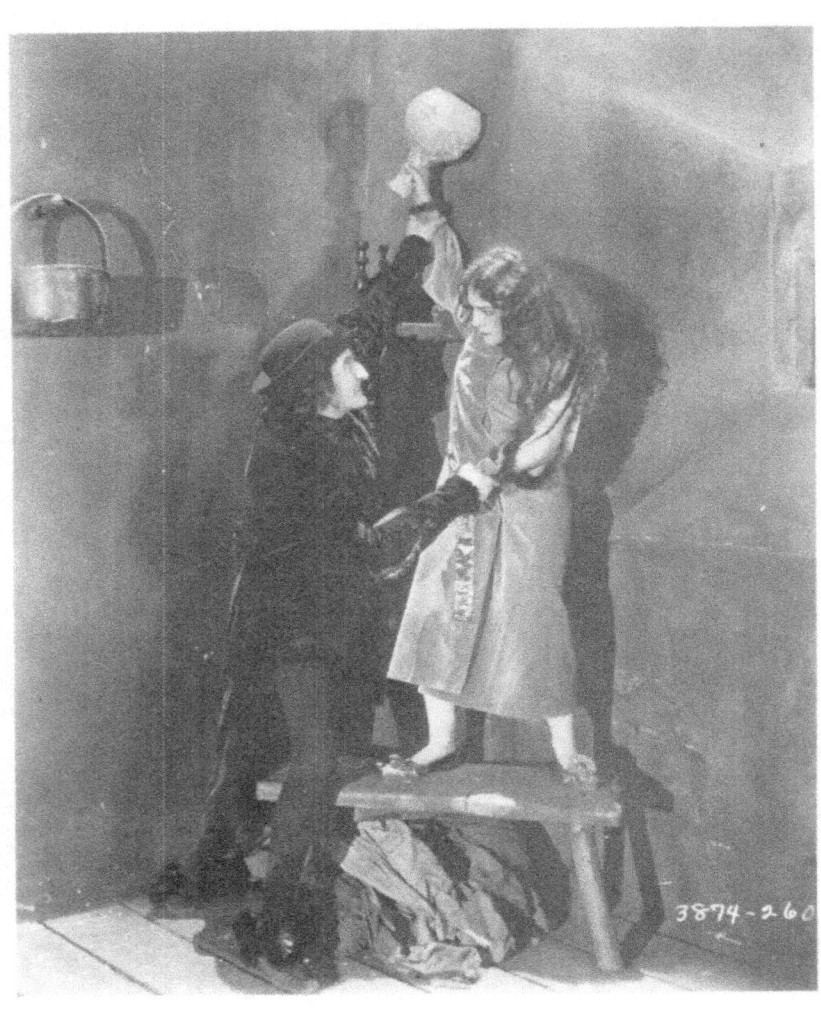

198

417. EXT. PLACE DU PARVIS NEAR RIGHT HAND DOOR MED SHOT NIGHT
We see Clopin, the central figure of a crowd of his own people, with soldiers and other followers of Clopin struggling in b.g. Phoebus is established in the f.g. CUT TO:

418. GALLERY NOTRE DAME MED SHOT QUASIMODO NIGHT
This shot establishes the second fire, and picks up Quasimodo as he turns with sudden purpose after seeing Clopin. He runs toward fire and hurls on roll of lead. He now returns to the parapet with dreadful expectancy, waiting for the effect of the lead. CUT TO:

419. INT. QUASIMODO'S CELL
Jehan has now got Esmeralda into a corner and is beginning to paw her a bit as she struggles to fence him off and to avoid all contact with him. He is sneeringly sure of himself. CUT TO:

420. EXT. PLACE DU PARVIS. IN FRONT OF RIGHTHAND DOOR OF CATHEDRAL
This is medium shot of Clopin close to camera. He has just seen one of the surviving knights massacred in the near b.g. Now as he gives an exultant shout of terrific laughter, the lead strikes him. His laughter turns into a scream of rage and agony. His giant form is twisted in anguish. With his last strength he raises his arms and face toward Quasimodo and curses even as he succumbs under the deluge of scalding metal. He falls writhing, and dies. CUT TO:

Changed

Clopin with broken spear head through him

"My children, I would have set you free, Fight on! Fight on!"

421   EXT. NOTRE DAME   CD. SHOT OF QUASIMODO
       Quasimodo registers ferocious glee as he sees the ~~effect
       of his defense~~. CUT TO:

422.   EXT. PLACE DU PARVIS   LONG SHOT FROM PARAPET OF NOTRE DAME
       This is a down shot and shows the route of the mob as the
       battle practically comes to end. There are dead and wounded
       all over the place. The able-bodied followers of Clopin are
       fleeing with the soldiers in pursuit. CUT TO:

423   EXT. NOTRE DAME.   MED. SHOT ON PHOEBUS AND GRINGOIRE.
       As we pick up the action, Phoebus, who is now on foot,
       has just completed successfully his fight with his last
       assailant, whom he runs through with a sword. Phoebus
       is on foot and is disheveled, but practically unhurt.
       With him established, Gringoire rushes into scene, also
       on foot. He has been looking for Phoebus. Gringoire
       cries out for Phoebus to follow and he will lead him to
       Esmeralda. Gringoire indicates the big central door
       which has been partly smashed open. As Phoebus eagerly
       moves to follow up Gringoire's suggestion, CUT TO:

424.   PLACE DU PARVIS   LONGER SHOT NEAR CATHEDRAL CENTRAL DOOR
       This follows up action of Gringoire and Phoebus in preceding
       scene and establishes the dead and dying on the Cathedral
       platform. Gringoire and Phoebus rush toward center door and
       scramble through. As they disappear into Cathedral, CUT TO:

200

425. INT. QUASIMODO'S CELL MED. C.U. ESMERALDA AND JEHAN
Jehan has forced Esmeralda down to the mattress where she has shrunk from him as he seizes her. He is struggling to bring her close enough to him to kiss her. Esmeralda is still using all her strength to hold him off, but she knows that her efforts will shortly be unavailing. As Jehan overcomes her, she speaks title:

SUBTITLE (172) "GOD WILL PROTECT ME FROM SUCH AS YOU."

BACK: Jehan sneers as he presses Esmeralda to him. He indicates that God Himself cannot help her now. Jehan slowly brings his lips to Esmeralda's neck in a straining embrace. As she reacts to this and struggles from his kiss, CUT TO:

426. GALLERY OF NOTRE DAME MED C.U. QUASIMODO
He is at the parapet waving his arms in wild delight at the route of the mob. He thinks of Esmeralda - he wants to tell her the good news. He turns and runs toward the closed door of the cell. CUT TO:

427. INT. QUASIMODO'S CELL MED. SHOT NIGHT
The action between Jehan and Esmeralda has continued. As Esmeralda has wrested herself somewhat free from Jehan's grasp and is leaning against the wall fighting off Jehan, Jehan gets to his feet and attempts to seize her again. The door of the cell is thrust open just as Jehan once more gets his arms about her and draws her struggling to him. This is the spectacle that meets Quasimodo's eyes. Quasimodo pauses for a moment, as his recent delight is succeeded by amazement and speechless rage. At the same time, Jehan gets Quasimodo's presence and recoils somewhat as Quasimodo - his face become terrible - starts forward. Jehan relinquishes Esmeralda who recoils with horror. Jehan is now face to face with Quasimodo, preparing himself to resist Quasimodo's attack. Quasimodo's action has been slow, until with sudden ferocity, he seizes Jehan, just as Jehan is tugging at his dagger. As Quasimodo closeson Jehan. CUT TO:

428. INT. CORRIDOR NOTRE DAME.
This shot is toward the stairs leading down. We pick up Phoebus and Gringoire as they come running along the corridor. In the middle f.g. is the open door of Dom Claude's cell, with the light streaming through. Phoebus, with all his thoughts fixed on Esmeralda, runs on past the door. Gringoire is about to follow him, but gives a glance into the cell and pauses with a start of horror at what he sees. As Phoebus runs out of scene and Gringoire, touched with fear and awe, enters the cell. CUT TO:

429. INT. DOM CLAUDE'S CELL MED SHOT NIGHT
The shot is toward door as Gringoire with awe and pity approaches Dom Claude who is just struggling up from the floor, where he has recovered from the knockout Jehan gave him. CUT TO:

430. INT. QUASIMODO'S CELL MED SHOT NIGHT
Quasimodo is now carrying the struggling Jehan to the door. As he starts to drag Jehan up over his head. CUT TO:

431. GALLERY NOTRE DAME LONG SHOT TOWARD CELL DOOR
The shot is from a point in space in front of the gallery, taking in the parapet, the cell door and side of tower. As Quasimodo staggers with the struggling Jehan toward camera. CUT TO:

432. GALLERY NOTRE DAME C.U. JEHAN & QUASIMODO NIGHT
This gives the action as Jehan stabs Quasimodo twice and Quasimodo ignores his wounds as he continues forward. CUT TO:

433. MED. SHOT GALLERY NOTRE DAME NIGHT
The shot is a different angle so that the parapet is in and cell door is left out. We pick up Quasimodo as he carries the still struggling Jehan to the parapet and makes a final display of strength and energy as he prepares to hurl Jehan into space. In the midst of this action, Jehan stabs Quasimodo for the third time. Then instantly Quasimodo with a supreme effort throws Jehan over the parapet and into space. CUT TO:

434. MED. SHOT ON CELL DOOR TOWARD BACK OF GALLERY NIGHT.
This shot shows Esmeralda in the door of the cell. She is horrified by what she has just seen. She covers her face with her hands and wilts back a little. On this action we bring Phoebus around the rear corner of the tower. He pauses for a moment of eager scrutiny before he sees Esmeralda. Then he discovers her and calls her name. As she hears his voice, she turns somewhat. Phoebus takes her into his arms. CUT TO:

435. C.U. QUASIMODO GALLERY NOTRE DAME NIGHT
Shooting toward the Place. As we pick up Quasimodo, his back
is to camera as he watches the fall of Jehan. Now he turns.
He is wounded to death - death is already on him. But as
he sees Esmeralda and Phoebus in each other's arms, there comes
into his face a look of pitiful contentment and joy.
CUT TO:

436. MED. SHOT DOORWAY QUASIMODO'S CELL NIGHT
This shot picks up Phoebus and Esmeralda unconscious of
everyone else except themselves. Each has believed the
other dead. Now they are in each other's arms. Esmeralda
almost swoons with joy as she looks up into Phoebus' face.
Phoebus with a very reverent joy in his own bearing,
supports Esmeralda into the cell, leaving the door open.
CUT TO:

437. C.U. QUASIMODO GALLERY NOTRE DAME NIGHT
Quasimodo has a wonderful look of happiness and of
approaching death in his face as he sees the lovers disappear. He is now all alone. He is as if deserted by the
whole world. He has lived his life. There is only one
thing in the world that still has a place in his heart
and mind. He lifts his face toward the belfry. The
thought brings to him a measure of consolation and of
inspiration. With his dying strength, he leaves the
parapet, and still clutching his wounds, starts weakly
forward.   CUT TO:

438. MED. SHOT GALLERY NOTRE DAME NIGHT
Cell door is in f.g. and shot is toward rear corner of the tower. Around the corner come Dom Claude and Gringoire. Dom Claude is not yet quite fully recovered from his recent violence, but is gentle and spiritual. Gringoire is guiding him and imparting information as to the events of the night. They stop at the open door of Quasimodo's cell and look in.   CUT TO:

439. INT. QUASIMODO'S CELL   NIGHT
This is a flash of Esmeralda and Phoebus as seen from the exterior of the door. Phoebus kisses Esmeralda passionately. CUT TO:

440. MED. SHOT GALLERY NOTRE DAME NIGHT
The shot is toward Dom Claude and Gringoire. As they see what transpires within, Dom Claude smiles benignantly and turns to Gringoire. Just as he starts to turn, he hears..
CUT TO:

441. FLASH OF BIG BELL
Just moving sufficiently for the clapper to hit the bell.
CUT TO:

442.   INT. BELL-RINGER'S ROOM   NIGHT   C.U. QUASIMODO
The Hunchback is using his last strength to pull the bell
rope. He hears the bell. The sound is a blessing to him.
He sinks, dying. CUT TO:

443.   LONG SHOT GALLERY NOTRE DAME   NIGHT
This is as long a shot as possible, showing not only the
door to the cell but also the front of the tower. In response to the sound of the bell, Dom Claude pauses a moment
in thought, gets a meaning of the sound. He beckons to
Gringoire. They start with quickened stops toward front
of tower and exit. CUT TO:

444.   INT. BELL RINGER'S ROOM C.U. QUASIMODO NIGHT
The Hunchback gives one final pull at the rope and
collapses, face down, with a smile on his death stricken
face. CUT TO:

445.   INT. BELL RINGER'S ROOM   LONG SHOT   NIGHT
Quasimodo lies face downward on the floor of the room,
with his hands still on the rope. He is motionless. At
the door of the room, appear Dom Claude and Gringoire,
Dom Claude with swift concern hurries forward and kneels
at Quasimodo's side. Dom Claude tenderly turns Quasimodo
over so that his face is up. Dom Claude sees Quasimodo
is dead and makes the sign of the cross on Quasimodo's
forehead, before lifting his face in prayer. In the
course of this action, Gringoire is seen in the immediate
b.g; slowly bows his head. FADE OUT.

Finis

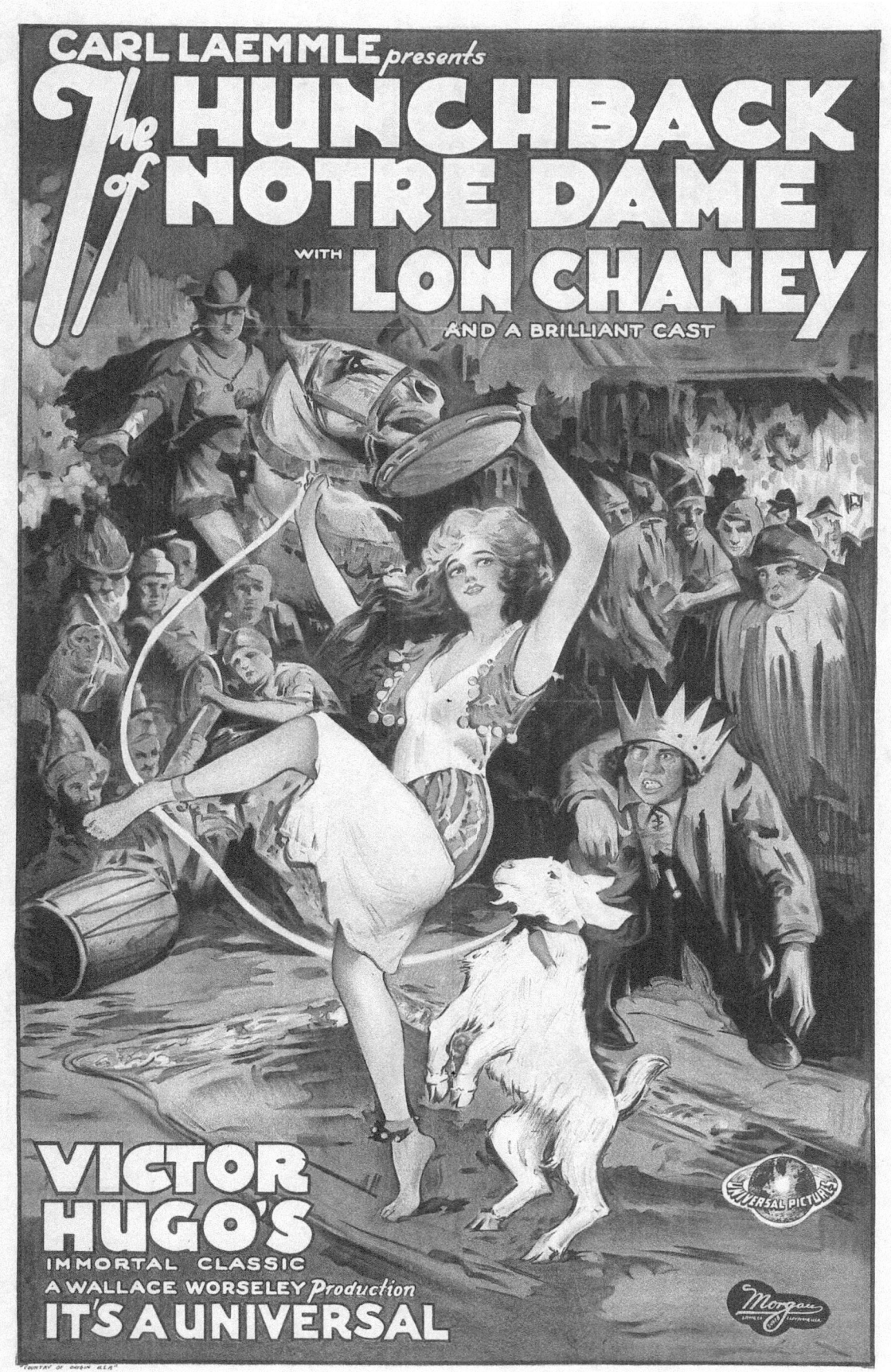

One-sheet for the 1929-30 Sound re-release of The Hunchback - orchestral track only.

Lon Chaney's great-grandson Ronald Chaney, with his two daughters. Notice the family resemblance.

Forrest J Ackerman and make-up artist Michael Spatola with the original Creature from the Black Lagoon costume on display at the Ackerman Archives.

ACKNOWLEDGEMENTS

The author wishes to thank the following individuals and institutions for their generous assistance:

Wallace Worsley Jr. - For allowing us to reproduce in facsimile his father's script and personal photographs
Christopher Worsley
Academy of Motion Picture Arts and Sciences, and Robert Cushman
Corine DeLuca, Universal Studios and The Billy Rose Library, Lincoln Center
Marc Wanamaker, Bison Archives
William K. Everson Collection
Andrew Lee, Universal Studios
Ernest Goodman, Universal Studios
Michael Sington, Universal Studios
Patsy Ruth Miller
Kevin Brownlow
Steven Jochsberger
George Turner
Tod Firetag, Poster City
Wes Shank
The Museum of Modern Art, Mary Corliss
Special photography by: Alexander Anton Studio 53

Introduction by George Turner originally appeared in American Cinematographer, June 1985 and is reproduced with permission of the author.

Also many thanks to:
Ron Chaney
Lon Chaney Jr.
Christopher Consalvo
Michael Flemming
Michael Spatola, make-up artist

Susan E. Suwalsky, Mechanical Artist

Main Entry under title:
THE HUNCHBACK OF NOTRE DAME (Motion Picture)
Includes the original script: The Hunchback of Notre Dame
by Perly Poore Sheehan.
Includes index:
I. Riley, Philip J., 1948-
II. Miller, Patsy Ruth, 1904-
III. Chaney, Lon, (Actor) 1883-1930
IV. Hugo, Victor Marie, comte 1802-1885

Pictures, Filmscript from the Universal 1923 Motion Picture *The Hunchback of Notre Dame* used with the permission of and by special arrangement with the owners; after extensive copyright search all materials presented in this volume are from the private collections mention above. The editor and publishers make no claim to copyright except in the format of this presentation for historical preservation.

4

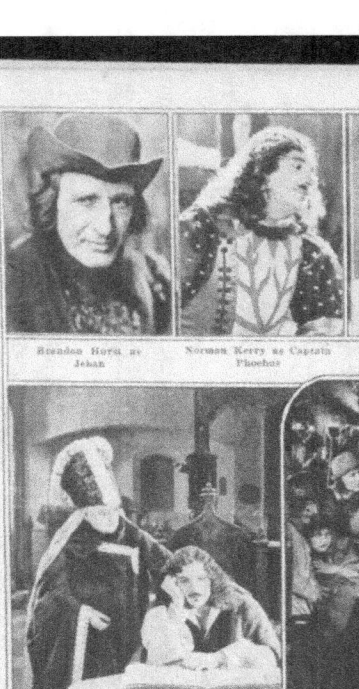

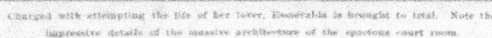

1988

Philip J. Riley began his career as a rock-and-roll musician, but film has always been his first love. When he got the opportunity to work as a "film archeologist" for Forrest J Ackerman, the world's foremost authority on science fiction and fantasy films and literature it was an easy career change. The influence of Ackerman and Mr. Riley's contact with the directors, actors and authors who would gather in the Ackerman museum developed his interest for writing and journalism. Soon his knowledge of film history especially the horror fantasy genre became second only to Mr. Ackerman's.

Philip Riley has acted as consultant on several major film releases, has composed more than fifty songs and still performs at selected seminars around the country. His articles have appeared in film and non-film related magazines and his is preparing a college filmfest lecture series on lost films. His first book *London After Midnight* won the Anne Radcliffe Award for Best Book of the Year and received an additional award for journalism from Europe as well as praise from the world's major film archives.

The Hunchback of Notre Dame follows his second book *A Blind Bargain* ironically in the same time sequence by which they were filmed.

He is currently working on a filmbook reconstruction of *The Divine Woman*, MGM 1928—Greta Garbo's only lost film and Laurel and Hardy's only color film *The Rogue Song*, MGM 1930 for publication—and is preparing the score for the recording of his children's ballet based on *Lord of the Rings*.

Of his past accomplishments it has been said:

"Philip Riley is setting the Industry standard for preserving the great silent film history in book form."

Kevin Brownlow,

"With 'Phantom of the Opera' a hot item, Lon Chaney's version is getting attention again. But the non-Phantom Chaney is virtually, as the title of one of his pictures puts it, 'The Unknown'. Philip J. Riley is trying to rectify that. Following Riley's marvelous book on the legendary 'London After Midnight', comes 'Blind Bargain' completely forgotten (at least, to me). It's fun to reconstruct the film through effective text and generous pictures. Besides the kick of discovering a 'new' Chaney, it's pleasant to again meet one of the great beauties, Jacqueline Logan. Let's have more, Mr. Riley."

John Springer

"'A Blind Bargain' is a lovingly reconstructed version of the film on paper. Since the film no longer exists it's the next best thing to seeing it."

Martin Scorsese

"Another lost Chaney! Wonderful! The Ackerman Archives provide another treasure for posterity."

Ray Bradbury

"I've been waiting for a book like this for 20 years."

Dan Woodruff,
Academy of Motion Picture
Arts & Sciences Library

"Lon Chaney is one of America's most important actors, and Phil Riley's book on Chaney's 'London After Midnight' becomes an instant classic in cinema literature."

John Landis

www.ingramcontent.com/pod-product-compliance
Lightning Source LLC
Chambersburg PA
CBHW080549230426
43663CB00015B/2766